MILITARY
TECHNOLOGIES
of the WORLD

MILITARY
TECHNOLOGIES
of the WORLD

VOLUME

1

T.-W. LEE

Praeger Security International
Westport, Connecticut • London

Library of Congress Cataloging-in-Publication Data

Lee, T.-W. (Tae-Woo)
    Military technologies of the world / T.-W. Lee.
        p. cm.
    Includes bibliographical references and index.
    ISBN 978-0-275-99535-5 (set : alk. paper) — ISBN 978-0-275-99537-9 (vol. 1 : alk. paper) —
ISBN 978-0-275-99539-3 (vol. 2 : alk. paper)
    1. Military art and science—Technological innovations—History.   2. Weapons systems—
History.   3. Military history.   I. Title.
    U39.L42 2009
    623—dc22   2008034976

British Library Cataloguing in Publication Data is available.

Library of Congress Catalog Card Number: 2008034976
ISBN: 978-0-275-99535-5 (set)
        978-0-275-99537-9 (vol 1)
        978-0-275-99539-3 (vol 2)

First published in 2009

Praeger Security International, 88 Post Road West, Westport, CT 06881
An imprint of Greenwood Publishing Group, Inc.
www.praeger.com

Printed in the United States of America

The paper used in this book complies with the
Permanent Paper Standard issued by the National
Information Standards Organization (Z39.48-1984).

10   9   8   7   6   5   4   3   2   1

Contents

CHAPTER

1

AIR SUPERIORITY

TECHNOLOGY CHANGES the way battles are fought. The rarity of notable air battles involving dogfights in the post–Vietnam War era can be attributed to the advances in air-to-air missile technology where longer range and better lock-in guidance have continuously increased the engagement distance between aircrafts. The U.S. Air Force, for example, has not had an ace (five aerial kills or more) since 1972. In many instances, the battle is already decided on the radar long before visual contact is made. In recent conflicts in the Middle East, air superiority was quickly established by the United States and allied air forces, and the opposing fighters were mostly destroyed on the ground after their radar and communication installations were knocked out in preemptive, stealth strikes or they simply elected not to engage the U.S. fighters. The advances in technology, at least in aerial battles, quickly made the prior-generation aircraft and armaments obsolete and resulted in lopsided advantages for the side in possession of the superior technology. The Israel-Syria conflict back in 1982 and U.S.-Iraqi conflicts from 1991 onward have shown that Russian-built MiG-29s and their equivalents were not of much threat to the F-15, F-16, and other western counterparts. While it is true that a large part of the western superiority also lies in the preparedness and training of the pilots, the training itself requires many technological advances in flight simulators and battle scene reconstruction using computers. More advanced Russian Sukhoi Su-30s and MiG-35s, on the other hand, are viable weapons with potent sets of armaments and are making their way into the air forces outside of Russia. The United States has in the meantime produced probably the most advanced aircraft in history in the F-22 Raptor that embodies state-of-the-art technologies in stealth, armaments, and battlefield management electronics. The more compact and utility-oriented (less expensive) F-35 "Joint Strike Fighter" is also in the works.

To find an example of aerial combats involving U.S. aircraft, one needs to look as far back as 1989 in the Mediterranean region off the coast of northern Libya, a country in North Africa next to Egypt. At the time, the Libyan strongman Muammar al-Qadhafi led a rogue state of anti-American dictatorship. Using oil money, he had equipped his air force with Russian-made jets including the MiG-23 Flogger. With the advent of long-range anti-ship missiles and sophisticated air strike jet fighters, the U.S. aircraft carrier John F. Kennedy operating in the area was on high alert. The tensions that existed between Libya and the United States in preceding years, along with the unpredictable nature of Qadhafi, fueled the prospect of an armed encounter in this region. A naval battle group, while carrying a tremendous range and punch through its carrier-launched fighters (F-14 Tomcats), also is vulnerable to missile and air attacks. For this reason, a battle group always moves with an airborne early warning capability, in this case in the form of E-2C Hawkeye surveillance aircraft. The long-range radar coverage of the E-2C allowed the intercept controller aboard to detect two Libyan aircraft taking off from the Al-Bumbah air base more than 100 miles deep in Libya and approaching the two F-14 Tomcats then on patrol in the air space above the Gulf of Sidra off the Libyan coast. One of the patrol mission objectives was to protect the air space near and above the carrier, and the F-14s took an air path to intercept the bogeys from a rear, threat position. Instead of holding their course, the Libyan MiGs made a counter move to circumvent the F-14s. Apparently the Libyan ground-based radars were closely monitoring the situation, and instructions were being sent to maneuver against the Tomcats. This cat-and-mouse jockeying of position repeated, with each side attempting to gain an advantage by taking a pursuit position from the rear. From this pursuit position, the forward-looking radars and also the heat-seekers can lock on to the opposing aircrafts without the possibility of that favor being returned. At twenty miles and closing fast from a head-on position, it became evident that the Libyan MiGs had no intention of being escorted out of this air space and every intent of engaging the F-14s. It is unclear whether the Libyan MiGs were locking on to the F-14 Tomcats, but the WSO (the weapons system officer, also referred to as radar intercept officer, RIO, at this time) onboard one of the F-14s was advising the lead pilot to move the aircraft in position for an optimum launch. At this distance and speed, the two opposing sides are fair games for the air-to-air missiles and under intense pressure of oncoming MiGs, one of the F-14s fired two Sparrow missiles that did not come close to the target. In the heat of battle, the WSO had the radar in a track-and-scan mode, which did not provide radar illumination to guide the Sparrow missiles with passive radar guidance. The Sparrows pursue the target in response to the radar signal illuminated by the launch aircraft. All of this transpired without the two sides having visual contact of the other. Now, the MiGs appeared as specks in the sky, and the Tomcats split up with the wingman heading directly into the MiGs while the lead Tomcat veered to gain a rear position. The Tomcat approaching the MiGs this time successfully locked the radar onto one of the bogeys and fired, resulting in a spectacular explosion. Incredibly, the pilot escaped in an ejection chute. The lead Tomcat finally gained the pursuit angle on the remaining MiG and fired a short-range, heat-seeking Sidewinder that tracked the jet exhaust heat and made contact. The entire sequence lasted approximately four minutes, and most of the battle was fought in the radar space without visual contact. Not a single shot of the Vulcan cannon was fired.

A new era in the use of the air force in highly coordinated, precision attacks was opened during the Operation Desert Shield in 1991. Although only 5 percent of all the munitions delivered during this operation was of the guided type, it proved that optimal use of the air power could debilitate the entire defense infrastructure of the opposing side, starting from the command and control down to the infantry level dug in foxholes. The lopsided superiority of the coalition aircraft and pilots were proven at the outset by the fact that thirty-nine of the outdated Iraqi MiGs were promptly shot down. In the next days, some of the remaining Iraqi aircraft sought refuge in Iran to become permanent properties of Iran, and the brief phase of the air-to-air encounters ended without much drama. Although there were some 800 Iraqi aircraft, few of them challenged the coalition air force. U.S. Navy and Air Force AWACS airplanes located and identified Iraqi threats from the outset, in some cases alerting the nearby coalition aircraft to fire their SAM missiles to destroy Iraqi aircrafts just as they cleared the runway during takeoff. In another instance, a Navy F/A-18 pilot was alerted of an approaching Iraqi fighter and using a Sidewinder missile recorded a beyond-the-visual-range kill forty seconds after the AWACS alert. The overall result was a complete control of the air space from which coordinated, multidimensional attacks on the Iraqi targets could be made at will and with minimal losses, human or machine, to the coalition side. During the second operation against Iraq ten years later, Operation Enduring Freedom, a similar approach was taken except with much increased size and performance of the guided munitions delivered either by aircraft or cruise missiles. In both instances, the first strikes were targeted against radar defenses and command/control sites so that the air space could be cleared for subsequent operations.

Although the first of the bombings on Baghdad was broadcast live a little before 7 PM EST on January 17, 1991, the real war had started in the darkness of the southern Iraq-Saudi Arabia border about two hours before the first wave of F-117 stealth fighter-bombers reached Baghdad. Iraq had built one of the most extensive air defense systems in the world by this time, following the 1981 Israeli air raids on its nuclear reactor facility. This heavy air defense network consisted of seventy-three radar sites, 400 observational posts, sixty surface-to-air (SAM) missile batteries, and close to 2000 anti-aircraft guns, all of them linked to seventeen regional command posts, four sector operator centers, and the Air Defense Headquarters in Baghdad. The heavy volume of communication was handled through microwave relays and fiber optic cables to and from a central command computer installed by a French contractor, Thomson-CSF. This modern air defense in principle would detect any encroachments by foreign aircraft, and appropriate measures could be quickly deployed to defeat them. As described in Chapter 3, a small gap in this dense network of radars was identified, and a squadron of AH-64 attack and USAF Pavelow helicopters slipped in at low altitude to knock out the two forward radar installations forty miles apart from one another without raising alarm to the rest of the network. This operation allowed streaming of massive waves of aircrafts through the corridor thus created.

The first wave to follow the helicopter attack was a fleet of twenty-two F-15E Strike Eagles along with EF-111 Ravens electronic warfare aircraft. This wave focused on high-priority targets such as fixed Scud missile launch sites, while the EF-111 Ravens jammed the Iraqi air defense radars so that they could not find a fix on the F-15E's locations. As the flyable corridor was yet quite limited, only the F-117 Nighthawk stealth fighter-bombers and Tomahawk cruise missiles made bombing raids on Baghdad. The primary targets in Baghdad again were sector operation centers, command bunkers, power grid sites, telecommunication centers, the Ba'ath Party Headquarters, and the presidential palaces. At 3:45 AM Baghdad time, a formation of thirteen-ft-long unmanned drone aircrafts was sent over key radar installations, making themselves appear as heavy bombers making a run to Baghdad. Soon, the Iraqi radars locked on to guide hundreds of SAM and anti-aircraft artillery (AAA) fires to fill the sky, except that the only real flying objects were the coalition HARM (high-speed anti-radiation missiles) that locked on to the lit radars and promptly knocked them out. At one point during this bait-and-hit operation, there were close to 200 Iraqi SAM missiles in the air jabbing wildly at the drone decoys, and roughly one-quarter of the Iraqi SAMs were expended in this manner during the first day of combat with minimal effectiveness. This pattern continued for several days with the F-117s attacking Baghdad during the night, the Tomahawks during the day, and decoy/HARM combinations at any time.

Modern fighter aircraft today are a culmination of many technological breakthroughs in diverse engineering disciplines ranging from avionics, flight control, material, and aerodynamics to propulsion system. Control of the air space in modern battles gives the army unprecedented freedom and authority on the ground. The ability to monitor the troop and weapon movement and deployment, combined with the air-to-ground strike capabilities to destroy the military and high-priority targets such as command and control sites, essentially assures a lopsided battle for those who can command the air space. In addition, movement of aircraft through the air is fast and far-reaching. Aerial refueling allows strategic bombers to stay in the air for extended periods of time. Ground troop support from carrier-based aircraft in response to evolving battle situations has become a standard tactics of the U.S. forces deployed in faraway locations. For this reason, all of the world's major powers have invested their technological and economic assets into developing ever more potent jet fighters and bombers. In this chapter, we examine the technological advancements found in some of these aircrafts.

UNITED STATES AIRCRAFT

The F-15 Eagle fighter aircraft that once was the mainstay of the U.S. Air Force in maintaining air superiority is shown in Fig. 1.1. The F-15 Eagle has several versions from F-15A to F-15E and represents the main all-weather tactical fighter for the U.S. Air Force and also for several ally nations (Israel, Japan, Saudi Arabia, and South Korea). Developed in response to the alarming improvements in Russian fighters such as the MiG-25 Foxbat, F-15 Eagles lived well up to their expectations by continuously outperforming any contending aircraft in various air battles. In fact, on record no F-15 fighter was lost in an aerial combat. Although two F-15Es were brought down by ground fire in the Iraqi theater in 1991, its superiority in aerial engagements is unprecedented as given by the accumulated statistics of 104 kills against 0 losses in aerial battle. Since 1979, F-15s have been deployed in battle mainly by the Israeli and U.S. forces, and they continuously overwhelmed adversaries with superior electronic and maneuver capabilities, shooting down mostly Russian-made aircraft ranging from MiG-21 "Fishbeds," MiG-23 "Floggers," MiG-25 "Foxbats," and MiG-29 "Fulcrums," to Su-25 "Frogfoots," Su-22 "Fitters," and French Mirage F1s flown by the Iraqis.

Given the success of the F-15 and subsequent, more advanced fighters produced by the American aerospace industry, it may come as a small surprise that the F-15 emerged as a replacement for the F-4 Phantom jets, which were clearly outclassed by the Russian jet fighters of the time. It is no coincidence that the size and even the exterior of the F-15 aircraft resembles those of MiG-25 because it was the aim of the U.S. military to combat the threats posed by the class of Russian jet fighters at the time. Further revelations of the

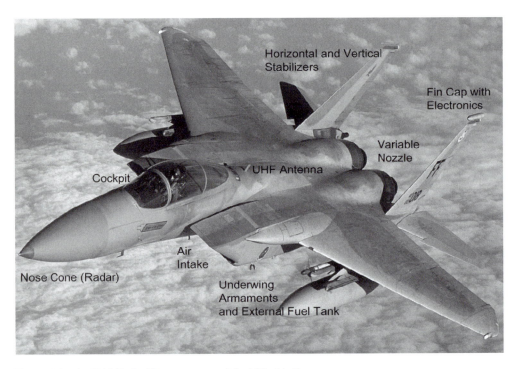

Figure 1.1. An F-15 Eagle. Photo courtesy of the U.S. Air Force.

actual performance, however, have proven that in spite of the Russian jets' record-breaking speed and rate-of-climb, their size and weight made these heavyweights vulnerable in dogfights due to lack of maneuverability. F-15s, however, made extensive use of titanium in the airframe to lower their bulk weight. Adding to this formula was the then state-of-the-art power plant, Pratt and Whitney F-100-PW-100 turbofan engines. These engines provided a 25,000 lb thrust with the afterburners running, which was eight times the engine weight. Also, the small wing area and advanced control systems allowed the F-15 then unprecedented maneuverability in addition to its range and armament capacity.

The letter designation for F-15 follows its evolution from its introduction to the U.S. Air Force in 1976:

F-15A: The version introduced in 1976, single seat.

F-15B: Two-seat trainer version of F-15A.

F-15C: Improved version of F-15A. 2000 lb of additional internal fuel capacity, external conformal fuel tanks, and improved power plant allowing for maximum takeoff weight of 68,000 lb.

F-15D: Two-seat trainer version of F-15C.

F-15E: Two-seat, all-purpose version for deep strike and interdiction. Improved weapons control and electronics.

Although, the F-15E Strike Eagle is based on the same airframe as the preceding F-15 series, it is perceived as an aircraft in a different class both by its pilots and military analysts. It has capabilities far exceeding its predecessors. To handle the advanced weapons control systems, the F-15E allows for a weapon system officer (WSO) to sit behind the pilot. The added capabilities allow F-15Es to carry out long-range ground assault missions under any conditions. Table 1.1 gives some of the main characteristics of the F-15E Strike Eagle. F-15E armaments include air-to-air missiles like AIM-9, AIM-7, various guided bombs such as CBU-10, -12, -15, and -25, and an air-to-ground missile, AGM-65. Some of the key electronic gears are the synthetic aperture radar, head-up display (HUD), and LANTIRN (Low Altitude Navigation and Targeting Infrared for Night).

Although the F-15's prowess was well recognized, it was a large and expensive aircraft. Though many of the shortcomings of the F-4 Phantom were overcome using superior technology, the F-15 got big and costly to give heavy armament capabilities and flight performance. Proponents within the U.S. Air Force for small, agile aircraft more suitable

Table 1.1. F-15E Specifications.

Length	63.8 ft (19.45 m)
Wingspan	42.8 ft (13.05 m)
Height	18.5 ft (5.64 m)
Maximum Take-Off Weight	81,000 lb (36,818 kg)
Power Plant	2 Pratt & Whitney F100-PW-229 afterburning turbofans
Total Thrust	58,200 lb
Maximum Speed	High altitude: Mach 2.5 or 1650 mph (2655 km/h) Low altitude: Mach 1.2 or 900 mph (1450 km/h)
Ceiling	65,000 ft (20,000 m)
Range	3500 miles (5600 km)
Rate of Climb	50,000 ft/min (255 m/s)
Thrust-to-Weight ratio	1.30

for air combat got what they wished in the F-16 Fighting Falcon. Smaller and less expensive than the F-15, the F-16 would have unparalleled maneuverability at the time of its introduction, transient performance including acceleration and climb at all speed ranges, along with effective armaments for air combat. The Lightweight Fighter (LWF) program out of which the F-16 originated had objectives of developing a highly capable aircraft of 20,000-lb weight (about half that of the F-15), low cost of production and operation, and high performance at Mach 1.6 and below and at altitudes of 40,000 feet and below. The cost for the F-16A/B would turn out to be about $15 million per airplane, about half the cost of the F-15 and one-tenth that of the ultramodern F-22 described next. Yet, the F-16 featured many of the technological advances, some beyond even those of the F-15. The F-16 was intentionally designed to be aerodynamically unstable with the center of gravity well behind the center of lift at the main wing. The natural tendency for the aircraft then is to pitch up and go out of control. Thus, the aerodynamic surfaces like the horizontal stabilizers need to be constantly engaged to maintain the aircraft's level motion. This stabilization is performed by onboard quadruple-redundant computers in what is known as fly-by-wire. As opposed to direct hydraulic control of the aerodynamic surfaces by the pilot's control stick, the computer receives the pilot input digitally (i.e., by wire) and computes the necessary configurations for the desired aircraft attitude and motion. The configuration data are then transmitted again via wire to the hydraulics, which in turn rotate the aerodynamic surfaces. The fly-by-wire has much quicker response, and because the aircraft is naturally unstable its ability to go into unusual flight angles is much greater (i.e., the aircraft becomes much more agile). The higher agility means that it can make high-G turns, which was limited to about 7 Gs in previous aircrafts. By reclining the pilot seat to thirty degrees instead of the usual thirteen degrees and placing the control stick to the right side with an armrest, F-16 pilots could withstand and control up to 9-G turns. Also, the blended body design where the wing gradually merged with the aircraft body reduced the aerodynamic drag while increasing the available space for internal fuel storage. The increased fuel capacity and an efficient turbofan engine (General Electric F110-GE-100) give the F-16 an exceptional range (2435 miles) for an aircraft of its size.

We can see the next plateau in the military aircraft technology in the recent addition to the U.S. Air Force fighter fleet, the F-22 Raptor shown in Figs. 1.2 to 1.4. The F-22 Raptor design originated from the need to replace the aging F-15 Eagles and provide the USAF with a dominant super-fighter that will ensure air superiority for the next several decades. In spite of the F-15 Eagle's modern look, they were introduced to service back

Figure 1.2. F-22 Raptor. Photo courtesy of the U.S. Air Force.

Figure 1.3. The underside of the F-22 Raptor. Most of the armament is carried in the interior bay. Photo courtesy of the U.S. Air Force.

in 1976. Even with all the successes of the F-15 program, vast advances in military aircraft technology have taken place. Many of these advances and several new ones are embedded in the F-22 Raptor, which entered service in 2005. New materials such as advanced alloys and composite material are used in the Raptor airframe, aerodynamic surfaces, and engine components. The control is vastly improved for both routine and high-G maneuvers using fly-by-wire system. The computerized control of the F-22, as opposed to direct pilot control, allows the aircraft to perform highly unstable maneuvers. For example, the F-22 can fly at an angle of attack of sixty degrees, well beyond the stall limit of the aircraft. The power plant gets an even higher efficiency thrust, along with advanced thrust vectoring, using Pratt and Whitney pitch-vectoring turbofans. The electronic equipment is so far advanced that the F-22 can serve as an advance airborne station for electronic warfare and battlefield intelligence management. The complex radar and sensor inputs are synthesized and displayed to the pilot in integrated avionics displays to maximize the situational awareness and decision abilities of the operator. The sensitive suite of sensors is designed to always give the F-22 the first-kill option long before the opposing aircraft or targets are even aware of the presence of this stealth fighter. The airframe geometry, material, and the exhaust section have all been designed for reduced visual and electromagnetic observability, essential for survivability and preemptive strike roles. Two Pratt and Whitney engines propel the F-22 to supersonic cruise speeds and give unmatched agility with vector thrust nozzles.

Figure 1.4. F-22 showing its vertical flight capability. Photo courtesy of the U.S. Air Force.

All of the previously mentioned technological advances did not come without a high price tag. Many of the new technologies were researched and developed as part of the F-22 project. If all the development costs are added in, each F-22 carries a price tag of over $300 million. In fact, the next-generation joint strike fighter (JSF), the F-35, is under development so that these advanced technologies can be furnished at lower cost and in larger volume. The high cost of the F-22 also makes some of the existing aircraft such as the F-15, F-16, and F-18 indispensable elements of the American airborne capabilities. Table 1.2 shows some of the main specifications of the F-22.

The F-22 airframe can be divided into three major sub-frames that are manufactured by different companies. The forward fuselage along with the fins (vertical and horizontal stabilizers), flaps, ailerons, and leading-edge flaps in the wings comprise one sub-frame group that is made by Lockheed Martin in Marietta, GA. Lockheed Martin in Fort Worth, TX, constructs the complex mid-fuselage that measures 17 feet in length and 15 feet in width, prior to assembly with other sub-frames. This section houses the core of the hydraulics and electronic networks. The aft fuselage section is built by Boeing and includes the main wings, power supplies, auxiliary power units (APUs), and other sub-components. Much of the structural load on the aircraft is supported by the five titanium bulkheads in the mid-fuselage. The clipped delta wings are designed for efficiency at high speeds and have ailerons, flaperons, and leading-edge flaps to give an enlarged flight envelope. The leading-edge flaps, for example, maintain controlled flow over the wings at high angles of attack over sixty degrees. The internal space of the wings, as in other aircraft, serves as fuel tanks. The ailerons operate in opposite directions in both wings to provide roll force, while the flaperon increases lift and controls the flow at high angles of attack. The horizontal stabilizers also shield the engine exhaust radiation, in addition to performing as a pitch-control aerodynamic surface. The vertical stabilizers are angled in the same direction as the sloped aft fuselage. The heavier armaments like the AIM-120 AMRAAM GBU-30 1000-lb bombs are kept in an internal weapon bay with retractable covers, and the two AIM-9 Sidewinder missiles are also stored internally near the air intake. The internal storage decreases both the aerodynamic drag and radar reflection signatures. M61A2 20-mm-caliber Vulcan rotating cannon gives the continuous fire capability of 480 rounds. The primary airframe, the mid-fuselage, is a unified structure manufactured using an advanced casting process. Using a high-pressure injection of molten titanium in an autoclave, the complex mid-fuselage is constructed as a single structure with no welds or joints.

Table 1.2. F-22 Specifications.

Length	62.1 ft (18.9 m)
Wingspan	44.5 ft (13.56 m)
Height	16.8 ft (5.08 m)
Maximum Take-Off Weight	80,000 lb (36,288 kg)
Power Plant	2 Pratt & Whitney F119-PW-100 pitch-vectoring turbofans with afterburners
Total Thrust	70,000 lb
Maximum Speed	High altitude: Mach 2.42 or 1600 mph (2570 km/h) Low altitude: Mach 1.72 or 1140 mph (1826 km/h)
Ceiling	65,000 ft (20,000 m)
Range	2000 miles (5600 km)
Rate of Climb	N/A (classified)
Thrust-to-Weight Ratio	1.26
Maximum G-load	−3/+9.5

This method achieves high-strength integrity with reduced weight and machining time. Composite materials and specialized alloys are used for critical components to provide strength at low weight and radar signatures.

The stealth capability encompasses minimizing radar, visual, infrared, and audible signatures, with the radar being the most critical. The radar cross-section, or RCS, is a measure of the aircraft's visibility when illuminated by a radar beam and basically means the equivalent cross-sectional area of a surface if that surface were to reflect all of the incident radar energy. A large bird, for example, has an RCS of 0.01 m^2, much smaller than its actual cross-sectional area because a bird's feather does not reflect radar energy efficiently. The B-2 bomber, with somewhat earlier stealth technologies and larger dimensions, has a RCS of 0.75 m^2. The RCS of the F-22 is estimated to 0.01 m^2, about the same as a large bird and essentially invisible to the radar. First, all of the F-22 surfaces tend to form acute angles, so that the incident radar does not bounce back to the source to reveal its presence. For example, the F-22 has a cross-sectional shape of a flat triangle and straight-line features on the aircraft are replaced with W-shaped lines. Radar-absorbing paints and materials are used for all of the exposed surfaces. The rotating engine fans are a significant contributor to RCS, and in the F-22 the serpentine inlet duct does not allow the radar beam to make contact with the engine fan. Even the radar reflection from the pilot's helmet through the canopy has been taken into account. The glass canopy is plated with radar-insulating thin film while maintaining 85 percent transmission of the visible light. Thus, the entire canopy can be considered as a radar filter. The exhaust is the most critical component in minimizing infrared signatures that can be imaged by FLIR (forward-looking infrared) or IR sensors in heat-seeking missiles. The exhaust of the F-22 is designed to absorb the heat by using ceramic components, rather than conduct heat to the outside surface. Also, the horizontal stabilizers are placed to shield the thermal emission as much as possible. The camouflage paint schemes blend the aircraft into the sky when viewed from below and into the ground when observed from the top. Vapor trails and other tell-tale contrails are aerodynamically suppressed.

The Pratt and Whitney F119-PW-100 engine is another component in the F-22 that is arguably the most advanced in aircraft technology. Each of these engines generates more thrust without the afterburner than conventional engines with full afterburner power on, and its supersonic thrust is also about twice the other engines in the class. Using two of these engines to develop a total thrust of 70,000 pounds, the F-22 can travel at supersonic speeds without the afterburners for fuel-efficient high-speed cruise to the target area. This level of thrust is more than the aircraft weight and enables the F-22 to fly vertically upward much like a rocket. The F119 engine is also unique in fully integrating the vector thrust nozzle into the engine/airframe combination for a twenty-degree up/down redirection of thrust for high-G turn capabilities. The thrust vectoring is designed to enhance the turn rates by up to 50 percent in comparison to using control surfaces alone. The engine achieves all these functional characteristics with 40 percent fewer parts than conventional engines to furnish exceptional reliability and maintenance and repair access. In a design method called integrated product development, inputs from assembly line workers and air force mechanics were incorporated to streamline the entire sequence of engine production, maintenance, and repairs. These design innovations are expected to reduce the support equipment, labor, and spare parts in demand by approximately one-half. Similar to the mid-fuselage airframe, the turbine stage consisting of the disk and blades is constructed in a single, integrated metal piece for high integrity at lower weight, better performance, and thermal insulation for the turbine disk cavity. The fan and compressor blade designs went through extensive permutations and modifications using computational fluid dynamic (CFD) simulations, resulting in unprecedented efficiency in both sections. Hardware cut-and-try of different designs would have cost way too much time and money. High-strength and degradation-resistant "Alloy C" was used in key components like the compressors, turbines, and nozzles to allow the engine to run at higher temperatures, one of the important contributing factors to the increased thrust and durability of F119 engines. The combustor, the hottest component in the engine, uses oxidation-resistant, thermally insulating cobalt coatings. A digital electronic engine control device called FADEC (dual-redundant digital engine controls) not only fine-tunes the engine operating parameters to deliver the highest performance at the maximum efficiency, but also establishes responsive and precise engine operating parameters with inputs from the pilot control of the throttle and the engine/flight sensors.

The F-35 Lightening II Joint Strike Fighter (JSF) Program represents the effort to provide a capable, multi-mission aircraft while containing the budget. The F-35's price tag is about half of the F-22 Raptor's. The argument for wide adoption of this scaled-back aircraft is that the F-22's capabilities are best directed against opponents with similar technological capabilities, and with the changed geopolitical environment in the United States, F-22 Raptors are less likely to be involved in such encounters. On the other hand, emerging powers like China could in theory bring more capable aircraft into the picture, and by moving away from the F-22 production the United States may lose the capability to put a significant number of the advanced F-22s on the scene. Though somewhat smaller than the F-22 and with a single engine, the F-35 (Fig. 1.5) does contain many of the stealth technologies and has a weapons capacity of 15,000 pounds. The JSF is designed to be used across the military branches, and in addition to the standard conventional take-off and landing version (CTOL) F-35A for air force use, there will be an F-35B, the short-takeoff and vertical landing (STOVL), and an F-35C for carrier-based (CV) missions. The air force version F-35A is expected to replace the F-16 and A-10 and to augment the F-22. The navy version F-35C will augment the F/A-18E/F and will have larger wing and tail surfaces for carrier take-off and landing. The F-35C will also overcome one shortcoming of the F/A-18 by being capable of twice the range on internal fuel alone. The unique variants are in the marine STOVL version, F-35B, also planned for adoption by the British Royal Navy to replace the Sea Harrier. The short take-off is facilitated by a number of auxiliary nozzles to divert the thrust. In a normal engine, the

Figure 1.5. F-35 Lightening II, the Joint Strike Fighter. Photo courtesy of the U.S. Air Force.

jet exhaust is pushed out the nozzle at the rear of the engine to provide only forward thrust. In engines with thrust reversers, the fan stream is redirected to the forward direction to generate negative thrust. The same concept can be used to redirect the thrust to other directions by using auxiliary nozzles. For the F-35B, there is a lift nozzle that takes the fan exhaust and directs it vertically downward. Also, the pitch nozzle at the main nozzle can be turned to add a vertical component in the thrust. For control of the aircraft during this tricky maneuver, there are four additional nozzles. Nozzles control the roll angle by sending a small fraction of the main exhaust at off-horizontal angles, while two yaw nozzles generate thrust in the forward and backward off-set angles.

Reliability-driven components and manufacturing are intended to lower the maintenance costs, and advanced avionics and sensors (AN/APG-81 AESA radar) are embedded in the aircraft. A large panoramic cockpit display (PCD) and direct voice input enhance the pilot's ability to multitask. The AN/APG-81 Fire Control Radar consists of an active electronically scanned array (AESA) and is an improvement over the original radar installed on the F-22 (AN/APG-77). This sensor has both the air-to-air and air-to-ground scan/track capabilities at high resolutions and can acquire multiple targets while engaging in counter-electronic functions. Electro-optical sensors are embedded at various points on the aircraft body to detect missile and other threats, and the inputs are integrated into the AN/AAS-37 infrared search and track system. This sensor network is referred to as EOTS (electro-optical targeting system) and provides a new level of situational awareness by using multiple sensors to cover the entire spherical periphery of the aircraft and facilitates the detection, day/night vision, and fire control.

The cannon on the F-35, a 25-mm GAU-12U, is actually of larger caliber than that on the F-22 but carries less than 200 rounds with somewhat larger ammunition loads in the F-35B and C. The missiles can be mounted internally or on external pods and include up to six AIM-120 AMRAAM or AIM-132 ASRAAM. Other deployable weapons include JDAM, JSOW, HARM, SDB (small diameter bombs), and WCMD (wind-corrected munition dispenser).

Following the heavy-weight, variable-geometry-winged F-14 Tomcat, the F/A-18 Super Hornet (shown in Figs. 1.6 and 1.7) is the United States Navy's most advanced carrier-based aircraft. The current trend in military aircraft development is to fill multiple mission requirements from a single aircraft and its variants, and in this regard the F/A-18 functions as an air superiority, day/night air strikes, reconnaissance, and long-range air space control aircraft. The first series in this aircraft was introduced as the F/A-18A/B Hornet out of the Naval Fighter-Attack Experimental (VFAX)/Navy Air Combat Fighter (NACF) program in the 1970s in an effort to replace all of the aging F-14 Phantom II, A-4 Skyhawk, A-7 Corsair II, and expensive F-14 Tomcat aircraft. Advanced sensor, weapons control, and avionics including multifunction displays to switch between different attack modes allow multirole capabilities in a relative compact and cost-effective (est. $55 million per aircraft) airframe. The digital fly-by-wire control, good thrust-to-weight ratio, and aerodynamic controls offer excellent agility for this aircraft, at the expense of range that needs to be extended using organic or external fueling options. The leading edge extension (LEX), for example, are small protruding vanes on

Figure 1.6. U. S. Navy's F/A-18 Super Hornet taking off from an aircraft carrier. Its flaps are fully extended for maximum lift. Photo courtesy of the U.S. Navy.

Figure 1.7. F/A-18 carrying two 500-lb laser-guided (GBU-12) bombs under the wing and an AIM-9 Sidewinder missile at the wing tip. Photo courtesy of the U.S. Navy.

the front edge of the wings to cause turbulent vortices to be formed, energizing the flow over the wing so that it will remain attached to the wing surface at high angles of attack. This works much like the dimples on golf balls that keep the flow from separating from the surface, and thus reducing the drag of the golf ball. Other aerodynamic controls include an oversized horizontal stabilizer, trailing-edge flaperons, and vertical rudders that can translate as well as rotate. Digital fly-by-wire is a method to control the aerodynamic surfaces and therefore the aircraft movements using computer-generated outputs based on the pilot and sensor inputs. Complex and unstable flight conditions can be harnesses into highly agile maneuvers using this control method. Two General Electric F404 engines provide a maximum of 17,750 pounds of thrust per engine with the afterburner running to propel the aircraft to Mach 2 (1200 mph) at 40,000 feet. With the fully loaded aircraft weight of 37,150 pounds, this gives a thrust-to-weight ratio of just under 1. The power and agility of the aircraft have been well documented in battle situations—during the Operation Desert Storm, for example, two F/A-18s each with four 2000-lb bombs were still able to outmaneuver and destroy two Iraqi MiGs and go on to deliver the bombs on target. The integrated design and manufacturing methods also significantly improved the aircraft reliability and operability, with F/A-18s setting record levels of around-the-clock aircraft-launched delivery of munitions.

To fulfill its multi-mission roles, the F/A-18 can harness a wide range of armaments of up to 13,700 pounds at nine external hardpoints (two at wingtips, four underwing, and three fuselage). The AIM-9 Sidewinder, AIM-132 ASRAAM (advanced short-range air-to-air missile), AIM-120 AMRAAM, and AIM-7 Sparrow along with one 20-mm M61 Vulcan gun with 578 rounds are used for aerial targets. For surface targets, the AGM-45 Shrike, AGM-65 Maverick, AGM-88 HARM, SLAM-ER, JSOW, Taurus, and AGM-84 Harpoon missiles can be launched from the Hornet. The GBU-12, GBU-16, and GBU-24 laser-guided bombs and CBU-87 and CBU-89 unguided bombs are also deployed for stationary targets.

After production of nearly 400 F/A-18A and B models, upgrades were added in 1987 in the F/A-18C (single seat) and D (dual seat) versions. The night attack capability was improved by installing the NAVFLIR (navigation forward-looking infrared) pod, pilot night vision goggles and compatible cockpit lighting option, digital color moving map, and an independent multipurpose digital color display. In addition, with the F/A-18C advanced synthetic aperture ground mapping radar was added to generate the ground terrain map below under all-weather conditions for exact tracking of the aircraft flight path and target locations. A modified version of F/A-18D RC (reconnaissance version) uses the space vacated by the removal of the M61A1 cannon to mount a multifunction electro-optical suite consisting of roll-stabilized visible and infrared imagers.

The F/A-18 E/F Super Hornets overcome some of the limitations placed on the original F/A-18 on avionics, ordnance carriage, and range. The E/F aircraft are over four feet longer, have 25 precent larger wing area, and carry one-third more fuel internally than earlier versions, with the resultant increase in range by 40 percent and endurance (the amount of time that the aircraft can stay in the air) by 50 percent. The armament weight is also increased to 17,750 pounds and the newest weapons like JDAM (joint direct attack munition) and JSOW (joint standoff weapon) can be adapted for delivery. The increased weight and hardpoints allow various combinations of air-to-air and air-to-ground armaments that can be carried for versatile attack profiles. The total thrust is raised to 44,000 pounds, and low observable (stealth) features were enhanced as well. The ATFLIR (advanced targeting forward-looking infrared) was introduced in the E/F versions for night attack capability and also now used as upgrades in earlier versions.

If the above fighters are agile machines that can fly at extreme speeds and altitudes, then modern bomber aircraft like the B-1B Lancer represents a new breed of giant flying machines. B-1B Lancer is the one of the U.S. military's primary bomber aircrafts, but it has gone through a long and tumultuous history involving several cancellations of the production and changes in its mission objectives. The origin of the variable-geometry wing design for an aircraft of this size goes back to the early 1970s, where the contract was given to North America Rockwell for production of 240 of these bombers to replace the gigantic B-52 bombers. One of the mission requirements was to penetrate the opponent's air space at supersonic speeds and be able to deliver both nuclear and conventional munitions. Both low-level flight at tree-clipping 200-ft altitude and high-speed flights at Mach of 2.2 were demonstrated by the B-1A armed with AGM-69A SRAM (short-range attack missiles). The B-1 bomber production plans were cancelled by the Carter administration in 1977 in view of the escalating costs and the advances in long-range, precision missile strike capabilities. However, the flight test program continued to develop the use of synthetic aperture radar and other advanced avionics that may assist in the bomber's penetration capabilities in the future. When President Reagan took office in 1981, $20.5 billion was provided to the U.S. Air Force as a part of the Strategic Modernization Program to acquire and operate 100 of the modified B-1B bombers. The high speed was deemed less critical than the bomber's radar signature, and the inlet and wing structures were simplified along with an increase in the take-off weight from 395,000 to 477,000 pounds. The result was a final maximum speed down to Mach 1.25, but the radar cross-section was reduced significantly. As the nuclear arms negotiations reduced the number of aimed threats between the United States and Russia, the B-1B has been transitioned out of its nuclear missions since 1997 and now serves as conventional munitions launch platform. Now, the bomber is equipped with upgrades for effective delivery of guided and unguided bombs, JDAM, JSOW, WCMD, along with advanced electronic countermeasure suites including ALE-50 towed decoy countermeasures. The large capacity of the B-1B, with its defensive electronics, has been put to good use in recent years—in Afghanistan B-1B bombers were responsible for 70 percent of the JDAM delivery although they flew only 5 percent of all the sorties. Similarly in the Operation Iraqi Freedom, the B-1B carried out 22 percent of the guided weapon drops at 1 percent of the combat sorties.

The B-1B shown in Figs. 1.8 and 1.9 is designed to perform many different roles, ranging from ground-troop support, gravity bombing (unguided), precision bombing, and cruise missile launch, to strategic and tactical nuclear weapon strike capabilities, although the latter are not currently deployed in these bombers. As shown in the photograph, the B-1B features a complex variable-wing geometry. The wing is extended during low-speed flights, including take-off and landing, and retracted during high-speed, supersonic flights. The variable-design wing was implemented as one of the original tasks envisioned for the B-1B bomber was to fly intercontinental missions and then fly under the radar at extremely low altitudes to reach the target. Such a large flight envelope required the aircraft aerodynamics to be tailored depending on the flight phase, and thus the variable-wing geometry.

Figure 1.8. B-1B Lancer, the U.S. multi-role bomber with many advanced technological capabilities. Photo courtesy of the U.S. Air Force.

Figure 1.9. A photo of B-1B Lancer showing the variable-wing geometry. Photo courtesy of the U.S. Air Force.

Large, advanced electronic gears are carried by B-1Bs, including avionics and threat/weapon management systems. Since the B-1B is an air-to-ground attack aircraft, the sensors and electronics are oriented toward defense against AAM and SAM. Included are electronic jamming for illuminating radars, infrared countermeasures to thwart heat-seeking missiles, and radar location and warning systems. These components are integrated in an AN/ALQ 161A comprehensive defensive avionics package that can detect and offset missile attacks from all angles. The defensive measures include standard chaff and flares, but also include the ALE-50 AAED (advanced airborne expendable decoy). The vehicle can be remotely operated well away from the aircraft and is designed to bear a nearly identical radar signature. The avionics include inertial navigation and synthetic aperture radar with high resolution (down to one foot in planned upgrade) for finding, fixing, tracking, engaging, and assessing targets.

The weapons are stored in three bays, forward, intermediate, and aft, which have sufficient room to carry eighty-four Mk 82/Mk 62 500-lb bombs/mines, twenty-four JDAM, thirty CBU 85, twelve JSOW, and twelve Mk 65 2000-lb bombs.

The B-2 Spirit bomber is perhaps the most unique aircraft in the world; in fact, as shown in Fig. 1.10, it does not even look like an aircraft, more like a giant flying stingray with odd edges and no vertical surfaces. If the F-22 Raptor advanced all aspects of aircraft technology, the B-2 is at the forefront of stealth technology. The B-2 does not fly at supersonic speeds nor is it highly maneuverable, but its low-observable design allows it to penetrate all currently known radar-based defenses and deliver conventional and nuclear armaments. The stealth design encompasses not just radar signature but also infrared, acoustic, visual, and electromagnetic. Another bar set by the B-2 bomber is its price tag—over $2 billion, which is nearly fifteen times that of the F-22 Raptor and twice that of a

Table 1.3. B-1B Lancer Specifications.

Crew	4
Length	146 ft (44.5 m)
Wingspan	137 ft (41.8 m) extended, 79 ft (24.1 m) swept
Height	34 ft (10.4 m)
Empty Weight	326,000 lb (87,1000 kg)
Maximum Take-Off Weight	477,000 lb (216,400 kg)
Power Plant	4 General Electric F101-GE-102 turbofans with afterburners
Total Thrust	30,780 × 4 lbf (pound force)
Maximum Speed	950 mph (1529 km/h), Mach 1.25
Ceiling	60,000 ft (18,000 m)
Range	7456 miles (11,988 km)
Ordnance Capacity	3 internal bays for 75,000 lb (34,000 kg)
	Optional external hardpoints for additional 59,000 lb (27,000 kg)
Armaments	Up to 144 GBU-39 bombs,
	84 Mk-82AIR general purpose bombs,
	81 Mk-82 bombs,
	30 CBU-87 cluster bomb units,
	24 GBU-31 GPS-guided bombs,
	17 GBU-38 GPS-guided bombs,
	24 Mk-84 bombs,
	24 AGM-158 ground-attack missiles,
	Or 12 AGM-154 ground attack missiles.

Figure 1.10. Photographs of B-2 Spirit bomber. Photos courtesy of the U.S. Air Force.

Los Angeles–class nuclear attack submarine. This means that the B-1B crew of two is entrusted with a piece of equipment at about $1 billion per crew, including the training flights. There are as of 2008 only twenty-one of the B-2 Spirit bombers, and at a given time about fifteen of them may be operational after counting out routine maintenance, the permanent test aircraft, and training uses. This precludes the use of the B-2 for all but the highest-priority targets.

The B-2B constitutes the ultra-stealth component of the U.S. Air Force's large-volume bombing capabilities, along with B-1B and the classic B-52 bombers. B-2B's unparalleled stealth capabilities are best directed at high-value, heavily defended targets, such as sophisticated anti-aircraft radar installations, deep command and control centers, and key military targets. Without refueling, this aircraft can fly for 6000 nautical miles for intercontinental bombing missions. During Operations Enduring Freedom and Iraqi Freedom, the B-2B flew directly from Whiteman Air Force Base in Missouri to Afghanistan and Iraq. The wingspan of 172 feet is about one and half times the aircraft length of 69 feet. Without vertical stabilizers, a combination of ailerons, elevons, and the center stabilizing elevator control the aerodynamics of the aircraft. Maximum take-off weight with full fuel tanks and armaments is 336,500 pounds, out of which 40,000 is the weapons weight. Four General Electric F118-GE-100 engines of 17,300 pounds of thrust each power the aircraft, and these engines are well embedded into the airframe for low infrared and radar signatures. One of the B-2B mission requirements is to deliver nuclear munitions, and for that reason is mandated by the Department of Defense to be equipped with a survivable communication for receiving orders or recall of orders to launch. It is estimated that the advanced extremely high frequency (EHF) satellite communication constellation is used to provide a highly functional, highly survivable network for such purpose, with B-2B communication equipment integrated to this network. In spite of its futuristic appearance, the B-2 aircraft was developed in the 1980s and the first operational vehicle, the Sprit of Missouri, delivered in 1993. Some of the planned upgrades are a digital engine control system to monitor the engine health and operating parameters to optimize the engine performance and reliability. Although the details of the stealth technology are not available, the flat-wing shape with no vertical surfaces, full engine shrouds, non-reflecting composite materials, and coatings are attributed to the overall low observability. To counter future radar and detection systems, there are plans to yet reduce the observable signatures across all spectra.

The weapons bay can hold a combination of nuclear, conventional, and precision bombs up to a 40,000-lb payload. Nuclear weapons options include sixteen B61, sixteen B83, sixteen AGM-129, ACM, sixteen AGM-131, and SRAM 2. For conventional bombs, eighty Mk82 500-lb bombs, sixteen Mk 62 mines, sixteen Mk 84 2000-lb bombs, thirty-six CBU 87, thirty-six CBU 89, and thirty-six CBU 97 small weapons dispensers can be carried. For precision, guided weapons, the B-2B can deliver eight GBU 27, twelve JDAM, eight AGM-154, JSOW, eight AGM-137, and TSSAMs. Some of these ground-attack weapons are described below.

JDAM, JSOW, and Guided Munitions

Aside from air-to-ground missiles discussed in Chapter 2, there is an array of weapons for ground targets. A new genre in the use of air power in three-dimensional battlefield would be evidenced during U.S. operations against Iraq, first during Operation Desert Storm in 1991 through much televised footage of smart bombs going through the crosshair mark shown on the video screen. Due to the highlighted nature of this footage, the prevailing conception at the time was that the bombing was performed predominantly in this precision, surgical mode. During Operation Desert Storm only 5 percent of the munitions delivered were of the laser-guided type. However, that 5 percent accounted for 84 percent of the total ordnance cost. Moreover, all of the guided munitions required clear weather to enable the target-illuminating beams, and also the claim of "one target, one bomb" by the manufacturers of laser-guided bombs (LGB) would prove to be false—the average number of LGB released per target would turn out to be four. Other limitations arose in the damage assessments, and in the end more than 50 tons of both unguided and guided bombs would be expended on targets that were already destroyed and more on false targets such as Scud launcher decoy models. The performance and number of guided weapons of course significantly increased during Operation Enduring Freedom in 2001, as more LGB-sensor combinations and aircraft to deliver them were available. Still, the LGB required the target to be illuminated by the bomber aircraft, and thus the number of targets that could be engaged during a sortie was limited. For this reason, large, 2000-lb LGB tended to be used against high-priority targets.

Precision bombing was the dream of the World War II air campaign planners because exorbitantly large numbers of bombers were flown to ensure the targets were hit, often repeatedly over the same target. The idea behind precision bombing is a simple one— guide the bombs to within feet of the target as opposed to thousands of feet that was typical of bombs dropped from 30,000-ft altitude. The aircraft speed and altitude were the primary variables determining the bomb impact points but wind, poor aiming, and limited visibility contributed significantly to the uncertainty in the final outcome. Late in this war, radio-steered bombs called AZON (Azimuth Only) were successfully used against narrow targets such as critical bridges. As the name "Azimuth Only" suggests, the bomb path could only be controlled in the lateral directions, but by aligning the aircraft in the direction of the length of the bridge sufficient accuracy could be attained by radio control of the tail fins. During the Korean War, improved version RAZON with both the range and azimuth controls was again used successfully to knock out high-priority targets. The first laser-guided bomb idea was conceived by a forward-thinking defense steering committee in the 1950s, even before the first laser was actually built and demonstrated. The idea was passed to U.S. Army scientists, then to U.S. Air Force engineers, and finally to Texas Instruments in a $99,000 contract while the Vietnam War was going on. Texas Instruments came up with the prototype "Paveway" laser-guided bombs, in which the target was illuminated by a hand-held laser gun. Later, more user-friendly laser illumination using bore-sighted lasers and TV monitors would be used. The principle was identical to the modern LGB where the sensor on the nose of the bomb seeks the point of maximum laser light being reflected from the target and turns the tails fins to home in. In fact, with much improved sensors, illuminating pods, and control, the modern LGB manufactured by Raytheon Corporation still bears the name "Paveway." During the Vietnam War era, each Paveway LGB would cost about $8000 but due to their unprecedented accuracy was considered equivalent to about twenty-five conventional bombs in effectiveness. The American forces used a total of 25,000 Paveway LGBs during the Vietnam War; however, the impact of this technology was nearly completely lost as the rationale for the war itself was increasingly unjustifiable, and none of the methods succeeded in achieving the U.S. objectives in the final outcome.

As noted above, the Paveway-series LGB is the standard guided munition of the United States armed forces, with size ranging from GBU-12 Paveway-II at 500 lbs to GBU-15 and GBU-24 Paveway-III at 2000 lbs. These LGBs work in conjunction with various targeting pods such as LANTIRN and AN/AAS-35 Pave Penny. To filter out ambient light interference, the pulse repetition frequency of the illuminating laser is synchronized with the seeker sensor prior to launch. As noted above, LGB does require continuous engagement by the bomber aircraft, and to improve on this aspect autonomous guided munitions have been developed as in JDAM and JSOW.

JDAM (Fig. 1.11), or joint direct attack munition, for example is a cost-effective tailkit that can be adapted to existing conventional bombs to provide accurate delivery. The tailkit consists of inertial navigation system (INS) and GPS guidance along with an adapter interface and aerodynamic surfaces to direct the bomb to within 30-ft radius of the intended target coordinates. There is also a wraparound piece with aero-stabilizing strakes on the main body of the bomb. The INS and GPS can operate effectively regardless of the visibility conditions and altitude, and JDAM-equipped bombs can be released from up to fifteen miles away from the target at high altitudes. The bomb drops under gravity, and the JDAM guides the free fall toward the target by controlling the aerodynamic surfaces. The INS and GPS function autonomously based on its preprogrammed target coordinates and thus do not require further external inputs after release. 250-, 500-, 1000-, and 2000-lb bombs (Mk-80, Mk-81, Mk-83, and Mk-84) can be fitted with JDAM, at which time these munitions change designations to GBU-29, GBU-30, GBU-31, and GBU-32. JDAM can also be integrated with advanced warheads on heavier GBUs for hard-target penetration. For example, the boosted unitary penetrator (BUP) has rocket propellants around a dense metal warhead that are ignited on deceleration sensor input to maximize the acceleration into the hardened surfaces. WCMD is a simpler version of JDAM where only INS guidance is used to compensate for the wind drift during the free fall.

The AGM-154 JSOW (Fig. 1.12), joint stand-off weapon, is a similar concept except more range and control are afforded using small wings to allow the bomb to glide to the target, as opposed to simply controlling the gravity fall trajectory in JDAM. The range is enhanced to up to forty miles, and therefore the delivery vehicle can be away from the threat area. In addition, different sub-munitions of 1000- to 1500-lb range can be loaded

Figure 1.11. Joint direct attack munition (JDAM). Photo courtesy of the U.S. Air Force.

Figure 1.12. Joint stand-off weapon (JSOW) being lifted up to aircraft flight deck. Photo courtesy of the U.S. Navy.

on the JSOW so that JSOW functions like an independent bomber using sensor guidance on each sub-munition. The aircraft carrying JSOW releases this gliding device, and the INS/GPS guidance directs the JSOW path to the target area. On reaching the target coordinates, sub-munition release is autonomously performed. For example, multiple "bomblets" are delivered from the AGM-154A to be released at multiple target points. The AGM-154B version carries six armor-penetrating sub-munitions with individual infrared sensors to release shape-charged projectiles against detected targets.

ADVANCED RUSSIAN AIRCRAFT AND THE EUROFIGHTER

The major Russian counterparts in advanced fighter aircraft are the MiG-29 Fulcrum (shown in Fig. 1.13) and Su-30 Flanker-C. There is a later design, MiG-31; however, due to production and maintenance problems, the MiG-35 Fulcrum E are primarily produced and also exported by Russia. The Russian jet fighters are produced by two main manufacturers, Mikoyan and Sukhoi, and their fighters bear respective designations of MiG and Su. The MiG-29 and Su-30 programs were developed in response to the U.S. "FX" program that resulted in the F-15 Eagle. What started as the Russian advanced tactical fighter (*Perspektivnyi Frontovoi Istrebitel*) was divided into two separate development programs: a "heavy advanced tactical fighter" that became the Su-27 Flanker and the "light advanced tactical fighter" that is the MiG-29. The MiG-29 entered service in 1983 and has been exported to many countries such as India, Germany, Iran, Syria, North Korea, and the former Eastern Bloc nations. Su-30 is one of the modernized versions based on the Su-27 frame that include variants such as the Su-28 Trainer, the Su-33 Flanker-D for carrier version, and the

Figure 1.13. MiG-29 Fulcrum firing an air-to-air missile during a low-altitude flight. Photo courtesy of the U.S. Department of Defense.

fighter-bomber Su-34 Fullback. The Su-30 (Fig. 1.14) features many aeronautical technology advances such as vectored-thrust engine, high angle-of-attack capability, and powerful avionics. The Su-30 has a fly-by-wire control with relaxed stability (meaning that the aircraft will be out of control without the fly-by-wire system in place). The high maneuverability afforded by the fly-by-wire control allows Su-30s to perform impressive stunts in the air, such as Pugachev's Cobra (a full 360-degree turn in the pitch axis while turning a somersault loop). With a price tag of approximately $50 million as of 2007, these Russian aircrafts are widely adopted by the world's various air forces.

The Su-30 is a dual-seat multimission aircraft with advanced technologies. The main wing is made of titanium panels, defensive electronics are embedded in the leading edge, and on the right wing tip is the Gsh-301 30-mm cannon. In addition to the main wing and the tail stabilizers, Su-30 has a small canard (forward wing) spanning 6.4 m (21 ft) at a sweep angle of 53.5 degrees. The canard is automatically rotated at high angles of attack to optimize the aerodynamics and also adds to the lift of the aircraft during take-off and landing. The thrust vectoring, fly-by-wire, and aerodynamic surfaces produce exceptional agility. It can perform a maneuver called "Pugachev's Cobra" where the aircraft pitches up, tilts backward, and regains forward pitch angle to continue on a horizontal flight. The aircraft can also do several turns in a controlled flat spin on the horizontal plane. Such tailspins can occur without control in dual-engine aircraft when one of the engines flames out, but the Su-30 does these spin maneuvers under full aerodynamic control. The power plant is two Saturn AL-31FP afterburning turbofan engines with sufficient thrust and efficiency for Mach 2 and a 3000-km range. The unique aspect of the power plant is the dual asymmetric thrust vector control on each engine, with 15 degree pitch up or down angles. However, the pitch axes are different for the two engines by 32 degrees so that the thrust can be directed to any angle when operated with other aerodynamics surfaces.

At 72.8 ft (21.9 m) length and with a 48 ft (14.7 m) wingspan, the Su-30 is larger than the F-22 and seats two pilots in tandem. The cockpit is filled with modern displays and

Figure 1.14. Su-30 Flanker-C with the air brake applied during landing. Photo courtesy of the U.S. Air Force.

controls with seven LCD multifunction and HUD (heads-up) displays. The rear cockpit has the targeting displays and weapons control. A large pulse Doppler phase array radar (Phazotron N010 Zhuk-27) is in the forward radome, and a rear-facing radar is installed in the tail cone. To carry out multiple missions, a variety of armaments of up to 8000 kg can be loaded on twelve external hardpoints, along with one or two sensor pods. As noted in

Table. 1.4. MiG-29 Fulcrum and Su-30 Flanker-C Specifications.

	MiG-29, Fulcrum	*Su-30 Flanker-C*
Manufacturer	Mikoyan Design Bureau	Sukhoi Corporation
Crew	1	2
Length	57 ft (17.4 m)	72.8 ft (21.9 m)
Wingspan	37.3 ft (11.4 m)	48 ft (14.7 m)
Height	15.5 ft (4.7 m)	21.5 ft (6.4 m)
Empty Weight	24,450 lb (11,000 kg)	39,021 lb (17,700 kg)
Maximum Take-Off Weight	37,000 lb (16,800 kg)	72,752 lb (33,000 kg)
Power Plant	2 Klimov RD-33 K turbofans with afterburners	2 Saturn AL-31FL turbofans
Total Thrust	44,400 lbf	27,500 × 2 lbf
Maximum Speed	1518 mph (2445 km/h)	1320 mph (2125 km/h)
Range	1800 mi (2900 km)	1860 mi (3000 km)
Service Ceiling	59,060 ft (18,013 m)	57,410 ft (17,5000 m)
Rate of Climb	65,000 ft/min	45,275 ft/min
Guns	1 30-mm GSh-30-1 cannon (150 rounds)	1 30-mm Gsh-301 cannon (150 rounds)

Figure 1.15. Su-33 Flanker-D at a high angle of attack maneuver. Photo courtesy of the U.S. Department of Defense.

Chapter 2, Russia has an arsenal of capable missiles, and air-to-air and air-to-ground missiles, gravity bombs, and unguided rockets (80, 130, and 250 mm) are used on the Su-30.

The Eurofighter shown in Fig. 1.17 is Europe's answer to the American and Russian advanced fighter aircrafts. Designed by a consortium of the Italian Alenia Aeronautica, BAE (British Aerospace) Systems, and EADS (European Aeronautic Defense and Space),

Figure 1.16. German Panavia Tornado GRMk1 fighter. Photo courtesy of the U.S. Department of Defense.

Figure 1.17. The Eurofighter. Photo courtesy of the U.S. Department of Defense.

the Eurofighter is a sophisticated aircraft with most of the advanced technology found in U.S. and Russian aircraft and also a price tag near the level of the F-22 Raptor. This aircraft uses canard and delta wing configuration, similar to the Swedish Saab Viggen. Two afterburning turbofans power the aircraft to a maximum speed of Mach 2 and a supercruise speed of Mach 1.2 without afterburning, similar to the F-22. Many of the armaments used by the United States and European nations are common, and the Eurofighter carries AIM-9 Sidewinder, AIM-132 ASRAAM, AIM-120 AMRAAM, AGM-84 Harpoon, AGM-88 HARM, and JDAM, along with an assortment of missiles of European origin. The gun is a German 27-mm Mauser BK-27 cannon.

As seen by the armaments, the Eurofighter reflects the current worldwide need for fighter aircraft that can perform a variety of missions. The Eurofighter incorporates multi-role attack capabilities that include (1) air interdiction using a large weapons payload over long ranges and multiple sensor systems; (2) close fire support for ground operations based on long flight endurance, ground-target tracking, and air-to-ground armaments; (3) suppression of enemy air defense (SEAD) using sophisticated avionics and sensors; and (4) maritime attack again using a versatile set of armaments and sensors against surface and submarine vessels.

AIRCRAFT PROPULSION

We look briefly at missile propulsion systems in the next chapter, one of which is the gas-turbine engine for cruise missiles. Now, the gas-turbine engines are exclusively used in military aircrafts in various forms and also in helicopters, ships, and some tanks. Although

many industrialized nations can assemble military aircraft, the complexity and technological advances inherent in modern military gas-turbine engines limit the number of
sources to a handful. In the United States, General Electric and Pratt & Whitney are the
primary procurement sources for military gas-turbine engines, while Rolls Royce, Eurojet,
and CFM International supplies the European aerospace industry. Eurojet is a consortium
of partner companies including Rolls-Royce (Great Britain), Avio (Italy), ITP (Spain),
and MTU Aero Engines (Germany).

In turbofans, the air is ingested by the engine inlet, which in aerospace terminology is
also called a diffuser because one of its functions is to control the speed of air before it gets
to the compressor. The aircraft speed can be anything from zero (during start-up) to supersonic, but the engine components like the compressor, combustor, and turbines are designed to work only for a range of air speeds coming through. So the inlet is shaped or its
shape altogether varied in variable-geometry inlets to control the amount and speed of air
coming into the engine. The compressor, as the name suggests, sequentially increases the
pressure of air going through. Its operation is analogous to fans: By rotating aerodynamically shaped blades you can increase the pressure downstream of the blades. Compressors
in high-performance engines may have twenty or more stages of blades, so they constitute
a large bulk of the engine. The fuel is injected in the combustor, and with swirl vanes and
swirl injectors the fuel is mixed thoroughly with air and the flame stabilized. If the air
speed into the combustor is mismatched with the flame condition, then a potentially dangerous flame-out condition can occur. With flame-out, the engine thrust is completely lost
in that engine, which is not good either in single- or twin-engine aircraft. With engine
sensors and controls, along with combustor design, such conditions are infrequent; however, most aircraft engines are equipped with high-altitude (cold condition) relight capabilities. The turbine, in principle, is the reverse operation of the compressor, except that
the turbine aerodynamics are somewhat different since it is usually easier to turn turbines
using high-pressure, high-energy air.

A major feature of gas-turbine engines used in high-performance aircraft is the afterburner added to the turbofan (see Fig. 1.18). The afterburner adds yet more energy to the
flow through the engine to provide boost in the engine thrust, at a cost of very high fuel
consumption. During normal engine operations, you would not see the orange-color glow
of flame since all the burning occurs well inside the engine in the combustor. With
the afterburner on, the flame is stabilized just inside the nozzle making it highly visible.

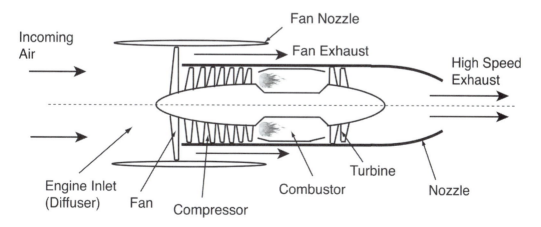

Figure 1.18. Gas-turbine engine with afterburner.

So running the afterburner is the high-throttle engine operation that can give the aircraft quick bursts of speed used in high-G maneuvers, take-offs, pursuits, or evasions. After-burners are essentially a large tube with fuel injectors and flame stabilizers. Since gas-turbine engines ingest much more air than is necessary to burn all of the fuel in the main combustor, there is still plenty of air mixed with combustion gas coming out of the main combustor. The gas temperature is already very high even after expending some energy in turning the turbine, and therefore adding fuel to this hot stream will automatically ignite the fuel and air mixture. All that is needed to continuously burn fuel in the afterburner is a metal frame to stabilize the flame (appropriately called flame stabilizers) as shown in the figure. Without the flame stabilizer to slow down the flow speed, the flame will simply blow out of the afterburner. Using this combination of afterburner fuel injection and flame sta-bilizers, much energy can be added to the gas stream, which is then accelerated out the nozzle, providing large thrust.

In contrast, the fan operation gives the gas-turbine engine efficiency and therefore range under cruise conditions. The fan imparts energy and momentum to the air flow to provide positive thrust. Since all aircraft need a certain range and speed to be effective, gas-turbine engines are designed with a balance of efficiency and maximum thrust.

The level of technology that goes into modern gas-turbine engines pushes the operating limits of the gas-turbine engines to a point where these power plants can generate thrust force in excess of the aircraft weight. To achieve this level of performance, engine compo-nents operate at extreme conditions, high rpms, and high temperatures. The compressor and turbine axes are connected and can rotate at speeds up to 10,000 rpm in modern gas-turbine engines. That is about 167 turns per second. As anyone who has visited typical amusement parks can attest, anything turning at high speeds tends to force everything outward. If that object is a compressor or turbine blade consisting of the weight of the metal alloy, then the rotation exerts tremendous stress on the material. Should even a small fragment break off into the whirling cascade of turbine blades, it will instantly spell the end of the engine. Moreover, everything from the combustor onward is subject to temperatures in excess of 2800 °F (about 1550 °C). The main combustor and the after-burner temperatures can actually be higher. Adding to all those effects is that throughout the gas-turbine engine the operating pressure is much higher than the ambient. In fact, the higher the pressure is raised by the compressor the more efficient the gas-turbine be-comes. All of these operations are precisely controlled using sensors and electronic control to give the desired engine response and performance.

The Pratt & Whitney F119-100 turbofan engine with a thrust-vector nozzle used in the F-22 Raptors is shown in Fig. 1.19. The F119-PW-100 is the most advanced gas-turbine engine at this time. Although variable inlets and nozzles were used in many previous military engines, they were only designed to expand or contract to maximize the nozzle flow acceleration. In the F119-100 engine, the nozzle geometry not only optimizes the jet acceleration but also can be used to turn the direction of the exhaust jet. This is analogous to turning the screw angle on small boats: It turns the boat a lot quicker than using the rudder. Similarly, aircraft maneuvers are conventionally made by using aerodynamic sur-faces—ailerons on the main wing and vertical and horizontal tails. The +/– 20 degree turn capability in the pitch direction for the vectored nozzle allows much more rapid turns.

The detailed geometry of the F119-PW-100 engine is not yet available, but we can look at a typical variable-geometry nozzle used in supersonic aircraft as in Fig. 1.21. The vari-able-geometry nozzles consist of pie-shaped metal plates that can be extended or retracted using multiple hydraulics. The main functions of the variable-geometry nozzle are to ad-just the flow area to optimize the thrust for the given engine operation and to provide re-verse thrust and thrust vectoring as in F119-PW-100. During cruise operation, the nozzle

Figure 1.19. F119-100 thrust-vectoring gas-turbine engine used in F-22 Raptors undergoing test. Photo courtesy of the U.S. Department of Defense.

Figure 1.20. F-35 engine.

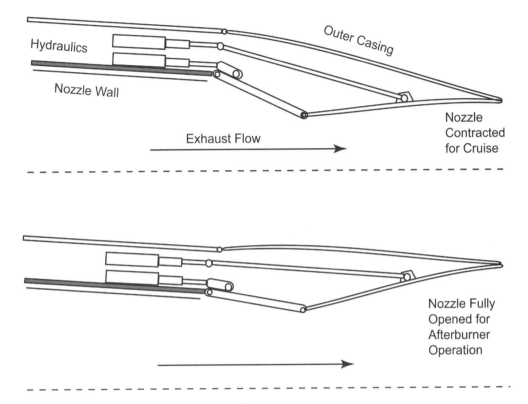

Figure 1.21. Details of variable-geometry nozzle.

is retracted because the engine flow is small. During afterburning operation, the nozzle is fully opened. Also, for supersonic exhaust the nozzle geometry converges first and diverges as shown by the shape of the internal nozzle wall in Fig. 1.21. The reason for this convergent-divergent shape is that although flow accelerates with decreasing flow area at subsonic speeds (convergent section), the reverse is true if the flow becomes supersonic. The flow accelerates when the flow area increases! Thus, the shape ensures that the maximum exhaust velocity is achieved through the nozzle.

If the variable nozzles on military jets are easily noticeable, the inlets in some of the advanced aircraft serve equally important functions but are harder to see because the engine inlets are merged with the aircraft body. The aircraft speed varies from zero (during startup and sometimes in mid-air) to supersonic, and the function of the inlet is to capture the air needed for the engine operation and also to tailor it so that the engine can operate smoothly. At supersonic speeds, shocks will form at any surface that is in the way of the flow, and therefore inlets must control these shocks so that the engine flow does not deviate from design conditions. One way to handle such a large range of airflow requirements is to again use variable-geometry inlet. Although not all aircraft are equipped with such inlets, they make the overall engine operation more efficient.

Again, we can look at the F-15 Eagle variable-geometry inlet in Figs. 1.22 and 1.23. It has three ramps that are controlled by a set of hydraulics to bypass doors and bleed exits to send out excess air. Of course, the pilot does not control any of these hydraulics. The sensors and controllers automatically determine and set the optimum configurations for the inlet ramps. Fig. 1.22 shows the schematic of the F-15 inlet system, and the bleed exits and the bypass door (in its closed position) are also shown in a close-up photo of the F-15 Eagle (Fig. 1.23).

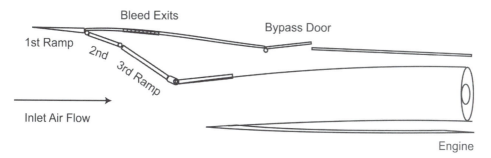

Figure 1.22. A schematic of the F-15 variable-geometry inlet involving three ramps and bypass exits.

Table 1.5 shows some of the specs for military gas-turbine engines. The engine designations are given first, then the maximum thrust at the sea level. TSFC stands for "thrust-specific fuel consumption" and indicates how much fuel is consumed per hour to develop one pound of thrust ((lbm/hr)/lbf). Lbf is the symbol for one pound of thrust, while lbm is the pound mass. OPR is the overall compressor pressure ratio. The higher the OPR, the more efficient the engine is, but it also makes the engine heavier and more expensive. The bypass ratio is how much air is being sent to the fan section in comparison to the airflow that goes through the core part of the engine. Turbine inlet temperature is the temperature of the air leaving the combustor and entering the turbine. It is indicative of the maximum thrust that the engine can deliver.

The smallest gas-turbine engine in Table 1.5 is the F107-WR-101 used for air-launched cruise missiles, and it is only 12 inches in diameter. Many of the features found

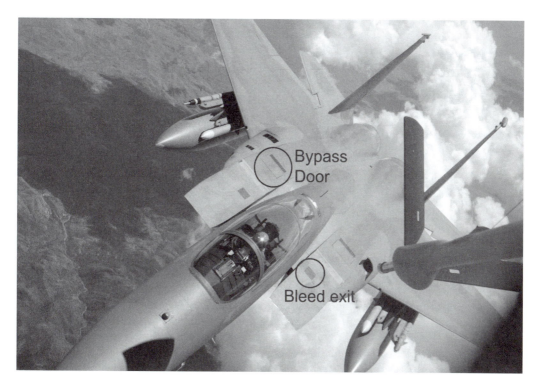

Figure 1.23. A close-up photo of the F-15 Eagle showing the details of the inlet. Photo courtesy of the U.S. Air Force.

Table 1.5. Specifications for Some Gas-Turbine Engines for Military Aircraft.

Engine Model Number	Maximum Thrust (lbf) at Sea Level	TSFC	OPR	D (in)	L (in)	Weight (lb)	Bypass Ratio	Turbine Inlet Temp(°F)	Aircraft
F100-PW-229	22,000	2.05	23.0	47	191	3036	0.4	2700	F-15, F-16
F101-GE-102	30,780	2.460	26.8	55	181	4480	1.91	2550	B-1B
F107-WR-101	635	0.685	13.8	12	48.5	141	N/A	N/A	Cruise Missiles
F110-GE-100	28,620	2.08	30.4	47	182	3895	0.80	N/A	F-16
F118-GE-100	19,000	N/A	N/A	N/A	N/A	N/A	N/A	N/A	B-2
TF30-P-111	25,100	2.45	21.8	49	242	3999	0.73	2055	F-111F
TF34-GE-100	9065	0.37	20.0	50	100	1421	6.42	2234	A-10

in other engines are skipped for this engine for reducing weight and cost. Not much information on the F118-GE-100 engines is available to maintain its stealth category for the B-2, where the engine is used. For the A-10 attack aircraft, the performance of the engine (TF34-GE-100) is exchanged for gain in range (large bypass ratio) and also survivability.

CLASSIC AIRCRAFT AND THEIR ARMAMENTS

Compared to the modern array of beyond-visual-range (BVR) aircraft-borne armaments, the classical air duels involved close-in daring maneuvers and simple weapons. Early weapons used in the 1900s included handguns, rifles, grappling hooks, and flechettes. The grappling hook was used in the hope of damaging the flimsy airplane structures or ensnaring the propeller blades. The flechettes were pointed steel rods dropped from the aircraft to puncture steel helmets worn by the ground troops. Daredevil acts seem to be the main discerning characteristics in men flying these early fighters. A U.S. Army pilot named Jake Fickel was known to fire his rifle from the aircraft wing, unharnessed, and hit ground targets. A RFC (Royal Flying Corps) Captain L.G. Hawker is credited with downing three German aircraft just using a single-shot Martini carbine that was mounted diagonally so that he could not possibly hit his own propeller blades with his bullets. Machine guns were available by this time, and their potential in aircraft battles was soon realized. However, for an aircraft armament to be effective it needed to be in line with the aircraft so that the pilot simply guided the aircraft toward the target and then commenced firing. It was for the same reason preferable to have the gun mounted directly in front of the pilot, to shoot through the front propellers. To avoid mowing down the blades, Sopwith-Kauper interrupter gear was invented. The mechanism had a roller that was turned by the propeller axis to actuate a lever to interrupt or synchronize the machine gun firing, so that the bullets would be fired only when the blades cleared the path. During World War I, the Hotchkiss 7.7 mm gun was the standard among the Allies' observer aircraft. This gun had a rotating bolt driven forward by a spiral spring, while the backward re-cocking was accomplished by the gas action from the barrel pressure tap. Since aircraft speed and altitude had a cooling effect on the gun, the heavy cooling jacket was discarded, and in its place more rounds (ninety-seven in comparison to forty-seven in the infantry version) were carried in the ammunition drum.

The aircraft provided an ideal platform for dropping bombs because direct visual contact of the targets could be made. Accurately hitting the targets with the bombs and returning safely was, however, fraught with extreme dangers both from ground fire and aircraft attacks. As a precursor to the heavy bombers to come in later wars, the bi-plane bombers during this period were stocked with multiple machine guns and gunners to man them apart from the pilot(s). Sikorsky's Llya Muromets bomber, for example, had three forward machine guns pointing at different pitch angles and one rear-facing gun, so that it took a crew of two gunners and one pilot. A heavy German bomber, the Zeppelin-Staaken R VI, with four engines was manned by a crew of seven: commander, pilot, copilot, radio operator, fuel attendant, and two mechanics, some of whom doubled as gunners to fire five machine guns. The four engines (either Mercedes D.Iva or Mayback Mb.Iva) were mounted on the wings with two facing forward and the other two rearward for push-pull operation. The aircraft maximum speed was 84 mph, but it could carry 4400 pounds of bombs over a range of 500 miles. The bombs were stored either internally or externally in these bombers and released manually while flying at relatively low altitudes to improve accuracy. In 1914, there weren't any bombs weighing more than 22 pounds that ware dropped from aircraft; however, by the end of World War I the aircraft bombs proliferated to include the 16-lb Hale and Cooper, a 65-lb high explosive, 230-lb anti-submarine bombs, and a huge 3,307-lb bomb.

By World War II, the aircraft were much better but the basic armaments were still machine guns and cannons for the fighters. The stronger engines and airframes meant that bigger and more of these could be carried. The German Focker-Wulf Fw190 "Wurger," for example, had a twelve-cylinder inverted-V engine (BMW 801 D-2 radial) and could fly at 450 mph over a range of 520 miles. This aircraft could pack a punch of up to seven guns and cannons, two 13-mm MG131s fired from the fuselage, two 20-mm MG151 underneath, and another two MG151 from the wings, where one of the wing guns could be replaced by a twin MG151 pack. The Wurger was a lesser known aircraft from this era but was a highly successful fighter with 20,000 manufactured between 1941 and 1944. MG131 was made by the famed Rheinmetal Werks, and the electrical firing mechanism made the synchronization extremely accurate even at a firing rate of 900 rounds per minute. Armor-piercing and standard bullets could be fired at muzzle velocity above 710 m/s (2330 fps). The British Spitfire was also heavily equipped with multiple guns—eight 7.7 mm Browning machine guns with 350 rounds each in the early versions and two 20-mm Hispano Mk II cannons and four Browning machine guns in the later versions. Hispano cannons were widely used by the Allied aircraft, in which the dual action of gas-pressure and blowback automated the firing mechanism to provide a high firing rate and muzzle velocity of 800 m/s (2625 feet per second [fps]). The Spitfire had a light alloy monocoque fuselage, meaning that the fuselage was essentially a thin-walled shell with the stressed skin bearing the structural load along with some bulkhead rings. The wing also used stressed-skin covering along with a single spar, while the fabric-covered control surfaces were used for tail stabilizers. The single-spar design refers to one vertical load-bearing beam in the wing. Other possible wing structural designs are a box beam with two spars and multi-spar structures for larger aircrafts. Pure aluminum was predominantly used for stressed skins, and where strength was required an aluminum alloy called Duralumin with added cooper was used. For exposed elements, Duralumin with pure aluminum coating on the outside was also frequently applied to resist corrosion. The stressed skin on monocoque, for example, could be less than a millimeter thick, and for the wing covering the thickness could vary from 0.7 to 1.4 mm. A two-blade fixed-pitch DeHavilland wooden propeller was first used on Spitfire but was later changed to a three-blade propeller that could alter the blade pitch angle from high to low, and then finally to a fixed-pitch three-blade propeller. The propulsion, with this propeller being rotated by Rolls-Royce Merlin supercharged V-12 engine, developed a top speed of 397 mph and higher during dive.

The American fighter aircraft design during the early part of World War II emphasized ruggedness, or survivability in modern terms. The P-47 Thunderbolt shown in Fig. 1.24, for example, had a beefed-up structure that weighed 4000 pounds more than comparable single-engine fighters. To propel this aircraft, an equally large engine—the Pratt & Whitney Double Wasp XR-2800-21—was placed in a fat cowling. This engine had eighteen supercharged cylinders that were radially arranged in two rows, and developed 2000 hp at take-off and 2300 hp at 31,000 feet. During battle, the P-47's toughness saved many pilots' lives—the aircraft could take multiple hits on wings and control surfaces and still fly. In one incident, a P-47 had about four feet of the wing torn off after colliding with a steel pole during a mission over France but still made the flight back over to the base in England. The size of the aircraft allowed six to eight 0.5-in Browning machine guns with over 400 rounds per gun and up to 2500 lbs worth of bombs or ten HVAR (high-velocity aircraft rockets). Also, it could fly at high altitudes and the aircraft range was over 900 miles, about twice that of the Fw190 and Spitfire. However, maneuverability was not one of the outstanding traits of this 7-ton beast, and the aircraft could not keep up with the German Fw 190 during dogfights. Thus, the pilots in the European theater improvised by attacking German fighters from high altitudes, making a high-speed dive pass against German aircrafts and disengaging back to high altitudes because tight-turning dogfights would be too much for P-47s. The P-51 Mustang (Fig. 1.25) that became available in the later parts of World War II immediately proved to be superior in many aspects. The powerful Packard engine had a two-stage supercharger for the twelve-cylinder engines, and this gave the aircraft an exceptional speed of 437 mph and a range of 1650 miles with external tanks. The Mustangs proved to be invaluable for bomber escorts over Germany but saw little action in the Pacific theater where the Mitsubishi A6M "Zero" aircraft wreaked havoc during the early parts of the war.

Figure 1.24. P-47 Thunderbolt. Photo courtesy of the U.S. Air Force.

Figure 1.25. P-51 Mustang. Photo courtesy of the U.S. Air Force.

As the range of engagements between fighter aircraft substantially increased due to much greater speed, it was just not possible to get into close range before the other airplane sped or dived away. This trend continues today in modern aerial battles where most engagements are decided beyond the visual range through the use of long-range autonomous missiles. Thus, getting in position to shoot down an opposing aircraft, as hard as that may have been, was not a sufficient condition for a kill. Since both aircraft would be moving at different speeds and angles, it took great instinct, skill, and an intrepid killer mentality to become proficient in this business (i.e., to become a fighter ace). To assist their shooting, various gun sights were devised. One crude device was a simple extension of a line of sight consisting of a fixed foresight with a small metal ring and a rear sight with a larger metal ring and some cross-hair elements fashioned into it. If the opposing aircraft was directly in front, then the pilot's task was to point his aircraft so that the target fell in the center of the foresight and across the cross-hairs. This of course almost never occurred, and there would be lateral motions involved. Thus, the outer ring served as the estimator of the deflection angle, the angle that the target aircraft would be at by the time the bullet arrived at the center of the cross-hairs. The pilot would trigger the gun as the target aircraft just fell on the rear sight ring. However, as the rear sight ring diameter was fixed, this aiming would be good for only one lateral speed of the aircraft, typically set at 50 mph, accounting for the relative velocity and angle between the aircrafts. Later, this device was modified to a "sighting graticule" that projected a small ring on a reflector glass to mimic the rear sight ring. The idea was to allow the pilot to see the sighting ring in night conditions and also to be able to see through the ring by adjusting the brightness of the projection light. The sighting graticule also could be used to better estimate the deflection angle needed to shoot down the target aircraft. If the pilot was skillful enough to keep the aircraft heading toward the target, then the turning rate was proportional to the deflection angle. This principle was used to read out the turning rate using a gyroscope, and the turning rate was converted to rotation of the projection angle for the sighting graticule. Thus, the deflection angle was converted to a translation of the center of the cross-hair in the reflector screen so that when the target fell on it the gun was to be let loose. To account for the range, a crude but effective method was used where the sighting ring diameter was adjusted using a separate knob to fit the target aircraft wingspan within this diameter. As most if not all of the opposing aircraft wingspans were known, this gave the range of the target, and an analog computer then geared out a compensation in the rotation to be made in the projection mirror. This device combining the projection sight and gyro-generated targeting was known as the "gyro gunsight." Although this was a valuable targeting tool that produced better results than expected, the gyro gunsight was cumbersome in installation and operation. The device was bulky, and of course the pilot had to range the aircraft by fitting the wingspan in the sighting circle, which many pilots did not have the leisure to do. Nonetheless, in the U.S. and British fighter aircraft the gyro gunsight was a common piece of equipment, while some experienced pilots simply went on using their gut instincts and reflexes to engage German fighters.

The early versions of the fighter aircraft on both sides were made with unprotected cockpits and fuel tanks, in pursuit of speed and performance by using light structural components. However, as battle damages accumulated, much effort went into protecting the air crews and the aircraft in spite of the fact that added weight would deduct from both the aircraft speed and the amount of ammunition it could potentially carry. For example, to protect against direct hits by 20-mm rounds would require steel plating of 45-mm thickness, which meant that about 350 pounds of armored steel would have to be added just to provide head and back protection. A compromise solution was typically applied by using 4-mm Duralumin deflector plates at selected locations such as around the cockpit and the engine. The American Grumman F6F-3 Hellcat was an exception in this regard in that its size and power allowed full steel plate back armor of 13-mm thickness for the pilot as well as the deflector plate on the entire bottom side of the engine. Up to 50-mm thick glass components were also used, particularly on the front side, to diminish the impact of the incoming rounds. In all, the Hellcats carried a total of 450 pounds of various armor materials. Oil and fuel tanks were also considered to have shock-absorbing effects and were placed around the cockpit (front and underneath), except of course for the fuel—any leakage could cause fire. Self-sealing fuel tanks were thus introduced, where the metal tank is fully covered with a layer of uncured rubber. Any bullet hitting the fuel tank would sail through the rubber layer, but when the leaking fuel came in contact with the rubber it initiated chemical reactions that would cause the rubber to swell up, thus constricting the leakage. Fuel tank inerting was also attempted in some Russian aircraft, where the engine exhaust gas, consisting mostly of inert nitrogen and carbon dioxide, was diverted in part to the fuel tank after cooling and filtering. This would replace the air that would otherwise be occupying the empty space in the fuel tank. This fuel tank inerting approach, though cumbersome and expensive, is employed in some modern military cargo aircraft. However, the oil and fuel systems remained as the most vulnerable points on the aircraft statistically, with 80 to 85 percent loss rates of aircraft when these components were hit. Any hits on the cockpit and the pilot of course also led to a large loss rate, as did hits on the hydraulics and the power plant. Structural damages including wings and control surfaces resulted in less than 12 percent lost.

Two types of engines were generally used in the aircraft during World War II: water-cooled in-line or air-cooled radial engines both using gasoline. Radial engines had the cylinders arranged around the crank in a circular pattern, which increased its cross-sectional area and therefore the engine compartment diameter. This meant that good overall aerodynamic design in the form of streamlining the aircraft would be impossible to achieve. However, the large cross-sectional area and spread-out pistons meant that there will be good airflow over all of the pistons making air cooling feasible. In-line engines, on the contrary, could be arranged with a small cross-sectional area but had to be liquid-cooled to reach all the corners of the engine. The liquid coolant and the circulating system including the radiator not only added weight but made the aircraft vulnerable. The coolant plumbing was very susceptible to damage when hit by machine gun rounds, and the loss of cooling led to dramatic engine failures. Some of the automotive engine technologies still in use owe their origin to this period. Both in-line and radial engines, for example, used supercharging or turbocharging to maximize the engine power given the limitations in the engine size and weight. Both methods increase the combustion chamber pressure, and the engine power output is proportional to the pressure and displacement of the combustion chambers. Supercharging refers to extracting some of the crank power of the engine to run an auxiliary compressor to pressure the intake air prior to sending it into the combustion chamber. Turbocharging accomplishes the same end, but it uses the hot exhaust gas from the combustion chamber to run a centrifugal turbine. The turbine power is then used to run the air compressor. However, air gets heated up when compressed. In short, compression adds energy to air which causes the air temperature to rise. This is undesirable in gasoline-fueled engines because the hot air mixed with fuel vapor can detonate causing "engine knocks" damages. To avoid the knocking condition, the air temperature is reduced through an intercooler, which uses a water-cooling jacket through which the compressed air passes. Rolls-Royce Merlin-series engines used in the British Spitfire are classic examples of supercharged in-line engines. The air intake was on the underside of the aircraft and sent the air through the two-stage centrifugal compressor, which rotated on the same axis as the engine crank. The hot, compressed air then passed through the intercooler at the top and back of the engine block before being forced into the combustion chambers. Supercharging had multiplicative effect on the engine power output. For example, in comparison to the Merlin III engine in 1939 with a 27-liter displacement that developed 1030 horsepower, a Merlin 130 engine with the same displacement and two-stage supercharging could punch out 2030 hp by 1933. The high-pressure engine operation meant that the fuel octane number was critical to sustained, stable burning of the fuel. The Merlin 130 engine required octane numbers in the range 100 to 150, as opposed to 87 for Merlin III. The P-47 Thunderbolt perhaps carried this concept to an extreme. Due to space constraints, its turbocharger could only be located in the fuselage behind the cockpit. Thus, the exhaust gas from the engine had to be diverted below the cockpit into the turbocharger, and then the compressed air was routed back to the engine requiring a total of sixty feet of turbocharging ducts.

Dive bombing was a technique that was developed to hit targets with high precision, before the advent of guidance weapons. High-altitude gravity bombing was inherently inaccurate for the obvious reasons of aircraft speed, visibility, and wind conditions. During dive bombing, the pilot would line up the aircraft directly toward the target at steep angles, release the bomb so that it would follow the same path, and pull the aircraft up. This air support concept was effectively used by the German army who had much better coordination between the army and air force. The blitzkrieg tactics required quick and precise attacks from the air in areas that ground forces had difficulty in overcoming, such as concentrated opposing ground forces, fortified positions and tanks, and supply convoys. Stationary targets such as roads, bridges, and ships were also easy targets for dive bombers. The German Ju-87 Stuka is a classic example of a dive bomber, and later models could carry one 500-kg bomb or four 50-kg bombs. The precision was to a point where Stuka bombers were attacking positions just 100 yards from the advancing German troops. The compressed pitch of the propeller noise and the siren attached to the landing gears added psychological effects in addition to already devastating precision bombing. Typical Stuka dive-bombing procedure started with locating the target through the bombsight window on the cockpit floor from an altitude of 15,000 feet. The throttle was then cut back and dive brakes extended. Then, the Stuka dived to an angle of 60 to 90 degrees, reaching speeds up close to 350 mph. The altimeter light was set at the release altitude of typically 450 meters (1500 feet), at which point the bomb was released by pressing a knob on the control stick. The bomb was sent on its way, while the automatic pull-out mechanism turned the elevators to initiate a 6-G turn away from the ground. Once the aircraft reached a pitch above the horizon, the dive brakes would be retracted, and the pilot would retake the aircraft control. One fault of the Stuka bomber was its lack of agility and speed after the bombing, and many fell prey to the Allied fighters with superior armament and speed.

In the Pacific theater, the dive-bombing had an important function: knocking out naval vessels, particularly aircraft carriers. Even if only the flight deck could be disabled through such attacks, a significant advantage was gained because the naval battles in the Pacific revolved around the ability to place as many of the right kinds of aircraft in the air. The main Japanese dive-bombers were Aichi D3A "Val" (Fig. 1.26) and Yokosuka D4Y Suisei "Judy," while the U.S. Navy used Douglas SBD Dauntless and later Curtis SB2C Helldiver. These aircraft took off from carriers with the primary mission of finding and attacking opposing carriers. The SBD Dauntless carried over 2000 pounds of bombs, along with four machine guns (two forward and two rearward). The Curtis SB2C Helldiver, intended to replace SBD Dauntless, actually turned out to contain some problems. Instability at high-angle, high-speed dives made the bombing path less accurate, and poor stalling characteristics were high risks for carrier operations. Nonetheless, Helldiver was the sole carrier-based dive-bomber after the Dauntless aircraft had been phased out, and they did fly successful missions, including destruction of three Japanese carriers during the Battle of Midway in 1942.

Figure 1.26. Japanese Val dive-bomber. Photo courtesy of the U.S. Department of Defense.

Other bombing techniques were horizontal bombing, shallow glide bombing (less than 20 degree dive angle), and steep glide bombing (20 to 60 degrees). The horizontal pattern bombing from high altitudes was the norm for heavy bombers while they maintained formation flights. The pattern bombing ensured that a large area around the target was saturated with bombs to probabilistically ensure that the actual target would be hit. Higher accuracy from individual bombing was possible when the bomber flew at altitudes as low as fifty feet to release the bomb with a delay-action fuse. To aim the target from high altitudes, so-called vector sight was used. The bombardier dialed in the aircraft speed, altitude, and the bomb type along with the estimated wind speed and direction. The vector sight then mechanically geared out the point of release and displayed it using a cross-hair through the bomb sight. All that was needed was for the bombardier to communicate with the pilot to guide the aircraft so that the target point fell under the cross-hair, at which instant the bombs would be released. However, the vector sight assumed that the aircraft would be flying perfectly level, and any bank angle would throw the target line way off course. A tachometric sight was an alternate device where the sighting telescope was rotated by an electric motor. The motion to hold the telescope vertically pointed to the target was electrically read by an analog computing machine to indicate the corrections to the flight path toward the target. When the required corrections were zero and the telescope was vertically on the target, the electrical signals were generated to release the bombs automatically.

In a preview to the massive air power to be constructed by the United States, the Boeing B-17 Flying Fortress (shown in Figs. 1.27 through 1.29) represented long-range, large-payload bomber aircraft with heavy, multiple-gun defensive armaments to earn its name. Similar to other aircraft manufactured in the United States, size and structural toughness were discerning features of this aircraft. During World War II, operating out of bases in England and Italy, the B-17s were used in strategic bombing over industrial and civilian targets, delivering more bombs than any other aircraft during the war. Between the Royal Air Force and the U.S. Air Force that used this aircraft, over 640,000 tons of bombs were

Figure 1.27. B-17 Flying Fortress. Photo courtesy of the U.S. Air Force.

Figure 1.28. A formation of B-17 Flying Fortress. Photo courtesy of the U.S. Air Force.

dropped. The number of missions and persistent attacks by the German aircrafts, however, took the toll of 4750 of these B-17s being lost. In modern air campaigns, conventional bombing missions are conducted only after clear air superiority is established along with near total destruction of the anti-aircraft defense facilities on the ground. However, in the early phase of the strategic bombing campaign in 1942, these bombers were pretty much left to themselves to fend off ferocious anti-aircraft fire and German fighter attacks that could pursue the slow B-17s at will. As in several other military duties during World War II, flying in bombing missions was a high-risk, high-fatality job that men undertook none-theless. Attrition rates of 25 percent were not uncommon in a single mission, leading to many tactical and armament changes. The number of guns was increased to thirteen 0.5-inch M2 Browning machine guns, along with armor plates to gunners. These guns were located at the nose, tail, top, bottom, and sides of the aircraft. The top and bottom guns were mounted in a dual-gun turret to maximize the coverage. However, due to bombing requirements and lack of maneuverability there were always blind spots that the attacking fighter could use to make impudent approaches to isolated bombers. A tactical solution was sought in staggered box flight formations where the aircraft could pour concentrated machine gun fire over wider angles and at the same time protect other aircrafts within the box formation. However, such a concentration of B-17s made them more susceptible to anti-aircraft barrages from the German 88-mm guns, and the German fighters made sweeping, high-speed strafing passes to minimize their losses. It wasn't until the relatively simple idea (in retrospect) of fighter escorts was implemented with superior aircraft like P-51 Mustangs that the bomber loss rates became marginally acceptable. Four Wright R-1820-97 Cyclone turbo-supercharged radial engines powered the bomber to a maximum speed of 287 mph, although the cruise speed was down to 182 mph over a range of 2000 miles. Typical bombing missions involved delivering 8000 pounds of bombs for 400-mile radius missions and 5000 pounds for 800 miles.

Figure 1.29. Engine on the B-17 Flying Fortress. Photo courtesy of the U.S. Air Force.

The Boeing B-29 Superfortress (Fig. 1.31) was a heavyweight of a bomber with a maximum take-off weight of 135,000 pounds. Its production cost of $640,000 per airplane was more than twelve times that for P-51 Mustang; but a total of close to 4000 of these bombers was built, a huge number by today's standards. For example, only twenty-one of the modern B-2 Spirit stealth bombers have been built at a cost of $2 billion each, and one

Figure 1.30. Forward gun compartment in the B-25 Mitchell bomber. Photo courtesy of the U.S. Department of Defense.

Figure 1.31. B-29 Superfortress. Photo courtesy of the U.S. Air Force.

recently (February 2008) crashed to reduce the fleet to twenty. A typical bombing mission by a B-29 would involve take-off and a climb to an altitude of 5000 feet. With all the weight of the fuel and bombs, it would be counterproductive to try to go up to higher, rarefied altitudes. At its economic cruising speed of 220 mph, most of the journey would involve getting to and back from the target, unless of course the enemy fighters unfortunately engaged the bomber fleet. Its combat range with nominal bomb load was 3250 miles, so that a seven-hour one-way flight to the target would be a typical duration. At about 150 miles from the target, they would start the climb to 20,000 feet to avoid anti-aircraft fire and other air defenses. After unleashing the bombs at the target from a 20,000-ft altitude, the protocol was for the bombers to clear sixty miles prior to descending to a cruise altitude of 15,000 feet. At lower density and therefore aerodynamic drag, the return trip would be one to two hours shorter. By the time of landing, the consumption of fuel and bombs would bring the aircraft weight back to its empty weight of 74,500 pounds plus the crew and reserve fuel weight.

As noted previously, such textbook flights were nearly nonexistent during World War II, and much thought and work were expended to make the bombing missions acceptably survivable against German fighter attacks. Again, the formation flights and fighter escorts were the main solutions, but they were easier to draw up than implement. The bombers with heavy loads of fuel and armaments were not the most agile aircrafts for formation flying, particularly at higher altitudes. To provide concentrated firepower against incoming fighters, tight formation was essential. One approach was to bring the bombers into formation at low altitudes where the aircraft were easier to control, which was adopted except under cloudy conditions. It was too risky to attempt to cross cloud cover in close formations where the visibility might be nearly zero. Thus, in such weather conditions the aircraft were allowed to penetrate the cloud separately and form up above the cloud cover at an altitude of about

8000 feet using radio signals. It could take up to one hour for the formation to be completed, which consumed time and also precious fuel. Once in formation, the pilots needed to be vigilant to keep the level, distance, and speed to maintain formation, leading to extra pilot fatigue. Another operational difficulty was making turns, as the entire formation needed to be coordinated to avoid running into one another and the aircraft on the wings had difficulty seeing the lead aircraft in some formations. Thus, flight routes to avoid flak (anti-aircraft fire) zones were preplanned with a minimum amount of maneuvers to get to and from the target area.

A number of flight formations were experimented with to optimize the defense and flight maneuvers. The U.S. 8th Air Force used different formations as the air battle situation evolved. In one formation, for example, eighteen bombers were designated as a bomber group and divided into three squadrons of six aircraft each. Each squadron of six bombers flew in a 1 (front, lead)-3(middle)-2 (rear) staggered formation with the lead aircraft at the center left and front of the formation. The lead squadron flew ahead of the two squadrons that were 500 feet below and above the lead squadron. This formation allowed wide gun coverage, while affording visual contact among the aircraft. Later, such bomber groups could be combined, where four groups would be sent in a bombing mission. Each group would then be separated by a distance of 1.5 miles from one another, and also staggered in altitude by 1000 feet.

CLASSIC FIGHTER TACTICS

The range and lethality of modern air-to-air missiles tend to decide aerial battles well beyond the visual range. However, during World Wars I and II and in many conflicts afterward, the dogfights in the air frequently determined the fate of one pilot or the other. As the speed and performance of the aircraft increased, it took a level of physical and mental acumen as required by few other tasks to become proficient in shooting down opposing aircraft while being exposed to the same risk. Mastery of tactics and maneuvers during direct engagements are still emphasized in most pilot training programs, although in recent years there have been few conflicts in which opposing air forces with similar level of aircraft and pilot preparedness have met in the air. Some of the maneuvers originate from World War II or even earlier in spite of the dramatic changes in the aircraft performance. Also, a modern aircraft gun or cannon is capable of firing 20 mm rounds at 6000 rounds per minute with a muzzle velocity of 3300 ft/s. In addition, the pilot is equipped with an array of close- and long-range air-to-air missiles. The weaponry, speed, and maneuverability of modern jet fighters combined with the skills of the pilots make the modern dogfights an extreme test of human and machine capabilities.

Table 1.6 shows some of the major aircraft guns used by different jet fighters. We can see that the U.S. jet aircraft are superior in terms of the rounds carried, rate of fire, and the muzzle velocity. The GE M61 cannons are the primary gun on U.S. fighter aircraft, used by nearly all of the major fighter aircraft in the last five decades. M61 is also known as the Vulcan or Gatling gun, with the latter name in reference to the multibarrel design by Dr. Gatling back in the mid-nineteenth century. The original design was hand-cranked to rotate the barrels so that each barrel could independently undergo a firing cycle. This has the effect of multiplying the rate of fire as well as reducing the heating and wear on the barrels. The aircraft guns are of course mechanically driven, using hydraulics or electrical motor, requiring 35 hp at the full rate of fire. The maximum rate of fire is 6600 per minute, but the fire rate of either 6000 or 4000 is used. Six identical barrels are mounted on a drum breech base that rotates in the counter-clockwise direction when viewed from behind the gun (the preferred position when facing this weapon). The rotating drum breech is set in

Table 1.6. Aircraft Guns.

Aircraft	Guns	Caliber (mm)	Projectile Weight (g)	Number of Rounds Carried	Rate of Fire (per min)	Muzzle Velocity (m/s)
F-14	GE M61	20	98	675	6000	1030
F-15A-D	GE M61	20	98	950	6000	1030
F-15E	GE M61	20	98	512	6000	1030
F-16	GE M61	20	98	515	6000	1030
F/A-18A-D	GE M61	20	98	570	6000	1030
F/A-18E/F	GE M61	20	98	400	6000	1030
F-111	GE M61	20	98	1000	6000	1030
F-104	GE M61	20	98	725	6000	1030
F-22	GE M61	20	98	480	6000	1030
F-35	GAU-12/U	25	180	220	4200	1097
F-5E	Colt M39	20	98	280	1500	1030
A-7	GE M61	20	98	1000		
A-10	GAU-8/A	30	390	1174	3500	1067
Harrier GR.7	Aden 30	30	_	250	1500	800
Mirage 2000	DEFA 554	30	275	250	1800	840
J 35J Draken	Aden 30	30	_	150	1500	800
Tornado ADV	BK	27	_	180	_	_
Su-24	Gsh-6-23	23	109	500	8000	_
Su-27	Gsh-6-23	30	109	150	8000	_
MiG-27	Gsh-6-30	30	_	260	5400	850
MiG-29	Gsh-30-1	30	_	150	1800	850
MiG-31	Gsh-23-6	30	109	260	3500	890

contact with the stationary breech housing with a six-cam follower mechanism for loading, firing, and extracting the rounds. As each barrel is aligned with the cam follower, the round is electrically primed (ignited) to blast it down the barrel. At the muzzle, the six barrels are clamped with adjustable barrel angle settings to give different dispersion patterns. Due to the high feeding rate of ammunition, the feed mechanism is individually tailored for different aircrafts but the cannon itself is the basic M61 design. The M50 20-mm caliber ammunition can be fitted with high explosive, armor-piercing, or other charges. The rounds are arranged on a helical plate (somewhat like a screw or staircase) in a large drum, and an enclosed conveyor belt transports the ammo to the gun while a second conveyor brings the spent shells back to the ammunition drum.

The lethality of the rounds from the gun is measured by the kinetic energy of the projectiles; the kinetic energy is the one-half the projectile weight multiplied by the square of the muzzle velocity. It is analogous to large, speeding trucks being exceedingly more dangerous than a scooter moving among pedestrians, except that the effect of the velocity is much greater. In that aspect, nothing exceeds the lethality of GAU-8/A "Avenger" guns carried on A-10 attack aircrafts. Due to high fire rate and muzzle velocity, its total power output at the muzzle exceeds that of World War II vintage 75 or 105 mm howitzers. One wouldn't wish to be at the receiving end of 30-mm caliber bullets weighing close to a pound each flying in at a velocity of close to 1000 m/s (3300 ft/s) at rates of 60 hits per second. The weight and velocity of the rounds were originally intended for attacks on tanks or other hard-shelled targets. Each bullet fired from this gun weighs 1.5 pounds, with armor-piercing rounds weighing just under 1 pound. The complete GAU-8/A gun system with full ammunition load weighs close to 4000 pounds, and in the A-10 attack aircraft the entire lower fuselage forward side is used for the gun and the ammunition drum over a total length of some twenty-one feet. The ammunition is stored radially with the tip pointing inward, and the ammunition drum rotates to place the rounds on the slotted conveyor. The ammunition is transported to the gun from the ammunition drum on the slotted conveyor, so that there are no links between the rounds that tend to cause problems at high fire rates. Again, the empty aluminum (for reduced weight) shells are sent back to the drum for later disposal. The seven-barrel drum driven by dual hydraulic motors generate a firing rate of either 2100 or 4200 rounds per minute.

The rules of engagement in aerial combat vary from the air force to air force, squadron to squadron, mission to mission, and from one pilot to the other under the given constraints of the battle. One obvious approach to making a kill without becoming one is to fire long-range air-to-air missiles with active homing guidance from an unobserved distance and disengage from the battle. AMRAAM missiles, for example, are such long-range weapons with a maximum range of over 100 miles, but that decreases very quickly at lower altitudes. The next level of engagement is to fire the missile with semi-active homing guidance and remain engaged in battle by keeping the radar locked on to the target so that the missiles can track the opposing aircraft. Although modern short-range missiles like the AIM-7 Sidewinder have an autonomous, infrared homing guidance, they need to be fired from a visible distance and at optimum pursuit angles to be effective. If the above options have been exhausted or the opposing aircraft are in close range and interspersed with friendly ones, then the battle may transition into an old-fashioned dogfight. The classic close-range pursuit maneuvers and evasive moves are where some of the most intense training for military pilots is focused.

Some of the basic moves during an aerial combat are shown in Figs. 1.32 to 1.35. During pursuit, the defender (bogey) will make defensive moves to evade the pursuing aircraft, like a sharp turn into the path of the attacker. The idea is that the attacker will overshoot the defender and both aircraft will be at neutral positions. To maintain pursuit during a hard-bank turn by the bogey, either lead or lag pursuits can be made. Lead pursuit simply means that the attacker turns faster than the bogey and maintains the tail-pursuit angle. This does involve pulling a higher-G turn and also losing sight of the defending aircraft, since the turn is made by banking the aircraft so that the defender is at the outer circle beyond the underbelly of the attacker aircraft. A more standard approach is to turn outside the defender's turn circle and re-approach from the outer side, as shown in Fig. 1.32. As with all offensive moves, there are countermoves that can be taken by the defender. During a lag pursuit, the defender may see that the attacker is outside his turn circle and reverse his turn to gain an attacking position (Fig. 1.32). To avoid this situation, a variant of the lag pursuit is something called a lag displacement roll shown in Fig. 1.33. When the attacker sees the bogey beginning his defensive turn, he pulls up out of the pursuit plane and rolls into a turn (counter-clockwise roll). Coming down from the loop again places the attacker in the pursuit position. The pull-up move in the lag displacement roll accomplishes two things: One, it makes it difficult for the defender to pursue the attacker, and two, the pull-up slows down the aircraft speed so that a tighter turn can be made. Coming out of the loop, the attacker aircraft dives back to the initial pursuit plane to regain the speed. A barrel roll attack is a similar maneuver, except it is performed during a lead pursuit to avoid overshooting the bogey. In fact, using such looping moves to control the aircraft speed is common in fighter tactics, and a set of maneuvers called "yo-yos" is another example.

A high yo-yo shown in Fig. 1.34 is used during a lead pursuit to close the turning radius. By nosing up out of the pursuit plane, the aircraft speed is reduced, making the turn easier,

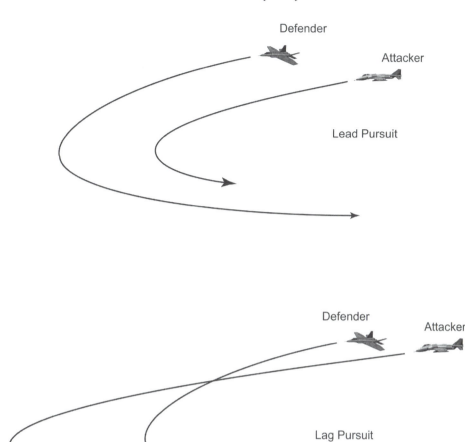

Figure 1.32. Lead and lag pursuits.

and also the attacker used the vertical space to close in on the bogey. A low yo-yo accomplishes the same relative position except the dive is followed by a climb up to the pursuit plane as shown in Fig. 1.34.

The real situation during the aerial battle usually is not as simple as the above examples. The defender will make various maneuvers to reverse the attacker-defender position. One of the ways for achieving this reversal is the scissors technique, shown in Fig. 1.35. During a flat scissors, the defender makes a sharp turn to cause an overshoot by the attacking aircraft, then turns back into the attacker to gain a six o'clock position. The attacker responds by turning into the defender, again causing an overshoot by the defending aircraft. This sequence can go on until one of the fighters makes a mistake or disengages. The flat scissors maneuvers are made in a horizontal pursuit plane, where the turns are made by banking the aircraft 90 degrees and pulling up on the control stick. To make the reverse turn, the aircraft needs to bank at –90 degrees. To make a more effective turn and also slow the aircraft, a rolling scissors technique is used. As in high and low yo-yos, aircraft will lose speed during pull-up climbs and gain speed during dives. This is exactly what happens on the ground as well, when a vehicle is going up-slope it will lose speed and vice versa during

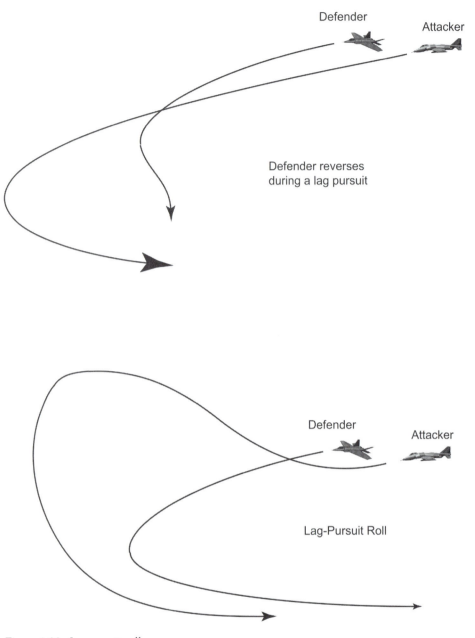

Figure 1.33. Lag-pursuit roll.

downhill runs. During a rolling scissors maneuver, the defender pulls up and at the same time turns into the attacking aircraft's trajectory, to cause an overshoot. This maneuver requires the aircraft to roll and follow a curve along the surface of an imaginary barrel, and therefore this maneuver is sometimes called a barrel roll. The attacking aircraft again responds by making a similar barrel roll, to regain the advantage. A defensive barrel roll pointing vertically downward to gain speed and therefore movement away from the attacking aircraft is called a defensive spiral.

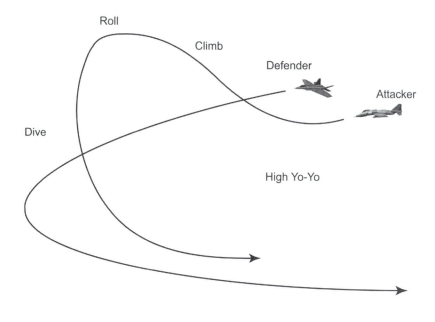

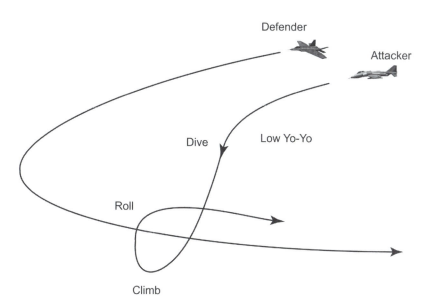

Figure 1.34. High yo-yo and low yo-yo maneuvers.

So the pilot does what is in his skill set to gain an attacking position or evade the attacking aircraft using a variety of moves. Once he gets into an attacking position, he can now make use of the weapons control technology embedded into the cockpit. The pilot's eyes will be locked on the target through the heads-up display (HUD) directly in front of him. Let us therefore look at some of the electronic and control technologies in military aircrafts.

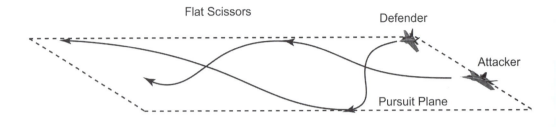

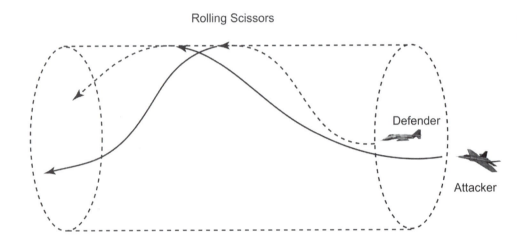

Figure 1.35. Scissors maneuvers.

AVIONICS AND CONTROLS

The cockpit of modern military aircraft is a busy place with all the instruments, weapons control, navigation, and communication gears. Fig. 1.37 shows the cockpit of a high-altitude reconnaissance aircraft, the U-2 "Dragonlady." It has some of the modern digital displays such as the artificial horizon and multifunction display showing the navigation map. A few back-up analog gauges are also seen for essential instruments.

The layout and the instrumentation vary from aircraft to aircraft, and many of the gauges are now embedded into the multifunction digital display. However, the essential components can be found in all the aircrafts. We can start by looking at a classic instrument panel of the F-4 Phantom jets, in Fig. 1.39. Starting from the left-hand side of the pilot, the armament safety override switch (1 in Fig. 1.39) is found near the pilot's seat. Number 2 is the anti-G suit control valve. To overcome the effect of high G-forces, fighter pilots wear a pressurized suit to prevent blood from being pushed to one side of the body. The panel that controls the suit air vent is next on the left instrument panel (3). Number 4 is the fuel control panel, to select from different fuel tank locations for center of gravity adjustments or to eject the fuel altogether. Number 6 is the eject light and switch. There are two engines on the F-4 Phantom aircraft, and therefore two engine controls (7 for the outboard engine and 11 for the inboard one). The throttle handle is controlled by the left hand (8). Numbers 9

Figure 1.36. Flight simulators. Photo courtesy of the U.S. Air Force

Figure 1.37. A modernized cockpit of U-2 Dragonlady. Photo courtesy of the U.S. Air Force.

and 10 are the left utility and vertical panels. Number 12 shows the handle that deploys the drag chute for short landing situations. The automatic controls are found on panel 13, while the intercom controls are on panel 14. Number 15 shows the controls for the auxiliary armaments. There are many dials and gauges on the classic F-4 cockpit: true airspeed indicator (16), angle-of-attack indicator (17), landing gear warning light (18), airspeed and Mach number indicator (19), attitude-direction indicator (20), magnetic compass (22), altimeter (24), and fuel quantity indicator (25). Number 21 is the optical sight unit for aiming the cannons. On modern aircraft, the optical sight is replaced by the heads-up display (HUD) discussed later. The main radar scope is in the middle of the instrument panel (23). Numbers 30 to 33 are the engine gauges—engine fuel flow indicator (31), tachometer (32), and exhaust gas temperature indicator (33). Since there are two engines, there are two of each gauge. The vertical velocity indicator gives the rate of climb or descent in feet per min. Number 36 is a clock. The remainder of the components is listed below.

37: Navigation function selector panel
38: Horizontal situation indicator
39: Multiple weapons control panel
40: Oil pressure indicator
41: Rudder pedal adjustment crank
42: Pneumatic pressure indicator
43: Hydraulic pressure indicator
44: Accelerometer (shows the number of Gs the aircraft is pulling)
45: Bomb control panel
46: Standby altitude indicator
47: Missile control panel

Figure 1.38. Cockpit of now-decommissioned SR-71 Blackbird. Photo courtesy of the U.S. Department of Defense.

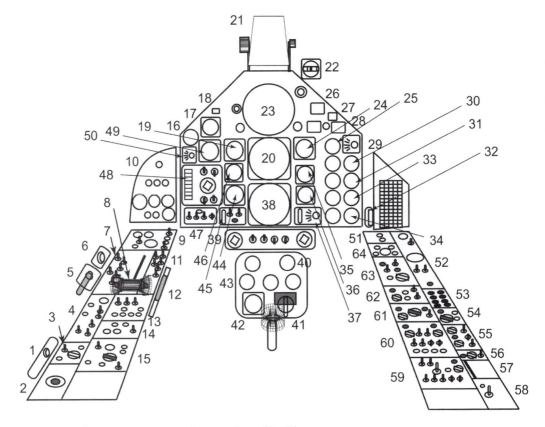

Figure 1.39. Instrumentation on a classic cockpit of F-4 Phantom.

48: Missile status panel
49: Radar altimeter (give the altitude using the radar reflection signal from the ground)
50: Landing gear checklist
51: Generator control panel
52: Defog/foot heat control panel
53: Essential circuit breaker panel
54: Temperature control panel
55: Cockpit lights control panel
56: Indexer light control panel
57: Wing fold control panel
58: Utility electrical receptacle
59: Exterior lights control panel
60: IFF (identification friend or foe) control panel
61: Compass system control panel
62: Com-nav group control panel
63: Emergency brake handle
64: Fuse function control panel

So quite a lot is packed into a small space, and the use of dialed gauges is pretty much the same as in World War II aircraft. The airspeed, altimeter, and rate of climb gauge are called barometric instruments because they rely on pressure measurements. For example, the standard air pressure is a known function of altitude with some minor adjustments depending on the local pressure. For example, from the standard 1 atmospheric pressure (101.325 kPa or 14.7 psi), the pressure decreases by approximately 10 kPa for every 800 meter increase in altitude to about 4000 meters, beyond which it decreases more gradually. Thus, at 30,000 feet, for example, the pressure is less than one-third of the pressure at sea level. This pressure change is measured by pressure transducers and calibrated back to altitude in modern digital altimeters. The rate of change of pressure, and therefore altitude, is converted to display the rate of climb or dive. The air speed gauge is based on the so-called Pitot-static probe measurements of static and stagnation pressures. The static pressure is the pressure of the moving air, while the stagnation pressure corresponds to the pressure reached when the incoming airspeed rams into the pressure sensor and thus increases the pressure. The stagnation pressure probe, or the Pitot tube, is thus oriented toward the incoming air. The difference in the static and stagnation pressure is proportional to the square of the air velocity, which is calibrated to give the air speed after accounting again for the altitude effect on air density. The artificial horizon, or the attitude indicator, give a visual display of the aircraft pitch and roll angles based on the gyroscope references. The artificial horizon is a demarcation between the blue and brown backgrounds to indicate sky and land, respectively, and pitch scale marks move up and down with respect to the aircraft symbol at the center to indicate the pitch angle. The rotation of the artificial horizon then is the measure of the aircraft roll angle. The horizontal situation indicator gives the aircraft heading information by using the gyroscope or magnetic compass. Typically, distance readouts from beacon signals is embedded on this indicator.

The use of the analog, dialed gauges was prevalent even in the early versions of the F-15 Eagles, as shown in Fig. 1.40. Nowadays, most of the gauge readings are incorporated into the multifunction display (MFD) except for a few backup gauges for critical indicators (see Figs. 1.41 to 1.43). MFD combines many of the functions of the classic dials and gauges, and much more, so that the pilot can select and view the overall aircraft conditions for each category. The display modes include primary flight display, navigation, plan position indicator, engine, aircraft configuration, map, station keeping equipment, engine operation display, compass, radar/target display, and weapons control. For example, the primary flight display including the horizontal situation display (artificial horizon) and the compass are shown in the main MFD in the middle of the cockpit in the figure, while the left MFD shows the map display. To allow the pilot to maintain visual contact with the surrounding through the canopy while being able to monitor some of the critical information, a heads-up display (HUD) is mounted directly in front of the pilot, as shown in the figures.

A HUD is now an essential piece of display equipment in military aircraft, and a lot of information can be selected and displayed. Primary flight data, weapons targeting, and other information can be displayed on the HUD. The primary flight data include the flight path vector (also known as the velocity vector), the artificial horizon, speed, altitude, heading, vertical speed (rate of climb/dive), and angle of attack. The speed, altitude, and heading are shown either in numerical values or on a linear scale with a moving cursor. Navigation information is also shared between the HUD and MFD, and this includes lateral and vertical guidance to the preselected flight plan, the next waypoint latitude and longitude, direction, and range/time to the next waypoint.

Two examples of the HUD display are shown in Fig. 1.44. The left HUD display is for air-to-air gun mode. The horizontal scale at the top is the compass heading, now showing a 120° heading. A plus (+) sign below the heading scale shows that the master arm is turned on. The horizontal line with a "W" in the middle is the aircraft attitude or the bank angle. The velocity vector, the circle with three ticks, shows where the aircraft is headed (now showing a dive to the right). The left vertical scale shows the aircraft speed while the right vertical scale is the altitude scale (now showing 430 ft). The inner, right vertical

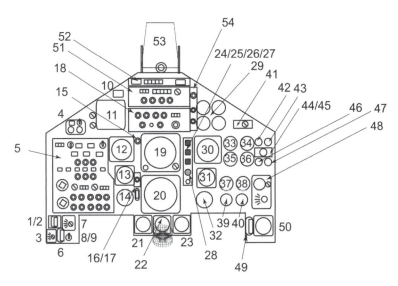

Figure 1.40. Cockpit of F-15A (1970s). 1/2. Hook switch/panel; 3. Flap indicator; 4. Fire warning panel; 5. Weapons control panel; 6. Gear handle; 7. Pitch ratio indicator; 8/9. Pitch ratio switch/panel; 10. Radio call panel; 11. Radar scope; 12. Air speed indicator; 13. Angle of attack indicator; 14. Accelerometer; 15. Emergency jettison switch; 16/17. Steer mode switch/panel; 18. HUD control panel; 19. Altitude indicator; 20. Horizontal situation indicator; 21. Air speed indicator (backup); 22. Altitude indicator (backup); 23. Altimeter (backup); 24/25/26/27. Master mode panel/AC mode button/ ADI mode button/V1 mode button; 28. Beacon light control; 29. TEWS displays; 30. Altimeter; 31. Vertical velocity; 32. Clock; 33. Left engine tachometer; 34. Right engine tachometer; 35. Left engine temperature; 36. Right engine temperature; 37. Left engine fuel flow; 38. Right engine fuel flow; 39. Left nozzle position; 40. Right nozzle position; 41. Display select button; 42. PC1 indicator; 43. PC2 indicator; 44/45. Utility indicator/ Oil hydraulics panel; 46. Left engine oil pressure; 47. Right engine oil pressure; 48. Fuel quantity indicator; 49. JFS panel; 50. Cabin pressure gauge; 51. UHF remote panel; 52. IFF remote panel; 53. Heads-up display (HUD); 54. Gun sight camera control panel.

Figure 1.41. F-16 cockpit. Photo courtesy of the U.S. Department of Defense.

Figure 1.42. Another photograph of the F-16 cockpit. Photo courtesy of the U.S. Department of Defense.

scale shows the radar ranging, with the arrow showing the current distance to the target of about 3000 ft. The range is also shown on the aiming reticle, where the solid line is at three ticks from the vertical. The small rectangle shows the target location, locked by the radar. The radar calculates the distance, speed, and relative motion of the target and aircraft, to locate the aiming reticle. In some HUD displays, the impact line of the gun is also continuously computed and displayed. Since the aircraft gun is fixed to the forward direction of the aircraft, the pilot must guide the aircraft until the aiming reticle coincides with the target rectangle. The number below the left vertical scale shows the number of rounds remaining (799). The HUD display in on the right shows the air-to-ground or the CDIP (continuous displayed impact point) mode used for basic bombing missions. Now the aiming reticle (called the "pipper") shows where the bombs will fall if released. This point is computed from the data on aircraft motion, height, bomb ballistics, bomb release velocity, and estimated wind speed and direction. Since an accurate height is essential, the barometric measurement may be replaced by laser or radar altimetry. So again, the pilot must guide the aircraft to overlap the pipper on the target, press the automatic bomb release button, and then pull up. The horizontal lines at the top and bottom of the HUD indicate the pitch angles. If the velocity vector lies at the horizontal line with number "5" next to it, it means the pitch angle is 5 degrees from the horizontal. Other display information includes the aircraft angle of attack, weapons mode, and safe pass height. The safe pass height indicates the fragmentation range, and the pilot should avoid releasing the bomb if the pipper comes too close to this height.

Photographs of the HUD displays on the F-18/A Hornet are shown in Figs. 1.45 and 1.46. It is in a primary flight display mode, simply showing the aircraft attitude line, with heading scale and pitch scales. For night flights, a synthetic image of the surroundings

Figure 1.43. Cockpit design in the F/A-18 flight simulator.

from the FLIR (forward looking infrared) or synthetic aperture radar can be superimposed on the HUD display to show the outside terrain and objects, as shown in Fig. 1.47.

The military does not seem to spare anything when it comes to assisting its pilots in maximizing their abilities to engage in battle through the use of emerging technology. The integration of the synthetic image onto the heads-up display gives the pilot an ability to carry out a mission regardless of the weather, day or night. If the pilot's pair of good eyes and a crude radio were the only link to the outside world for World War II pilots, nowadays the total sensory system of a jet fighter ranges from the radars, FLIR imager, jammer pods,

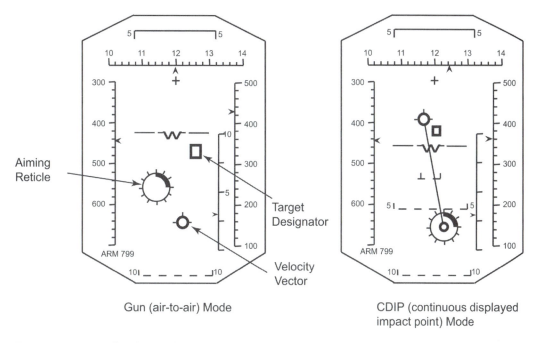

Aiming Reticle

Target Designator

Velocity Vector

Gun (air-to-air) Mode

CDIP (continuous displayed impact point) Mode

Figure 1.44. Examples of HUD displays.

RWR (radar warning receiver), IFF data links, ECM (electronic countermeasure) pod, to UHF radios.

Human vision, while being quite useful for daily tasks, is actually quite limited in its spectral range, meaning that we can only see from red to violet. In the broad scheme of things, red to violet covers the visible wavelength range of 400 nm (violet) to 760 nm (red). A nanometer (nm) is one-billionth of a meter. The total electromagnetic spectrum can go from gamma and X-rays of sub-nanometer wavelengths to microwave and radio waves with 1 to 1000 m wavelength. Radio waves are used for communications, and microwaves are used for radars. Microwaves have certain advantages for the probing of the sky. Microwaves are easily generated from oscillating electric

Figure 1.45. A heads-up display on F/A-18. Photo courtesy of the U.S. Navy.

fields and can propagate long distances in the atmosphere at the speed of light. But most importantly, most objects (rain drops, water surfaces, metals, etc.) reflect a lot of the incoming microwaves. Also, returning microwaves can be detected using the same apparatus. So, a radar scanning different directions will find a reflecting object, and the distance to the object can be determined by how long it took the radar signal to hit and return from the object. The radar signals, as well as other electromagnetic waves, travel at a constant speed (speed of light = 300,000 km/s) in air. Also, the speed of the object can be found

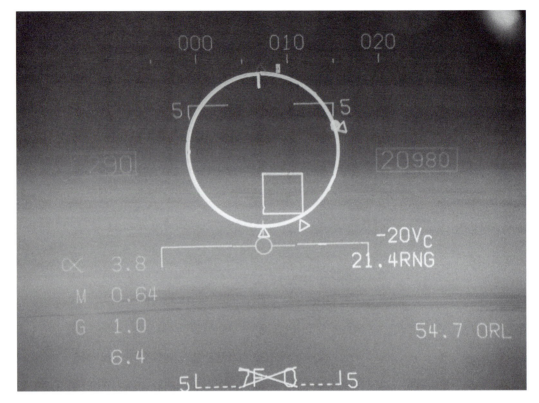

Figure 1.46. Another view through the HUD of the F/A-18. Photo courtesy of the U.S. Department of Defense.

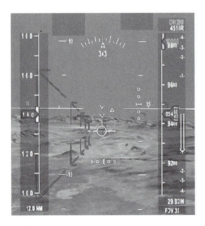

Figure 1.47. A heads-up display with synthetic image of the terrain. Photo courtesy of the U.S. Air Force.

because the radar wave frequency will be slightly shifted by the relative motion between the radar and the object. Radars are therefore active devices, producing and sending out probing signals. Typical military radars have ranges in excess of 100 miles, and horizontal coverage of 120 degrees (1/3 of the entire horizon) and vertical scan of +/– 9 degrees.

The FLIR system is essentially a digital camera, except it can see in the infrared range. As noted above, human vision works by looking at the visible light that is reflected from objects. The only problem is that when there is no sun or moon to illuminate the objects, human vision is quite limited. Infrared imaging works because even in the absence of any illumination all objects radiate in the infrared range (wavelengths greater than 760 nm). At typical ambient temperatures, most of the infrared radiation will be in the 5 to 20 μm range, and weak. So, IR-sensitive sensors with high gains are used to view the outside world even in the absence of illuminations. Why can't the normal digital cameras do this? The sensors in common devices only respond to visible light, and also the lenses will not transmit infrared radiation. In fact, IR cameras are expensive because of the high cost of the IR sensors and optical components.

The IFF is a radio transponder that sends out signals. An IFF unit responds on receiving a signal from another source by sending back a coded signal, which is interpreted by the sender to determine whether the aircraft in range is friend or foe without visual contact. More advanced identification systems have been or are being developed using specific radar signatures, and this is an active research and development area involving electrical and computer engineers.

AERODYNAMICS

Now that we have looked at a number of weapon technologies, let us look at something that is more fundamental to fighter aircraft, like how they fly and maneuver in the sky. As the Wright brothers proved for the first time in history, a wing or set of wings can generate an upward force or lift. This is due to the pressure difference between the flows at the top and bottom of the wings. Wings—more precisely airfoils—are contoured so that the flow must travel a longer path (and therefore must travel faster) around the top surface. For the air following these streamlines, the pressure goes down when the velocity goes up and vice versa. So the top surface is at a low pressure and the bottom at a high pressure, resulting in a net upward force called lift. The faster the air speed, the larger this pressure difference becomes and therefore more lift for the aircraft. Also, larger wing area, density, and shape of the airfoil affect the lift characteristics. So this lift force overcomes the weight of the aircraft to allow it to fly.

When we fly in commercial airliners, if we are seated at the row close to the trailing edge of the wing, we can see the wing flaps go down during take-off and landing and also hear the hydraulics to deploy these flaps. Flaps increase the wing area, but they are also designed to control the air flow to follow the wing contour at the take-off and landing conditions. For military aircraft, such elaborate flap design is both cumbersome and also not as necessary because the much more powerful engines can generate very large air speeds quickly. So they use different approaches to maximize lift during take-off and landing. The F-16, for example, has a fixed wing, but its wing profile can be changed both at the leading and trailing edge depending on the flight conditions. Fig. 1.48 shows the various profile changes controlled by an onboard computer for the F-16 aircraft. During take-off and landing, maximum thrust is required, and therefore the trailing-edge flap is down a full 20 degrees. During ground roll, the aircraft is moving parallel to the ground, and so the leading-edge flap is not deployed. Once off the ground, the aircraft noses up. That increases the angle of

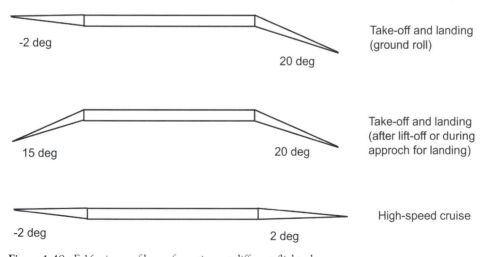

-2 deg

20 deg

Take-off and landing
(ground roll)

15 deg

20 deg

Take-off and landing
(after lift-off or during
approch for landing)

-2 deg

2 deg

High-speed cruise

Figure 1.48. F-16 wing profile configurations at different flight phases.

attack, the angle of the aircraft with respect to the incoming air. To accommodate this air flow coming from underneath, the leading-edge flap is down 15 degrees. During high-speed cruise, neither of the flaps is needed, and both flaps are retracted to pose minimum obstruction to the flow. During tight maneuvers (as in dogfights described above), the leading-edge flap is again deployed so that the aircraft is less likely to stall.

Another way to optimize the wing aerodynamics for the flight condition is to use the full variable-geometry wing, as in the F-14 Tomcat and the European fighter Tornado. The entire wing is rotated to a swept-back position during high-speed cruise to minimize and extended to a nearly straight position during take-off and landing to maximize the wing area. During maneuvers, the wing actually rotates to maximize its effectiveness. The variable-geometry wing thus provides the best of short take-off/landing, maneuverability, high-speed performance, and crew comfort in a single aircraft, at the expense of complex control and actuators.

The lift force counterbalances the weight of the aircraft, except that most of the time the lift is not exactly located at the center of gravity for the aircraft as shown in Fig. 1.49. This will obviously make the aircraft unstable and simply flip the aircraft. So aircraft have horizontal stabilizers, or the elevators, to balance the forces. In the horizontal direction, the aircraft also encounters aerodynamic drag which is balanced by the thrust force during constant-speed cruise. The balance force of elevators can be adjusted by changing their angles through rotation, and this will control the pitch of the aircraft. The F/A-22 Raptor is equipped with a clipped delta wing with the leading-edge flap, flaperons, and ailerons at the trailing edge. The leading-edge flap and the trailing-edge flaperon serve the same purpose as the ones shown in Fig. 1.49: They are rotated to optimize the aircraft's aerodynamic lift. The flaperons and ailerons also can be flipped in opposite directions on the two

Figure 1.49. Aerodynamic forces and surfaces on the F/A-22 Raptor (front) and F-15 Eagle (back). Photo courtesy of the U.S. Air Force.

Figure 1.50. Engineering testing of the F/A-18 Hornet aerodynamics at high angles of attack. Different liquid dyes are used to visualize the flow pattern. Photo courtesy of NASA.

sides of the wings (i.e., aileron up on the left and down on the right), and this will create a roll motion for the aircraft. Using both the flaperon and ailerons for this control motion adds to the flexibility and speed. The rudders shown on the vertical stabilizers control the yaw angle, the left-to-right attitude of the aircraft. The control of the angles, or more precisely the rate of turns in three aircraft axes of motion, then entirely dictates the path of the aircraft, along with the throttle to change the engine thrust. The aerodynamic surfaces are digitally actuated by an onboard computer, from input from the pilot through the control stick. Pulling the control stick backward toward the pilot will increase the pitch, and the sideways movement of the stick will start to roll the aircraft. In modern fighter jets, the weapons and display controls are also embedded into the control stick and the throttle lever through push buttons in an approach called HOTAS (hands-on throttle and stick). Visualization of the flow over the F/A-18 at high angle of attack is shown in a NASA test photograph in Fig. 1.50.

REFERENCES

Budiansky, Stephen. *Air Power: The Men, Machines, and Ideas that Revolutionized War, From Kitty Hawk to Gulf War II*. New York: Penguin Group, 2004.
Clancy, Tom. *Fighter Wing: A Guided Tour of an Air Force Combat Wing* New York: Berkeley Press, 1995.

Crawford, Steve. *Twenty-First Century Warplanes: The World's Most Potent Military Aircraft.* St. Paul, MN: MBI Publishing Company, 2002.

Laur, Col. Timothy M. and Steven L. Llanso. *Encyclopedia of Modern U.S. Military Weapons.* New York: Berkeley Books, 1995.

The New Face of the War: Air Combat. New York: Time-Life Books, 1991.

Price, Alfred. *Combat Developments in World War Two: Fighter Aircraft.* London: Arms and Armor Press, 1986.

Price, Alfred. *Combat Developments in World War Two: Bomber Aircraft.* London: Arms and Armor Press, 1986.

For further information on the B-1B bomber, see the following Web page:

www.fas.org/nuke/guide/usa/bomber/b-1b.htm and en.wikipedia.org/wiki/B-1_Lancer.

MISSILE TECHNOLOGY

MEDIA COVERAGE OF world events in the recent past, including the wars in Iraq, has shown the effectiveness of modern guided missiles and smart bombs zeroing on the target. Some of the broadcast footage included video transmissions from the missile itself or from the delivery aircraft as the guided projectile streams toward the laser-illuminated target. Targets as far away as 1000 miles and as small as a single-car garage have been hit with cruise missiles as if these missiles were individually guided by a human pilot. This kind of weapons technology gave rise to the term "surgical strikes." There are also missiles like the Patriot systems designed to perform high-speed intercepts of incoming missiles, and a substantial amount of research and development is being expended on so-called ballistic missile defense (BMD). BMD is a comprehensive defense program to provide a physical umbrella against ballistic missiles presumed to carry nuclear or other weapons of mass destruction, and one of the key components is the high-accuracy hypersonic projectile delivery toward the incoming warheads. Some of the air-to-air missiles launched from fighter aircraft are of the fire-and-forget type that lock on to the target from a distance of 100 miles or farther and guide themselves while the launch vehicle engages other enemy targets or simply disengages from the battle scene. One of the fire-and-forget armaments, the AIM-54 Phoenix missile shown in Fig. 2.1, has a range of greater than 100 miles and a speed exceeding 3000 mph. Shoulder-launched surface-to-air missiles like the U.S.-made Stinger (see Figs. 2.2(a) and (b)) are a legitimate threat for aircraft up to 15,700 ft (4500 m). Intercontinental ballistic missiles (ICBM) carry nuclear warhead(s) on a global scale and can be launched from the ground or from submarines. This array of airborne weaponry gives the commanders, and policy makers, unprecedented tactical and strategic advantages and options in conventional warfare.

The advantages gained from effective missile technology are evident. Large thrust can be generated from a relatively small and inexpensive propellant charge, so that a sizable warhead can be delivered over a long range and at high speeds. The missiles can thus be launched from the relative safety of long distances, minimizing the exposure of the launch vehicle or personnel. This class of weapon systems can offset much larger and much more expensive systems, for example, accurately fired rocket-propelled grenades can down light armored helicopters or land vehicles. An array of surface-to-air missiles, from shoulder-launched Stinger to ground-launched AMRAAM (Advanced Medium-Range Air-to-Air Missile) can in theory disable multimillion-dollar jets if these targets are locked onto by the missile guidance systems in range. A variety of warheads can be loaded on these missiles to suit the targets. For anti-tank missiles like the AGM-114 Hellfire missiles, the warhead contains a conical-shaped explosive charge in a copper liner cone to blast a jet of high-pressure gas through heavy armors in addition to the kinetic energy that the missile

Figure 2.1. AIM-54 Phoenix missile being launched from F-14 Tomcat. Photo courtesy of the U.S. Navy.

Figure 2.2 (a) and (b). Launch of a surface-to-air FIM-92 Stinger missile. Photo courtesy of the U.S. Army.

carries at a velocity of 950 mph. Since the end of the World War II, nuclear warheads installed on long-range ballistic missiles have continued to pose mutual threats among former Cold War adversaries and humanity. These nuclear weapons can be delivered from ground-launched ICBMs, submarine-launched SLBMs, cruise missiles, and even on artillery shells. The intercontinental ballistic delivery of the nuclear warheads involves high-altitude, high-speed trajectories that can only be provided using rocket thrusters.

The key components in missile technology are (1) the propulsion system, (2) the guidance unit, and (3) the armament. Rockets burning solid propellants are commonly used as the propulsion system because this type of propellants tend to be most stable, cost-effective, and easiest to maintain, but more sophisticated liquid-propellant rockets and gas-turbine engines are also used for long-range and cruise missiles, respectively. There are numerous passive and active guidance systems, ranging from heat-seeking sensors, active radars, and GPS (global positioning system) to terrain contour matching. Once the missile reaches the target, delivered by the propulsion and the guidance system, then it is the armament that determines the amount of damage. Conventional munitions are carried by a majority of missile weapons in use, although there still exists a large arsenal of nuclear and other weapons of mass destruction in the world deployable using tactical or strategic missile platforms. In this chapter, we look into these technologies, as well as see how the technology is used in various weapon systems. However, before we delve into these topics, let us look at how it all began.

A BRIEF HISTORY OF MISSILE TECHNOLOGY

Rocketry for military use is believed to have begun in China. The "black powder" was discovered before 900 CE in China and was used by the Chinese army to make crude flame throwers ("fire lance"), grenades, siege weapons, and other devices that delivered shock effects against the Mongols in the tenth century. There are references to the existence of black powder in Chinese documents dated as far back as 850 CE, and another Chinese document, "Wu Jing Zong Yao" ("Collection of the Most Important Military Techniques"), contains three different recipes for black powder—two for incendiary bombs to be used during siege and one for propelling bombs. A systematic military use of black powder is believed to have occurred in Kai Fung Fu, China, in 1232 CE through rack-launched bamboo rockets described as "arrows of fire." The Chinese also developed cannons and used black powder to launch heavy projectiles. When Mongols conquered China in the 1270s and acquired the technology, the use of cannons and rockets powered by black powder became widespread in the East Asian warfare. Like most other technology discussed in this book, when it came to technology on which survival depended the dissemination was quite rapid and widespread. The Arabs, being adjacent to Asia and also having been overrun by the Mongols, learned of the black powder in the thirteenth century. The Turks built an enormous ninety-cm-bore cannon that flung 320 kg cannonballs over a mile. In Europe some years later, the use of black powder was predominantly in guns and cannons, which developed rapidly through the inventiveness of the people and the metallurgical knowhow of that time.

Black powder consists of readily available ingredients—charcoal, sulfur, and saltpeter (potassium nitrate)—and was probably discovered by accident and perfected through trial-and-error. It acquires explosive characteristics only when finely ground and thoroughly mixed to the right proportions. Saltpeter is a naturally occurring substance with a white powdery appearance. It is an oxidation product of nitrogen-containing biological waste formed in the presence of water and oxygen and has a chemical formula of KNO_3 (K stands for potassium, N nitrogen, and O oxygen). As we can see in its chemical formula, it is rich in oxygen content and serves as the oxidizer. To burn any fuel, we need both the fuel and oxygen, and saltpeter releases the needed oxygen when heated. The burning of black powder goes something like this:

2 parts saltpeter + sulfur + 3 parts charcoal $\rightarrow$ combustion products + nitrogen + heat

As we will see later, both the volume of the combustion product and the amount of heat are important for generating thrust to propel rocket devices.

The invention of the black powder has had a long-lasting and profound effect on three major applications, missiles, guns, and fireworks. When packed inside a barrel, the black powder provided a near-instantaneous release of energy and high-pressure gas that hurled the projectile to great distances. By modifying the powder mix, early inventors of this technology discovered that the explosive characteristics could be controlled (i.e., the burning rate slowed down to sustain a steady thrust). Also, by dampening the mixture and slowly drying it, the black powder could be caked and packed into a desired shape. These are the same desirable characteristics in the solid-rocket boosters used in many of the modern missiles.

However, the use of the black powder in Europe was almost exclusively toward gunnery, to fire projectiles from long barrels such as muskets and cannons, therefore the common name "gunpowder" when referring to black powder. This was a natural development of the period because the most readily available technology to accurately guide the pellet trajectory was through the long muzzle of muskets. Plus the technology to fuse the warhead carried by missiles had not yet been invented. Military use of projectiles to deliver explosive warheads, interestingly enough, was reintroduced to the western world through another Asian nation, India. During a series of battles between an Indian kingdom, Mysore, and Britain in the late eighteenth century, a chieftain named Tippoo Sahib is known to have equipped his army with hundreds of rockets in cast-iron tubes. Cast-iron tubes, as opposed to bamboo tubes common in China and India, added weight but also to the strength of the tube, so that the powder charges could be packed in at higher quantity and density to withstand the pressure achieved during firing. It is believed that these rockets could be fired from a distance of one and a half miles. Although eventually defeated when British cannons, by luck, hit the rocket storage room inside Sahib's walled castle, the Indian rocket technology made a strong impression on the British troops, who shipped some of the intact rockets back to the Royal Arsenal at home.

The son of the comptroller of the Royal Arsenal at the time, William Congreve, was not only a Cambridge graduate with good connections to the British military through his father but also an inventive soul. By the time he finished, he would be responsible for patents for steam engines, canal locks, and printing techniques. The effectiveness of the Indian rocketry did not escape his keen interest because he was looking for a technology to destroy the troop-carrying barges that Napoleon was assembling for attack on Britain. One of the Congreve rocket designs is shown in Fig. 2.3 and is in fact quite similar to the Indian designs of Sahib. Thus began the modern development and military use of missile technology.

Congreve's rocket designs evolved into more sophisticated designs 1890s, incorporating metal casing, spin stabilization, and machine packing. However, there was a fundamental limit in the range of rockets using black powders. The use of black powder in rocketry up to this date owed to the ready availability of the ingredients. However, black powder generates a relative low thrust, or in technical terms, has a low specific impulse. Although we will get into some of the technical details later, specific impulse is the thrust force that you get when burning one pound of propellant in one second. Therefore, the larger the specific thrust the more thrust you will get. The specific impulse of black powder is about 80, compared to 150 to 300 for modern solid propellants. This of course means that you need a lot of black powder to

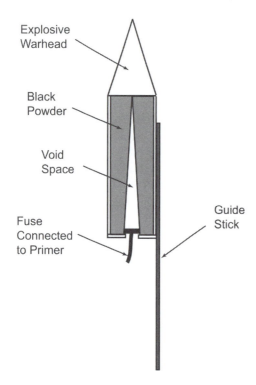

Figure 2.3. Early Congreve rocket design.

send the projectile a long distance or to a great height, and a lot of black powder in turn means more weight. So without the science and technological foundation, no further advances of black powder rockets were possible.

The basic scientific and engineering aspects of rocketry began to be formulated near the turn of the nineteenth century. A Russian named Konstantin Edvardovich Tsiolkovsky with little formal education read and taught himself physics, astronomy, and mathematics while attending public lectures and performing chemical experiments at home. In the midst of these self-absorbed activities, he published what is believed to be the first rigorous treatise on rocketry in the *Scientific Review* journal in 1903. In it, he presented logics and detailed calculations for a high-altitude rocket and showed that black powder had insufficient specific impulse for propelling an object, say, to a stable Earth's orbit or beyond (this would require a velocity of 18,000 mph, according to his calculations). Instead, he suggested the use of hydrogen and liquid oxygen, to be pumped into a metal combustion chamber. This is remarkable in the sense that he foresaw (through scientific calculations) the use of hydrogen as rocket fuel, as used in modern space shuttles, and also the design of liquid-propellant rocket engines. He also proposed the use of staging: jettisoning of spent fuel/oxidizer tanks and engines to reduce the system weight in flight. In spite of his pioneering theoretical contributions, however, he was a pure theoretician and made no attempt to turn his concepts into an operating rocket system.

The first realization of the modern rockets was made in the early 1900s by an American scientist and engineer, Robert Hutchings Goddard. A physicist by training, Goddard reached celebrity status when he published a sixty-nine page treatise called "On a Method of Reaching Extreme Altitudes." This was an age when space travel and rocketry were only fictional technologies found in novels by Jules Verne and H.G. Wells, and the public response to realizable space travel was sensational, leading in time to the formation of so-called rocket societies in the United States, Russia, Germany, and other places. A contemporary of Goddard, Hermann Oberth of Germany, also published pioneering works on rocketry but was not able to achieve the technical breakthroughs for an operational rocket. Goddard shunned publicity and kept most of his findings in modern rocket designs (see Fig. 2.4) within his own operation, consisting of assistants and mechanics; however, he and his ideas were charismatic enough to earn him continued and large support from public and private sponsors such as the Smithsonian Institute, the Carnegie Institute, and Charles Guggenheim. His work and technical innovations in valves, pumps, controls, and materials culminated in liquid-propellant rockets that he called the

Figure 2.4. Early designs by the American rocket pioneer, Robert H. Goddard. Photo courtesy of NASA.

"A-series." The A-series rockets were fueled by gasoline and liquid oxygen and generated 200 lbs of thrust for a top speed of 700 mph to reach altitudes up to 7500 feet.

The world's military powers at the time saw the potential for rockets and started establishing research and development plans. In Russia, it was the Reaction Propulsion Research Institute (RNII) under the direction of General Mikhail Tukhachevsky and later under an engineer named Segei Korolev when the general was purged and shot on Josef Stalin's orders. In Germany, the resurgent energy and finance of the then-Nazi state funded the rocket development and test facility at Peenemunde to the tune of $90 million, a tremendous amount in 1939. The German army, under the Treaty of Versailles restrictions for arms development and production following the World War I, had a free hand in the case of military rockets because there were no terms or limitations on yet unknown rockets. Wernher von Braun and a team of engineers developed advanced pumps for the fuel and oxidizers, cooling methods for the combustion chamber, and guidance systems to result in the infamous V-series rockets used during the World War II. So again, the major driver of the cutting-edge technology was the potential for military use. This indeed was also the case in the United States. Following the successes of Goddard's rockets, the U.S. Army established a research program at the California Institute of Technology (more often called Caltech) to a fluid mechanic professor named Theodore von Karman. Von Karman and the Caltech group developed new fuel/oxidizer combinations for both liquid and solid rocket propellants during this time. The specific aim of the U.S. Army in use of rocketry was directed toward rocket boosters for aircraft, as in jet-assisted take-offs for aircraft. The Caltech group eventually formed a corporation called Aerojet, named for the use of rockets.

The developments out of Peenemunde and later Mittelwerk were quite substantial. The precursor to the V-2 rocket, called A-4, flew to an altitude of 50 miles and a range of 120 miles in one of its early test flights in October 3, 1942. The first of the V-series weapons deployed during the World War II, V-1, however, was actually not a rocket but an unmanned aircraft powered by a gasoline-fueled pulse-jet engine. The V in the V-series weapons stood for the German word *Vergeltungswaffen*, or "weapons of vengeance." A pulse-jet engine is simply a jet engine with intermittent fuel injection, so that the combustion occurs at a frequency from 40 to 150 times per second (as opposed to a continuous operation). Pulse-jet engines were made without the complexity of compressors typically used in standard jet engines and therefore involved simple design and construction. Instead, the engine relied on so-called ram pressure, pressure that is attained when the air is ingested at a high speed. The high frequency of the combustion cycle caused a tremendous level of vibration and noise and therefore the nickname "buzz bomb." V-1s carried close to 2000 lbs of explosives. If one saw any photographs of the damage caused by a 1000-lb bomb during the recent Iraq war, one can imagine the physical and psychological horror that 2000 lbs of explosives may have caused, particularly in mostly civilian (or random) targets even after taking into account the change in the energy density of the explosives from then and now. V-1s were essentially unguided flying objects, with the only target control launching them in a certain direction and cutting off the pulse-jet engine, at which time it underwent a free fall to the ground below. V-1s flew at a speed of about 390 mph, close to the top speed of the propeller-powered fighter aircraft of the time, so they could be shot down by manned fighters. In fact, out of approximately 7500 V-1s launched toward England, approximately half of them were shot down by fighter aircraft and anti-aircraft artillery.

The V-2 was a different beast altogether. V-2s were 46 ft in height, 5 ft 6 in diameter, and carried a warhead of 2000 lbs of explosives. Below the warhead on V-2s was a section for guidance instruments (gyroscopes, steering controls), and a 20-ft section for fuel and oxidizer tanks. The fuel was a mixture of 75 percent alcohol and 25 percent water, while the oxidizer was liquid oxygen. The engine section contained the combustion chamber, oxidizer, and fuel pumps and a small steam turbine to drive the oxidizer and fuel pumps.

The steam turbine itself used a rocket fuel, hydrogen peroxide. Hydrogen peroxide in its pure state is a highly volatile substance that releases a large amount of heat when it decomposes into water vapor and oxygen. The high-temperature steam thus generated can be used to drive the steam turbines, which in turn turns the fuel and oxidizer pumps. The guidance was relatively crude. V-2s were launched at a predetermined angle and direction, and an onboard gyroscope detected a change in the launch angle, direction, and speed. When the gyroscopes detected deviations, then hydraulics were activated for the steering vanes in the exhaust section for the direction control. The steering vanes worked by slightly altering the direction of the rocket exhaust stream. The speed was controlled simply by shutting off the rocket engine when the set speed was achieved.

V-2s rose to a peak altitude of 50 to 55 miles, and covered a range close to 200 miles. They are what we call ballistic missiles, with a short, high-power boost phase immediately after launch. The boost phase is followed by a free fall trajectory from a high altitude reaching a great speed before impact on the ground. V-2s caused a great deal of physical and psychological damage during World War II, and they are also significant because they were precursors to the later American and Russian ballistic missiles.

In addition to the V-2 rockets deployed by the German army, rocket-powered weaponry began to take its place as an essential component of the armed forces arsenal during World War II. The U.S. Army bazooka was used against tanks as well as other fortified targets. The bazooka was essentially a rocket-powered grenade, launched from a cylindrical tube 4.5 ft long with a 3-indiameter in the version mostly used during World War II. The entire unit when loaded was only 13.3 lbs, and the projectile was 3.4 lbs, out of which 1.57 lbs was the explosive and the remainder mostly the rocket propellant. The rocket booster part derived from Goddard's pioneering work on rockets, and in fact was a side project of his funded by the Army Signal Corps during its early development from 1918 to 1923. Later, the design was knocked into shape by the army and navy engineers and also combined with a shaped charge (an explosive charge shaped to concentrate the force on a small area for hard targets such as tank armor) to become the bazooka, or the rocket launcher M1A1 by 1942. The early bazooka model used a 2.36-in diameter tube, but the tube length was 7 ft. However, soon the extra length was discarded in favor of the 3-in diameter tube of 4.5 ft length. The round was a modified mortar shell with an exhaust nozzle and stabilization fins. Instead of the mortar propellant pressurizing the launch tube, the addition of the exhaust nozzle forced the explosive gas to be ejected to provide speed for the bazooka rounds. An electrical current sent to the primer ignited the main propellant. These bazooka rounds could knock out medium-armored tanks from 200 yds or be aimed at the tracks and wheels of heavy-armor tanks, in addition to being very effective against hardened bunkers and building structures. German tanks, wary of bazooka attacks, started sporting vertical armor plates to cover the wheels and tracks. From captured bazookas, the Germans developed their own version called *panzershreck* (tank terror). However, the effective range of 200 yds seemed much closer when facing tanks, and also bazooka rounds left a telltale smoke trail that could be traced to the bazooka loader and shooter team. The success of the bazooka model during World War II led to a continuous evolution of LAW's (light anti-tank weapons), and follow-up models included the M9, M9A1, M20A1 (the "Super Bazooka"), and modern-day shoulder-fired SAMs (surface-to-air missiles).

The U.S.-made barrage rockets were another rocket-powered weapon widely used during World War II. Originally designed as aircraft-fired air-to-surface missiles, the deployment quickly spread to all branches of the U.S. military. Again, during launch the projectiles were guided along a tube of about 3 ft in length with a diameter of 3.25 or 4.5 in. In contrast to the heavy, complex artillery guns, the rocket-powered bombs could be transported and fired with much more ease. These rockets were given the M-8 designation by the U.S. military and could be deployed in many different launchers. The 8-tube or

60-tube launchers could be mounted and fired from the top of trucks or tanks, or a single M-8 could be launched from something as simple as a plastic tripod. The Navy version was called M-16, and these were fired from a ship-mounted 24-tube launcher called the "Honeycomb" or a 60-tube launcher called the "Hornet's Nest" toward land targets during landing operations. These barrage rockets had a range of up to 2 miles with top speeds of 600 to 900 mph, depending on the model.

Rocket-fired weapons, bigger and more powerful by this time, started to augment the typical cannon and dropped-bomb armament in aircraft. The British developed the so-called RP (rocket projectile) that was fin-stabilized and propelled by solid propellant in a 3-in diameter tube, to carry a 65 lb explosive in a 5-in diameter warhead. The American counterpart of this air-launched direct-fire weapon was the FFAR (forward firing aircraft rocket) that was used on slow or stationary surface targets. An upgrade version called HVAR (high velocity aircraft rocket) was 6 ft long and could penetrate 1.5 in of steel armor by impacting the target at a speed of 950 mph. Another aircraft-launched rocket called "Tiny Tim" was not tiny at all with a 12-in diameter and 1200 lbs of weight, out of which 500 lbs was armor-piercing warhead designed for use against Japanese warships.

After World War II, the use of the rockets expanded to non-military uses in high-altitude research, high-speed aircraft developments, and various space programs. All of these applications would, however, be intertwined in one form or another with military exploitations, such as in large rocket thrusters being converted for launching of nuclear weapons or satellites being used as reconnaissance platforms. Similarly, development of high-speed aircraft capable of breaking the sound barrier was pursued by the U.S. Army, Navy, Air Force, and NACA (National Advisory Committee on Aeronautics). The aircraft designed to pursue this interest in high-speed flight was the famed X-1, built by Bell Aircraft and powered by a four-chamber alcohol-oxygen rocket engine. Unlike other airplanes of the time (see Figs. 2.5 and 2.6), X-1 was shaped more like a bullet with a thin, flat wing and a horizontal tail that rotated in its entirety much like modern jet fighters. The liquid-propellant rocket motor could not be throttled, instead the pilot ignited a combination of four chambers in turn to apply some control over the total thrust. X-1 carried just enough fuel to propel itself for short durations, so it was carried underneath a B-29 bomber and released at high altitudes to begin its flights. On October 14, 1947, four days after reaching Mach 0.997, X-1 flown by test pilot Captain Charles "Chuck" Yeager was released from the B-29 bomber at an altitude of 20,000 ft. Igniting two of the rocket combustion chambers quickly accelerated the aircraft to an altitude of 40,000 ft. Igniting the third chamber at that altitude pushed the Mach number to 1.02 and then 1.06. Eventually, X-1 would reach a speed of Mach 1.45, and because the engine did not require any external air an altitude of 70,000 ft could be reached by the rocket aircraft.

Figure 2.5. X-1 rocket-powered aircraft that first broke the sound barrier. Photo courtesy of the U.S. Air Force.

The German V-2 rockets were the first ballistic missiles used for military purposes, and the rocket technology was quickly acquired by both

Figure 2.6. X-1 aircraft attached under B-29 bomber. Photo courtesy of the U.S. Air Force.

the United States and the Soviet Union after the downfall of the Nazi Germany. Up to 1950, the United States Army working with the Jet Propulsion Laboratory at Caltech used the V-2 as the primary booster for sounding rockets, high-altitude vehicles with various sensors to measure properties of the upper atmosphere. The V-2 rocket was combined with a smaller WAC Corporal upper-stage rocket and flew to a record 250-mile altitude in the first operational flights of multistage rockets. The U.S. Navy in collaboration with the Applied Physics Laboratory of Johns Hopkins University developed its own sounding rocket called "Aerobee," capable of lifting 150-lb payloads to an altitude of 60 miles. The Viking rocket design followed with a number of innovations. A more accurate guidance algorithm was put in place, light aluminum material was used in place of steel for major structural components, the fuel tank served as the outer rocket casing, and engines were mounted on gimbals to swivel back and forth for trajectory control in place of troublesome carbon vanes that deflected the rocket exhaust streams. The final versions of Viking rockets would be capable of sending 825 lbs of instrumentation to a height of 158 miles.

The Russians also used the German V-2 rockets as the starting point of their rocket program. From the R-1 (SS-1 Scud by the western or later NATO designation) to R-5 (SS-3 Shyster), these rockets were direct adaptations of the V-2 rocket engine technology, although improvements in the engine design and propellant formulation increased the final range to 700 miles and the payload to 3000 lbs. The upgraded version of R-5, designated R-5M, would also contain an improved guidance unit to be able to hit targets within a radius of about 1000 ft, whereas the V-2 was merely sent toward city-sized targets. The American counterpart of the V-2 adaptation rocket called the "Redstone" was developed by Wernher von Braun himself working with other German expatriates from Peenemunde and had similar accuracy except with a range similar to the original V-2 (200 miles). With such accuracy and a payload of several thousand pounds, these served as the first potential carriers of nuclear warheads for both countries. To achieve this level of accuracy, an inertial guidance system was used in conjunction with gimbaled engines. The inertial guidance system contained accelerometers and gyroscopes to detect the changes in the speed and orientation of the rocket, and by keeping track of these changes the guidance algorithm computed the deviation from the intended trajectory. Compensations were made by turning the engine gimbals to bring the rocket back to its intended line of motion. In addition, a separable warhead was designed to follow a stabilized motion away from the bulky booster during the approach phase. The Soviet R-5M was armed with a 1 MT (megaton or million tons) warhead, while the American Redstone was capable of delivering a 3.5 MT weapon. To give an idea as to the quantum leap in the destructive power of these weapons, the atom bomb dropped on Hiroshima was 15 kT (kiloton or thousand tons) and the largest conventional bomb used during World War II, called "Grand Slam," was 5 tons in equivalent TNT. Although the range of the missiles at this time was measured in hundreds of miles, not yet a threat as long-range ballistic missiles, these technologies would allow future missiles to become intercontinental carriers of nuclear warheads once boosters were developed to increase the range to thousands of miles.

The next-generation rockets would indeed bring both the payload and range close to the ICBM category. Using kerosene and liquid oxygen (LOX) in high-pressure combustion chambers enhanced the thrust of the American "Thor" and "Jupiter" to give a range of 1400 and 1600 miles, respectively. The Russians opted for the use of nitric acid as the oxidizer, under the calculated risk that even though nitric acid was highly corrosive it did not need cryogenic equipment as LOX did and therefore could be kept in a ready-to-launch state for much longer periods of time. The Soviet R-12 and R-14 had respective ranges of 1400 and 2000 miles, and this class of missiles was referred to as "theater weapons" or IRBMs (intermediate-range ballistic missiles). Due to their intermediate range, they needed to be based relatively close to the targets. For the American IRBMs, Italy and Turkey served as sufficiently close launch points, while the Soviets did not possess such logistic launch sites except for newly reformulated Cuba under Fidel Castro. The clandestine operation to base Soviet R-12s and R-14s was discovered by the American reconnaissance airplanes and led to the Cuban missile crisis in 1962. The ensuing confrontation was quite tenuous for about two weeks until the two sides made a covert agreement to pull their respective missiles from Cuba for the Soviets and from Italy and Turkey for the Americans. In the next several years, both sides would develop operational long-range ICBMs, obviating the need for such close-range launch sites altogether.

In fact, the work to develop rocket boosters capable of carrying heavier payloads over longer ranges was already underway in the late 1950s. The Soviet R-7 and R-7A, for example, had a range of up to 5000 miles with a payload of 12,000 lbs. On top of that, an improved guidance system using both inertial and radio control improved the accuracy as well. The R-7 rockets had a core booster surround by four additional boosters, and each booster had four small rocket engines for a total of twenty engines. There were separate small gimbaled vernier engines installed in the core booster for attitude control, while there were two such vernier engines on each side booster. The first ICBMs developed in the United States were the Atlas and Titan (Fig. 2.7), introduced in 1961 and 1962, respectively. The Atlas missiles were equipped with one main sustainer and two boosters, where the boosters were jettisoned after the main boost phase. The Titan had a more conventional two-stage design and could carry a larger payload than Atlas. Both of these missiles contained inertial guidance and separable reentry vehicle design to give a 600-yd radius of accuracy in delivery of 1 MT– class thermonuclear warheads. These rocket boosters would also serve both nations well in their respective space programs, with the R-7 booster being used to place the first artificial satellite, Sputnik I, in orbit. The American manned space flight programs Mercury and Gemini used the Redstone, Atlas (shown in Fig. 2.8), and Titan II missiles in the 1960s. The Titan series evolved from a 30-m long RP-1/LOX fueled Titan I

Figure 2.7. The early version of the Titan booster used for the Gemini manned space flights. Photo courtesy of the U.S. Air Force.

Figure 2.8. Atlas V launch vehicle evolved from the USAF ICBM program in the 1960s. Photo courtesy of the U.S. Air Force.

Figure 2.9. The Titan IV Centaur booster used for sending unmanned payload into earth orbit by the USAF. Photo courtesy of the U.S. Air Force.

booster, to Titan II ICBMs, to Titan III with two side solid rocket boosters, to the Titan IV Centaur whose combined length with all of its IUS (Inertial Upper Stage) components in place was close to 50 m. The use of LOX in Titan I meant that this cryogenic oxidizer needed to be pumped into the tank prior to launch, and this sequence would take fifteen to twenty minutes, diminishing its launch readiness capability. For this reason, Titan II and later versions would use hydrazine-based fuel with nitrogen tetroxide as oxidizer. The Titan IV could carry payloads equivalent in size and weight to those that could be delivered by the space shuttles and has been the most powerful booster for unmanned payloads for the United States. The launch was made with only the side solid boosters running, and the first-stage liquid propellant core engine fired up after two minutes of the solid rocket burning. The Titan IV liquid-propellant motors use Aerozine 50 as fuel and nitrogen tetroxide as oxidizer, which like nitric acid requires elaborate and expensive handling equipment. The use of the corrosive and hypergolic (ignitable on contact) substances again bypasses the need for the cryogenic equipment required for LOX and allows storage of the propellants for extended periods of time. The first and second stage engines burn from 164 and 223 s, respectively, while the third Centaur state has a burntime of 625 s. For low earth orbits (LEO), payloads of up to 47,800 lbs (lower for polar LEO) can be launched using Titan IV, while for higher-altitude geosynchronous orbits or interplanetary trajectories the limiting weight is approximately 12,500 lbs. The early Titan rocket fuel RP-1 is highly refined kerosene, while the Aerozine 50 used in Titan IV is a 50/50 mixture of hydrazine and UDMN (unsymmetrical dimethylhydrazine). The Titan III/Centaur combination would also be known for its role in sending the Viking Mars probe and Voyager probe to the outer planets and the Helios solar probe.

The emergence of spy satellite technology accelerated the pace of development and use of dedicated launch vehicles. The IRBM booster Thor was coupled with an upper stage "Agena" to launch a series of "Corona" spy satellites. The Thor-based multistage boosters evolved into NASA's Delta rockets that could be augmented with strap-on boosters to provide heavy payload and high altitude capabilities. Figure 2.10 shows the evolution of the Delta rocket from the lone Thor IRBM, to the Thor-Able combination with the Able upper stage added on top of Thor, to a Delta II with multiple side strap-on solid-propellant rockets, and to Delta IV with the core plus two liquid-propellant strap-on boosters. The Delta II and IV launch vehicles are used up as of the time of this book's publication

Figure 2.10. A sequence of images showing the evolution of the Delta rocket. Photos courtesy of the U.S. Air Force and NASA.

(see Fig. 2.11), and during 1980s, after the Challenger disaster and the stand-down of the space shuttle fleet, they served as able launch vehicles to uplift the backlog of orbital payloads.

MODERN MISSILE TECHNOLOGY

The use of missiles has multiplied to all branches of the military. Below are some of the weapon categories in which missiles are specifically deployed:

Air-to-air missile (AAM)
Air-to-surface missile (ASM)
Surface-to-air missile (SAM)
Surface-to-surface missile (SSM)
Ballistic missile (BM)
   Intercontinental ballistic missile (ICBM)
   Submarine launched ballistic missile (SLBM)
   Anti-ballistic missile (ABM)
Cruise missile
   Anti-ship missile (AShM)
   Anti-submarine Rocket (ASROC)
   Anti-tank guided missile (ATGM)
   Anti-satellite weapon (ASAT)
   Anti-radiation missile (ARM)

Air-to-Air Missiles

These missiles are typically fired from aircrafts or helicopters against other airborne targets. For some long-range air-to-air missiles (AAMs), the missile is sent to the coordinate where the target aircraft has been identified through an inertial guidance system, then a more precise guidance using radar or infrared (heat seekers) tracking may be applied to zero in on the target. Short-range AAMs may be equipped with a simple, multiwavelength infrared seeker to lock on to the exhaust of jet aircrafts.

Figure 2.11. Launch of the Delta rocket with an unknown National Reconnaissance Office payload from Vandenberg Air Force Base. Photo courtesy of the U.S. Air Force.

Table 2.1 shows the various AAMs used by various military forces in the world. As shown in the table, many of the AAMs are guided by a passive, infrared (IR) tracking system due to its compactness and simplicity. These infrared seekers detect the thermal exhaust from jet engines and guide the missile in the direction where the maximum infrared signal is detected. Heat from the exhaust is partially given off through infrared radiation that can be detected using infrared detectors. Active radar tracking requires the missile to carry a small-aperture radar antenna and send out radar signals to seek the target aircraft. These self-guidance methods are associated with the fire-and-forget missiles and can be used for medium- to long-range targets. Semi-active radar means that the missile only carries the radar receiver and homes in on the radar signal sent from the launch aircraft and reflected off from the target aircraft. Semi-active radars require the launch aircraft to remain engaged and lock its radar on the target. Although rarely used in AAM, sometimes optical tracking or "beam-riding" guidance systems are used. Instead of radar locks, the launch aircraft illuminates the target with a laser beam the reflection of which is acquired by the missile homing device. We will look at the technology behind different guidance systems in more detail in a separate section later in this book.

A photograph of AIM-120 AMRAAM, also known as the Slammer by the fighter pilots, is shown in Fig. 2.12. The missile is long and thin, contained in a 7-in diameter tube with a length of 12 ft. About half the length of the missile is used for the solid propellant, and the nozzle is movable to provide rapid control of the missile heading. An igniter wire runs through the center of the propellant and is fired up at missile launch. A data link is also located at the tail of the missile. A highly effective warhead of less than 50 lbs is located in the mid-section, just ahead of the fixed middle fins. A target detector device (TDD) and fuse are located next to the explosive charge, and when TDD senses the

Table 2.1. Some of the Main AAMs in the World.

Country of Origin	Name	Guidance Method
Brazil	Mectron MAA-1 Piranha	Short range IR
France	Matra R550 Magic, similar to the	IR
	American AIM-9 Sidewinder	IR
	Matra Magic II	Active radar
	Magic Super 530F/Super 530D, French	Inertial guidance and active
	counterpart of the AIM-7 Sparrow	radar (fire-and-forget)
	MBDA MICA—French counterpart of	
	the AIM-120 AMRAAM	
Italy	Alenia Aspide, Italian manufactured	Active radar
	version of the AIM-7 Sparrow	Medium-range, active radar
	MBDA Meteor	homing
	IRIS-T, replacement for AIM-9	Short-range infrared
	Sidewinder	homing
Israel	Rafael Python 4—medium range IR	Medium-range IR
	Rafael Python 5, improves on Python 4	Medium-range IR
People's Republic	PL-1, Chinese version of the Soviet	Short-range IR
of China	Kaliningrad K-5 (NATO reporting	Short-range IR
	name AA-1 "Alkali") PL-9	Semi-active radar
	PL-10, Chinese version of the Italian	Active homing guidance
	Aspide	system
	PL-11/AMR-1, similar to the Russian	Medium-range active radar
	Vympel R-27 (NATO reporting name	
	AA-10 "Alamo")	
	SD-10	
	TY-90, first air-to-air missile designed for	
	helicopters	
Russia	Kaliningrad K-5 (NATO reporting	Beam Tracking
	name AA-1 "Alkali")	Short-range IR
	Vympel K-13 (NATO reporting name	IR
	AA-2 "Atoll")	IR
	Kaliningrad K-8 (NATO reporting	IR
	name AA-3 "Anab")	Long-range IR
	Raduga K-9 (NATO reporting	Medium-range SARH or IR
	name AA-4 "Awl")	Short-range IR
	Bisnovat R-4 (NATO reporting	Long-range active radar
	name AA-5 "Ash")	Medium-range SARH or IR
	Bisnovat R-40 (NATO reporting	Short-range IR
	name AA-6 "Acrid")	Medium-range active radar
	Vympel R-23 (NATO reporting	
	name AA-7 "Apex")	
	Molniya R-60 (NATO reporting	
	name AA-8 "Aphid")	
	Vympel R-33 (NATO reporting	
	name AA-9 "Amos")	
	Vympel R-27 (NATO reporting	
	name AA-10 "Alamo")	
	Vympel R-73 (NATO reporting	
	name AA-11 "Archer")	
	Vympel R-77 (NATO reporting	
	name AA-12 "Adder")	

(Continued)

Table 2.1. Continued

Country of Origin	Name	Guidance Method
Brazil	Mectron MAA-1 Piranha	Short range IR
United Kingdom	AIM-132 ASRAAM	Short-range, IR
	Skyflash	Radar
United States	AIM-4 Falcon	Radar/IR
	AIM-7 Sparrow	Medium-range semi-active radar
	AIM-9 Sidewinder	Short-range IR
	AIM-54 Phoenix	Short-range IR
	AIM-120 AMRAAM	Long-range, semi-active and active radar
		Medium-range, active radar; replaces AIM-7 Sparrow

Figure 2.12. AIM-120 AMRAAM unleashed from an F-16 fighter jet. Photo courtesy of the U.S. Air Force.

proximity to the target it sends a signal through the fuse to detonate the warhead. The remaining forward section contains the radome for the active radar, battery, transmitter, and main guidance electronics. Its solid rocket motor propels the missile to supersonic speeds and for directional control uses vectored thrust and moving fins. As previously noted, it uses an inertial guidance system to get to the target vicinity and then turns on its active radar to home in on the target. Its unit cost is in excess of $386,000 as of 2003, and it is manufactured by Hughes/Raytheon. It is an improved AAM over the preceding AIM-7 Sparrow, envisioned as the beyond-visual-range weapon, and has a more advanced and lethal guidance system. AIM-7 missile guidance was via semi-active radar, as listed in Table 2.1, meaning that the aircraft must illuminate the target while AIM-7 can only guide itself based on the reflection of this radar signal from the target. This requires the aircraft to be fully engaged during the missile pursuit. In contrast, AIM-120 is installed with active radar, a radar transmitter antenna, and a pulse seeker. The pulse seeker searches for a specific waveform radar signal sent out by the transmitter to overcome interference, jamming, and other electronic countermeasures. This autonomous tracking allows the aircraft to pursue multiple targets and disengage after the missile launch. The active radar is activated on missile's arrival at the scene, and an inertial guidance unit with data update capabilities via signals sent by the launch aircraft takes the missile to the engagement scene. Also, the armament carried by AIM-120 is an improvement over AIM-7. AIM-120 carries a blast-fragmentation warhead with a proximity fuse, to enhance its kill probability.

AIM-120s are powered by the Hercules solid-propellant rocket motor. The ingredients of the solid propellant are not only proprietary but also classified, but they are designed for sustained high thrust and reduced smoke (to make visible detection difficult). The rocket motor propels the missile to a speed of approximately Mach 4 (four times the speed of sound at that altitude), and a maximum range of 46 miles. AMRAAM is compatible with most United States and NATO fighter aircraft, including the F-15, F-16, F-18A, F-22, and

British Sea Harrier. AMRAAMs can also be used as surface-launched CLAWS (complimentary low altitude weapon system) carried on HMMWV (Humvee) vehicles. Five AMRAAMs can be adapted for Humvee launch in the HUMRAAM adaptation program to provide mobile air defense.

AIM-54 Phoenix (Fig. 2.13) is another fire-and-forget type of missile, except with a much bigger range. It has an active radar guidance system and a maximum range of 127 miles at a speed of Mach 5. Most jet

Figure 2.13. AIM-54 Phoenix missile. Photo courtesy of the U.S. Department of Defense.

fighters have maximum cruise speed (without firing the afterburner) of just over Mach 1 and maximum speeds between Mach 2 and 3. For example, the U.S. Navy's F-14 Tomcat, which carries Phoenix missiles, has a maximum speed of Mach 2.34. At an altitude of 49,000 ft, Mach 2.34 is 1544 mph. So a missile speeding at Mach 5 toward a much slower jet fighter is a formidable threat. However, both AIM-54 and F-14 Tomcats have been retired from the United States Navy. A photograph of a Phoenix missile shows the size that was needed to carry sufficient propellant for the required speed and range. The long-burning Mk47 solid-propellant rocket motor was made by Rocketdyne and, along with the hydraulically driven tail fins, provided exceptional sustained thrust and maneuverability. The front section contained the radome for the planar array active radar and guidance electronics, and again the warhead of 60 kg of high explosive is found in the mid-section. Three proximity fuse antennas embedded equidistantly on the outside of the missile senses the presence of the target along with an impact sensor in the event of a direct hit. To the rear of the missile sits the solid propellant motor, and the rear section contains the hydraulic control for the tail fins. The last version of the Phoenix missile, AIM-54C weighed over 1000 lbs at a length of 13 ft and diameter of 15 in (the wingspan was 3 ft). The F-14 Tomcat carried up to six of these Phoenix missiles. A weapon control system interfaced with the onboard Phoenix missiles assigned individual target coordinates for each and launched them in a sequence as determined by the target priority or as input by the pilot.

The AIM-9 Sidewinders (shown in Fig. 2.14) are smaller, yet effective anti-aircraft missiles carried by the United States and many other of the world's jet fighters in various versions. The original design was made by the Naval Weapons Center (now Naval Air Warfare Center Weapons Division) at China Lake, California, but the production is now shared between Ford Aerospace and Raytheon. This is one of the most effective AAM in existence in terms of performance, size, and cost, and nearly all U.S. allies with a respectable air force use the Sidewinders. The simplicity in the design, with less than twenty-four moving parts in the early version, allowed low-cost production, reliable performance under rugged environments, and easy adaptation to a multitude of aircraft. The design goes as far back as 1949, to the days of vacuum tubes in electronic components, but a small team of engineers succeeded in designing an operation-passive infrared seeker head that would fit in the 5-in diameter body of the Sidewinder. Since then, advances in solid-state electronics have allowed much better sensor and guidance to be installed in the missile. The early versions of the missile performed erratically except in close range where the infrared signature was unmistakable, but the uncooled lead sulfide (PbS) infrared sensor had difficulty in low visibility conditions (cloud, rain, etc.) and also had a tendency to lock on the sun or reflections of the sun on lake or river surfaces in clear weather. However, by version AIM-9D nitrogen-cooled magnesium fluoride sensors permitted higher infrared sensitivity in inclement weather conditions, and the narrowed field of view also minimized false

Figure 2.14. A photograph showing the relative size of the AIM-9 Sidewinder (top row) and AIM-7 Sparrow (bottom) missiles. Photo courtesy of the U.S. Air Force.

lock-on problem. Subsequent versions proved to be highly successful based on this design, but modifications continued on the guidance unit to further enhance the missile's lock-on capabilities from longer range. In the later versions the IR sensor operates in two wavelengths to seek corroborating signals to defeat flares or other countermeasures. Increased tracking speed along larger fins moved by high-power actuators improved the hit ratio, while annular blast fragmentation ensured significant damage at contact. Due to its relatively small size, the Sidewinders are used for short-range targets and carry 25 lbs of blast fragmentation warhead, again with a proximity fuse. A separate optical target detector senses the presence of target in its potential kill radius and detonates the armament sending the high-impact fragments for either kill or severe damage. The current version, AIM-9X, encompasses design changes to place the missile to the forefront of short-range missile performance in comparison with similar missiles used by other nations. An infrared imaging sensor, higher tracking speed, better seeker signal processing and tracking algorithm, and more powerful warhead are considered essential components in the next-generation short-range AAMs.

The AIM-132 ASRAAM (advanced short-range air-to-air missile) represents a modern design from scratch. The British government invested close to $1 billion in its development in the late 1990s in an effort to counter the threat posed by the Russian Vympel R-73 (NATO reporting name AA-11 "Archer") missile with its large sensor field of view for off-axis target acquisition, acquisition range, and tracking ability. The target acquisition characteristics were significantly improved using the Raytheon-Hughes sapphire-domed infrared focal plane imaging sensor with a 128×128 pixel array. By not only registering the magnitude of the selected infrared wavelength signatures but also the shape and direction of the signal, the target identification is enhanced along with counter-countermeasure capability. Its speed of above Mach 3 also places the ASRAAM a step ahead of the Sidewinder and the Archer.

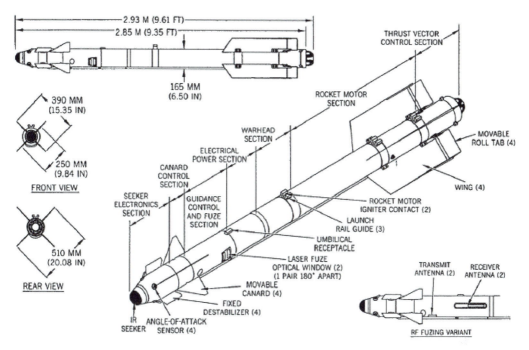

Figure 2.15. A detailed schematic of the Russian short-range AAM, Vympel R-73 (NATO reporting name AA-11 "Archer"). Schematic from the U.S. Department of Defense

Russia possesses highly effective AAMs in the Archer, a schematic of which is shown in Fig. 2.15. Although placed in a 170-mm-diameter, 2.9-m-long body, its range is rated at 30 km for R-73A and up to 40 km in later versions. AA-11 is carried by a fleet of modern Russian fighters including the MiG-29, Su-27, Su-32, and Su-35, as well as some of the older Russian jets. The missile guidance when coupled with the pilot's helmet input can be set to lock on targets in a +/– degree lateral directions from the aircraft axis, and with high maneuverability it can pursue a variety of airborne targets, fighters, bombers, attack aircrafts, helicopters, and cruise missiles, even undertaking high-G evasive maneuvers with a 12-G turn capability of its own. With exceptional counter-countermeasure and anti-jamming algorithms, it is a short-range fire-and-forget type of weapon in spite of the passive nature of the sensor device. Unlike the western counterparts with tail aerodynamic control, R-73 employs the forward surface control, or canards. The combination of the fixed forward stabilizer and control canards provide outstanding maneuverability. As shown in the schematic a laser optical sensor sends out a laser beam to look for reflected signals from the aircraft, which would set off the detonation fuse if the signal is above the set threshold. A miniature radar proximity sensor is also available, along with the standard impact sensor. A 7.4-kg high-explosive expanding rod warhead serves as the armament for the missile.

The stated ranges of the air-to-air missiles above are typically given for optimal conditions, such as head-on target pursuit and high altitudes where the air density is low and therefore the drag force on the missile is also small. For head-on targets, the distance between the target and missile rapidly closes due to the motion of the missile and the target. For tail chases, the missile obviously needs to cover much more range to acquire the target. Thus, the operating range of AAM decreases dramatically for hard pursuits involving steep turns, tail chase, and climbs and also at low altitudes. For example, the range of the Russian Vympel R-77 is stated to be 100 km for head-on targets, but this is known to decrease to only 25 km for hard pursuits. Even on head-on targets, the same missile only can fly in a 20 km range at sea level.

The Vympel R-77 (AA-12 Adder or unofficially "AMRAAMski") is the Russian counterpart to the AIM-120 AMRAAM medium-range missile. In addition to an accurate guidance unit, R-77 has an exceptional range of 90 km in the solid-rocket version and 175 km in the ramjet-powered R-77M1 version. The ramjet version is also powered initially by a small solid-propellant booster until the ramjet can start running at supersonic speeds. For the pure solid-rocket version R-77, the speed tops over Mach 4, and it can operate at an altitude of 25 km. Some versions of R-77 are suspected of high-altitude capability to the tune of 120 to 160 km, perhaps as a possible anti-satellite or anti-missile weapon. Similar to AMRAAM, an inertial guidance system sends the missile to the target area aided by mid-course adjustments, and then the active radar homes in on the intended target. A terminal infrared seeker is also available, as modern imaging sensors offer highly reliable short-range target lock-on capabilities.

Missile Guidance

We saw that IR (infrared) guidance is widely used for short-range AAMs. For missiles with longer ranges, more sophisticated active or semi-active radars are installed. In general, however, there are many different methods that are available to guide the missiles onto the target. The following are the various missile guidance methods.

1. Command-guidance
   A. Manual command line-of-sight (MCLOS)
   B. Semi-automatic command line-of-sight (SACLOS)
2. Beam-riding guidance
3. Radar
   A. Active radar
   B. Semi-active radar
   C. Track-via-missile (TVM)
4. Infrared guidance
5. Inertial and GPS guidance
6. Terrain contour matching (TERCOM)/Digital scene-matching area correlator (DSMAC)
7. Targeting by image contrast

Regardless of the guidance method, the missile guidance system consists of the following components. The sensor sends and/or receives radar, infrared, or other signals to track the target. The sensor unit typically includes a signal processing device to extract the true target signal in the midst of interference and noise. The signal is then fed to the onboard electronic hardware to generate commands according to sophisticated guidance laws. The onboard electronics involve a hardwired microcomputer (essentially a set of computer chips) dedicated to this kind of calculations. Electronically generated commands are then sent to the control unit, which activates various target adjustment devices, such as fins, tails or thrust vectoring. This loop is continuously operated, although as we shall see in the following discussions various guidance methods may be switched from one to the other depending on the flight phase of the missile.

The flight of the missile consists of the boost, mid-course, and terminal phases. The boost phase launches the missile away from the launcher, and no guidance is activated. Some long-range missiles may have a separate boost-phase rocket motor, to be jettisoned after they reach the mid-course phase. During mid-course phase, course guidance such as command guidance, inertial, or GPS is used to deliver the missile to the vicinity of the target. In the terminal phase of the flight, more precise, short-range guidance is activated to zero in on the target and to arm and detonate the missile armament. The detonation may be set off by the contact or when the guidance detects the target to be in the damage radius of the armament.

The command guidance is commonly used in surface-to-air and surface-to-surface missiles. It simply means that the missile is guided by an external command module, and the guidance signal is relayed to the missile via a radio or even a wire link. The command module tracks both the target and the missile, usually involving two separate radars—one for the target and another for the missile. Then guidance algorithms are used to generate command signals to the missile to guide the missile toward an intercept trajectory. The manual (MCLOS) and semi-automatic (SACLOS) line-of-sight guidance are different methods with which the command guidance is applied. MCLOS is a method in which signals are manually sent to the missile to keep it flying along the line-of-sight, the line between the target and the ground-based observation unit (typically a radar array or a laser). MCLOS tends to be ineffective against fast or maneuvering targets and are not used in modern missiles. SACLOS is a modern version of MCLOS and involves an automatic guidance algorithm that computes the trajectory correction necessary for the missile to intercept the target. Because the radars tend to lose accuracy at large distances, modern missiles combine the command guidance with other homing methods as the missiles close in on the target. The command guidance is only used to deliver the missile to the vicinity, and more accurate guidance is turned on near the target for the final target acquisition and armament detonation. The missiles that employ only the command guidance are therefore relatively outdated and include Russian SA-1, SA-2, SA-3, and SA-15 and U.S. Nike Ajax, Nike Hercules, and Nike Zeus (see Table 2.2).

Command guidance includes wire-guidance systems used in some anti-tank missiles fired from the ground or helicopters and also used in many naval torpedoes. For these systems, the target may be tracked visually in the case of anti-tank missiles such as M-220 tube-launched

Table 2.2. Missile Guidance Combinations for Mid-Course and Terminal Flight Phases.

Missile	Type	Guidance	
		Mid-course	Terminal
AGM-45, Shrike	Air-to-surface, anti-radar	Inertial	Passive radar
RIM-161, Standard Missile	Surface-to-air, anti-aircraft	Command guidance	Semi-active radar
AIM-54, Phoenix	Air-to-air	Inertial	Active radar
ASROC	Surface-to-sub-surface, anti-submarine	Inertial	Active sonar
BGM-109, Tomahawk	Surface-to-surface, anti-ship cruise missile	Inertial/GPS/ Scene Matching	Active and passive radar
AGM-84 Harpoon	Air-, surface-, or submarine-launched, anti-ship	Inertial	Active radar
Patriot	Surface-to-air, anti-ballistic missile defense	Command guidance	Track-via-missile
AIM-120 AMRAAM Slammer	Air-to-air	Inertial	Active radar

TOW missiles or using sonar in the case of naval torpedoes. The wire may be conventional electrical wires or fiber optic cables.

The beam-riding is another one of the simpler and older guidance methods. A target-tracking radar points the radar beam directly at the target to create a so-called line-of-sight. The missile guidance sensor detects the strength of this tracking beam, and tries to maintain a course that follows this tracking beam. Due to the spreading of the radar beam, beam-riding becomes ineffective at long ranges, and is no longer used in modern missile systems.

Onboard radar homing is referred to as "active" or "semi-active" depending on if the missile carries the transmitting radar (active radar guidance) or simply receives the radar reflection (semi-active radar guidance) as shown in Fig. 2.16. The active radar missile guidance allows the operator to disengage from the battle scene once the missile is launched, and for that reason often called the fire-and-forget missile.

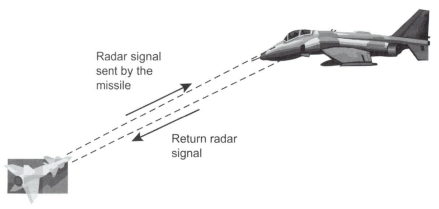

Radar signal
sent by the
missile

Return radar
signal

ACTIVE RADAR GUIDANCE

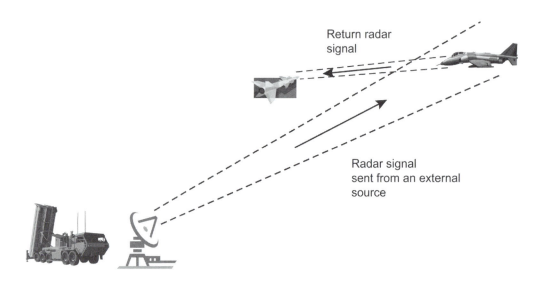

Return radar
signal

Radar signal
sent from an external
source

SEMI-ACTIVE RADAR GUIDANCE

Figure 2.16. Radar guidance.

Track-via-missile (TVM) is a form of semi-active radar guidance used in the Patriot missile system. An external radar illuminates the target, and the reflected radar signal is intercepted by a radar receiver onboard the missile. However, unlike the conventional semi-active systems TVM requires one additional step of downloading the received radar signal to the ground-based control station where the necessary trajectory corrections are computed and then uploaded back to the missile, all using high-speed communication links. The complexity of the TVM requires fast communication links that are viable only in short-range operations. However, the advantage of TVM is that most of the heavy and expensive electronics are not onboard the missile.

Infrared guidance is a passive method, where there are no onboard transmitters of any kind. Instead, infrared radiation or heat generated by the aircraft jet engines or other hot surfaces are identified by either point or imaging sensors. All objects at a given temperature emit characteristic radiation, one of the examples being the sun radiating from the solar surface temperature of about 6000 °C or about 11,000 °F. Objects at lower temperatures radiate much less energy and at progressively longer wavelength. In addition to this thermal radiation, jet exhaust contains lots of carbon dioxide and water vapor, which also emit in the infrared range at high temperatures (1500 to 4000 °F, depending on whether the afterburner is on or not). Carbon dioxide, for example, has a bright emission band at the 4.2 micron wavelength, which can be picked up be infrared sensors using materials such as lead sulfide (PbS), indium antimonide (InSb), and mercury-cadmium telluride (HgCdTe). These are the same materials used in night vision or thermal imaging sensors. Cooling these infrared detectors to low temperatures further increases their sensitivity by reducing sensor thermal noise, and liquid-nitrogen, thermoelectric, or other cooling methods are applied to keep these detectors at sub-freezing temperatures. Modern IR seekers use infrared imaging to scan a large area in the forward direction of the missile, which is essentially taking infrared camera shots of the air space in front and logging the direction from which the infrared signal originated from. Also, instead of looking at a single infrared emission band, modern heat-seekers may look for duplicating infrared signals at two wavelengths to discern the target from flares or other countermeasures. The IR seeker missiles thus have windowed domes at the nose that house gimbaled IR cameras of up to 4 megapixel resolutions. The dome itself must be transparent to the infrared (glass is not) and also be able to withstand the high temperatures encountered when the missile flies at Mach 2 to 3, similar to space vehicles heating up during high-speed reentry into the atmosphere. The gimbal system rotates the optical components to cover large scan angles and also stabilizes against any vibration to minimize the target image jitters.

For stationary targets or targets whose location is identified, missiles can be sent to specific locations using inertial guidance or GPS devices. Inertial guidance systems track the acceleration of the missiles using a set of gyroscopes and accelerometers. Accelerometers are devices that measure how fast the speed is changing with time. The data from the accelerometers can be integrated to give a time history of the missile speed, and that in turn gives the distance covered by the missile from the launch location. For keeping track of the missile heading or direction, gyroscopes are used. The gyroscope operates by the principle that any lateral acceleration causes the gyroscope axis to turn, which can be picked up by sensors. Thus, the direction and distance data from gyroscopes and accelerometers allow the onboard or external computers to calculate the location of the missile and use this information to guide the missile toward the target location. GPS is commonly used in both military and private sectors nowadays. GPS consists of a fleet of twenty-four geosynchronous (located at a constant location above the earth surface by moving at the same speed as the earth's rotation) satellites to provide a global coverage. A GPS receiver needs to receive valid signals from at least four of these satellites to triangulate its horizontal and vertical position. Long-range missiles such as cruise and other surface-to-surface missiles use the inertial or GPS guidance during the mid-course flight phase and deploy more accurate, target-specific homing guidance during the terminal, target-acquisition phase. In fact, many missile systems use dual or multiple guidance systems, one for the mid-course navigation to reach the target vicinity and another for the terminal phase. The reason is that the guidance required for the terminal target acquisition involves short-range, high-accuracy systems such as infrared or radar, while the mid-course corrections can be made with a less accurate but more compact systems. Table 2.2 shows some examples of the combinations of the guidance systems used in U.S. missiles.

Terrain contour matching (TERCOM) is used in cruise missiles, and is based on the topographic map data of selected patches of the terrain below. The altitudes of the terrain are stored in the onboard computer memory, and the missile's radar altimeter acquires the altitude data over the same terrain patch. The comparison of the acquired and stored terrain data then gives the exact position of the missile over that terrain patch. A more advanced method is the digital scene-matching area correlator (DSMAC). DSMAC involves an onboard digital camera that acquires the images of the land terrain below, and again the guidance processing unit compares the acquired and stored image data to locate the missile position.

The target data obtained from the various guidance systems above are used by the onboard computer (actually a compact, hardwired electronic unit that performs a fixed set of trajectory correction calculations) to make appropriate commands to the missile control. Various trajectory correction methods based on the target position and velocity are as follows:

1 Velocity Pursuit
2. Proportional Navigation
3. Command to Line-of-Sight
4. Beam Riding

The velocity pursuit has been used on first generation of laser-guided bombs and is effective only for slow moving targets. The idea behind the velocity pursuit is that the missile heading should always bear on the target position as illustrated in Fig. 2.17. Nearly all of the modern missiles with onboard homing guidance use proportional navigation. Proportional navigation involves turning the missile in the direction of the target motion at a rate proportional to the movement of the target, and therefore the name "proportional navigation." The missile tracks the bearing or the heading angle that the target makes with some reference angle (i.e., north) and turns its heading at a rate proportional to how fast the target bearing changes. Command to line-of-sight and beam riding are relatively simple concepts where a command is given to keep the missile in the line of sight between the observation radar and the target or in the midst of the guidance beam (beam riding).

Once the heading is determined, then the control unit actuates various aerodynamic control surfaces to implement the heading change. The control surface may be the tail fins, wings (located in the missile mid-section), or the canards (fins near the nose of the missile). Some missiles apply direct control through the vectored thrusts (i.e., there are movable vanes in the exhaust section to change the jet direction). The tail control is the most common, as found in missiles such as AIM-120 AMRAAM, AIM-54 Phoenix, AIM-9X Sidewinder, the Patriot missiles, RIM-66 Standard missiles, and many others. Canard control is used in FIM-92 Stinger, the Russian SA-13 Gopher, and so forth while AIM-7 Sparrow and AGM-98 HARM missiles employ wing control. Vectored thrusts are used in GWS-26 Sea Wolf and some versions of the RIM-66 Standard missiles.

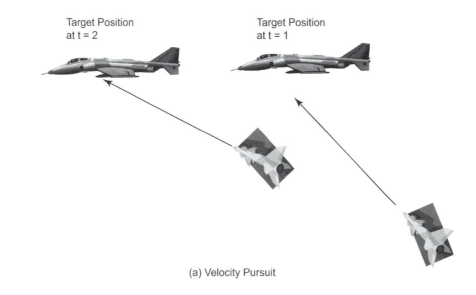

(a) Velocity Pursuit

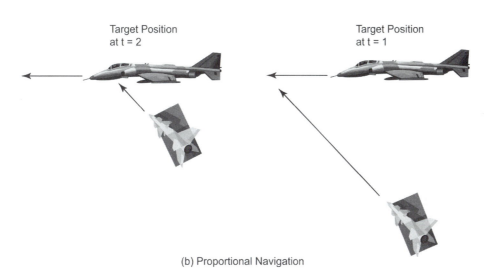

(b) Proportional Navigation

Figure 2.17. The concept behind the (a) velocity pursuit and (b) proportional navigation. For the velocity pursuit, the missile heading is updated based on the target position. For the proportional navigation, the ideal pursuit is when the target maintains a constant heading and therefore the missile also maintains a constant heading. If the target changes its bearing, then the missile will also change its bearing by a preset proportional rate.

Surface-to-Air Missiles

Surface-to-air missiles, or SAMs, have the same mission objective as the AAMs except that they are launched from the land or ships. The fact that SAMs are launched from the surface gives them more flexibility in the system weight and guidance system. In theory, much larger rockets can and need to be used as SAMs because these missiles must gain altitude to engage airborne targets, and much more elaborate guidance and tracking is possible using a network of ground-based radars. Also, highly effective portable systems such as the U.S.-made Stinger missiles and Russian 9K38 "Igla (Needle)" (SA-18 Gremlin) are available. Table 2.3 lists some of the major SAMs in the world.

The SA-series missiles are Russia's fleet of SAMs and range from long-range, two-stage missiles to portable shoulder-firing systems such as SA-7, SA-14, and SA-18. The SA- is actually the U.S. identification of the Russian missile, while names like "Guideline," "Gladiator," and "Giants" are used by NATO forces. The Russian designations vary depending on the type of the missile.

Table 2.3. Major SAMs of the World's Military.

Country of Origin	Military Designation, Name	Guidance Method
Canada	MIM-146, ADATS	Radar
France	Crotale	IR
	Mistral	IR
	ERYX	Visual
France/Germany	Roland	Radar
India	Akash Missile	Radar
	Trishul Missile	Radar
Israel	Arrow	Radar
Japan	Type 91	IR
Pakistan	Anza MKI	IR, Shoulder-launched
	Anza MKII	IR, Shoulder-launched
	Anza MKIII	IR, Shoulder-launched
People's Republic of China	HQ-9	Radar
	KS-1	Radar
	HQ-7	IR
Romania	CA 94	IR
	CA 95	IR
Russia	SA-1 "Guild"	Radar
	SA-2 "Guideline"	Radar
	SA-3 "Goa"	Radar
	SA-4 "Ganef"	Radar
	SA-5 "Gammon"	Radar
	SA-6 "Gainful"	Radar
	SA-7 "Grail"	IR, Shoulder-launched
	SA-8 "Gecko"	Radar
	SA-9 "Gaskin"	IR
	SA-10 "Grumble"	Radar
	SA-11 "Gadfly"	Radar
	SA-12A "Gladiator"	Radar
	SA-12B "Giant"	Radar
	SA-13 "Gopher"	IR
	SA-14 "Gremlin"	IR, Shoulder-launched
	SA-15 "Gauntlet"	Radar
	SA-16 "Gimlet"	IR
	SA-17 "Grizzly"	Radar
	SA-18 "Grouse"	IR, Shoulder-launched
	SA-19 "Grisom"	Radar
	SA-20 "Triumf"	Radar

(Continued)

Table 2.3. Continued

Country of Origin	Military Designation, Name	Guidance Method
United Kingdom	Blowpipe	Visual
	Javelin	Visual
	Rapier	Visual
	Sea Cat	Radar
	Sea Dart	Radar
	Sea Slug	Radar
	Sea Wolf	Radar
	Starstreak	Laser-guided
	Thunderbird	Radar
United States	Chaparral	IR
	FIM-43 Redeye	IR, Shoulder-launched
	FIM-92 Stinger	IR, Shoulder-launched
	Ground-launched AM RAAM-CLAWS (AIM-120 AAM)	Radar
	Ground-launched AM RAAM-SLAMRAAM (AIM-120 AAM)	Radar
	MIM-3 Nike Ajax	Radar
	MIM-14 Nike Hercules	Radar
	MIM-23 Hawk	Radar
	MIM-104 Patriot	Radar
	Nike Zeus	Radar
	RIM-2 Terrier	Radar
	RIM-7 Sparrow	Radar
	RIM-24 Tartar	Radar
	RIM-66 Standard Missile-1	Radar
	RIM-67 Standard Missile-2	Radar
	RIM-156 Standard Missile-2ER	Radar
	RIM-161 Standard Missile-3	Radar
	RIM-162 Eveolved Sea-Sparrow Missile	

The SA-2 (V-750 Russian designation) is one of the older SAMs that have two-stage rocket motors. The booster stage has a solid-propellant rocket motor with a casing fitted with four delta fins. The second- or the sustainer-stage rocket engine is fueled with liquid propellant consisting of nitric acid and kerosene. The payload weight of up to 195 kg can be carried, and this missile can be converted for delivery of nuclear armament. With a conventional high-explosive warhead, the missile has a kill radius of 65 m for jet fighters and 100 to 120 m radius for severe damage. It makes up for any guidance inaccuracies with a large warhead. These missiles can reach speeds of Mach 4.0 to 4.5, with a maximum range of 30 km. The SA-2 missiles are over 10 m (33 ft) in length, and the deployment unit consists of the truck-mounted transport and launch pad with an array of search-acquisition and guidance radars. A typical deployment involves six launchers arranged in a hexagon, and the radars and fire command operator van are hooked up with these launchers.

Figure 2.18. The Russian SA-14 shoulder-launched SAM. The tail fins are retractable and engage once the missile is ejected from the launcher. Photo courtesy of the U.S. Department of Defense.

Figure 2.19. The transport vehicle for the Russian SA-15 Gauntlet SAMs, complete with radar equipment and crew cabin. Photo courtesy of the U.S. Department of Defense.

The SA-7 (Russian designation Strela-2, 9K32) is a portable, shoulder-fired low-altitude SAM. Its U.S. equivalent is the FIM-43 Redeye. The SA-7 is a small, portable missile and has a small range of 4.2 km and an effective altitude from 15 to 2300 m. Once launched, it reaches a supersonic speed of Mach 1.75, which is approximately 500 m/s or 1500 ft/s at these altitudes. As with most portable SAMs, the SA-7 is equipped with a passive IR seeker (heat seeker). The SA-14 (Strela-3, 9K34) is an improved version of the SA-7 and consists of the launcher and the missile, as shown in Fig. 2.18. Although similar in appearance as its predecessor, the SA-14 (see Fig. 2.18) has a better range (4500 m), better altitude (3000 m), and more important a more sensitive heat-seeking guidance unit, using a cooled lead-sulfide infrared detector and a more accurate tracking algorithm.

A more advanced Russian system is the SA-15 Gauntlet. This system is complete with a transport/launch vehicle (see Fig. 2.19) that also carries radar and computer equipment. A three-man crew (commander, system operator, and driver) also ride in the vehicle turret. The vehicle is powered by a diesel engine but also is equipped with a 75 kW gas-turbine electric generator. The ranging radar operates in the E/F bands and provides complete coordinates (range, angle, and altitude) of up to forty-eight targets. The target type and range are fed to the onboard processing computer that can track and assess the threat levels associated with each target. The target tracking and missile guidance is performed by a separate radar operating in the G/H bands. The missile itself is 3.5 m in length and has a launch weight of 170 kg, out of which 15 kg is of high-explosive armament with a proximity fuse. To protect the launch vehicle, the missile initially ejected with a cold-launch device up to a height of 20 m and the solid-propellant rocket motor is turned on to reach a final speed of approximately 850 m/s. Effective range is believed to be 1500 to 20000 m at altitudes from 10 to 6000 m. At short range, this missile system is considered to be effective not only against aircraft but against incoming guided missiles as a missile defense unit.

As noted above, for the United States the AMRAAM can be launched from the air or the ground, and the latter version bears the designation SLAMRAAM (surface-launched AMRAAM) or HUMRAAM (HMMWV Humvee-launched). The SLAMRAAM is what the U.S. military refers to as CLAWS (complimentary low altitude weapon system), "complimentary" because these missiles are straightforward adaptation of the air-launch version and provide compact and mobile defense against airborne threats. Along with MIM-23 Hawk and MIM-104 Patriot, SLAMRAAM adds a low-altitude, short- to medium-range component to the spectrum of air defense weapons to guard against incoming aircraft, helicopters, and cruise missiles. The initial target acquisition and fire control is handled by the army's standard Integrated Fire Control Station, which receives signals from the MPQ-64 Sentinel radar. The turreted launcher with six AMRAAM missiles can be mounted on the Humvee (HMMWV, high-mobility multipurpose wheeled vehicle). Also, Raytheon in collaboration with the Kongsberg Defense Corp and the Norwegian army has developed a universal launcher consisting of six AMRAAM and three MIM-23 HAWK missiles to provide a versatile air defense system.

MIM-23 HAWK (shown in Fig. 2.20) is one of the classic SAMs in the U.S. arsenal since 1962, but through upgrades in guidance and propulsion units the viability of these missiles have been kept up to date. MIM-23 was designed as a ground-launch vehicle for delivering 120 lbs of blast-fragmentation warhead and thus is coupled with a ground radar for semi-active guidance. For the United States, the newer MIM-104 Patriot and the FIM-92A Stinger have replaced MIM-23, although such deployment leaves a gap in the range of engagement by either Patriot or Stinger. Raytheon and other licensed manufacturers have produced some 40,000 of these missiles, and they have been used in service by many U.S. allies. With a range of 15 miles and a nominal target ceiling of 45,000 ft (higher in high-altitude versions), HAWK has provided a solid platform for defense against airborne targets. The HAWK launch unit consists of a pulse acquisition radar to search high- or medium-altitude targets typically with a 20 rpm rotation, a continuous wave acquisition radar for low-altitude target search, two high power illuminator Doppler radar for target tracking and illumination, one back-up range-only radar, six launch vehicles with three missiles each, twelve missile transport vehicle with a total of thirty-six missiles, and a number of command/control and support equipment. This unit is manned by two officers and a crew of forty-nine men.

The Patriot (MIM-104) missiles are shown in Figs. 2.21 and 2.22 and have expanded their role from High to Medium Air Defense (HIMAD) to being the anti-ballistic missile weapon highlighted by the media exposure during the Persian Gulf War. The ground-based phased array tracking radar tracks and illuminates the target. The reflected signal is sensed by the passive radar on the missile head and transmitted to the ground engagement control station (ECS), which computes the intercept trajectory and sends it back to the missile for actuator control in what is known as TVM guidance. In the recent upgrades as in PAC-3, however, active radar guidance replaces the TVM. Patriot is associated with the acronym "Phased Array Tracking Radar to Intercept of Target" for the above reasons. The AN/MPQ-53/65 Radar Set includes the phased array radar for search and tracking, electronic counter-countermeasure, and IFF (identification friend or foe) and covers a 100-km radius area. The ECS is housed in a 5-ton tactical cargo truck and includes the data link terminal, the communication equipment, and the weapons control computer that runs the TVM intercept algorithm based on the radar signals. The data link connected to the M901 missile launching station allows remote control of the launch.

The Patriot missiles were introduced as the primary anti-aircraft missile to replace the Nike Hercules in 1976. As described above, along with phased array radar and ECS the Patriot was a complete and expensive system. Using the Patriot platform, advanced capabilities versions (PAC-1, -2, and -3) were developed to maximize the speed, range, intercept, and kill capabilities. Using the same 5.2-m length and 41-cm diameter missile casing up to PAC-2, the missile speed increased to Mach 3 in PAC-1 and Mach 5 in PAC-2.

Figure 2.20. Live launch of MIM-23 HAWK surface-to-air missile. Photo courtesy of the U.S. Army.

The PAC-3 upgrades, although still referred to as a Patriot missile, can be considered as a new missile with a much smaller diameter (25 cm), shorter range (15 km), and a completely different tracking method. PAC-3 was manufactured by Lockheed Martin, in contrast to Raytheon for prior versions, and now has a dedicated role of terminal defense against ballistic missiles. The guidance accuracy is improved against high-speed targets in PAC-3 so that its primary function is hit-to-kill while a "lethality enhancer" of 73 kg of high explosive blast and fragmentation warhead backs up the system with a proximity sensor.

The smaller diameter allows up to sixteen PAC-3 missiles to be fired from the launcher (eight for previous versions).

The media, the administration, and the manufacturer of the Patriot missiles depicted an exaggerated picture of the performance of the then–PAC-2 version in at least one instance, boasting forty-one out of forty-two Scud missiles destroyed by this anti-ballistic missile defense system. One known failure of the system involves the Scud hit of an army barracks in Dhahran, Saudi Arabia, that resulted in loss of twenty-eight soldiers. The cause of the "malfunction" in the Patriot launch was attributed to a software error in maintaining an accurate internal timing clock, which had drifted by one third of a second—equivalent to an error of 600 m in estimating the incoming missile location. This error caused the failure of the tracking radar to find the Scud missile and resulted in no intercept attempt (i.e., no launch). There have been counter-claims in which studies of the videotapes showed no direct hits on the Scuds by the Patriot missile. However, there are two extenuating circumstances to the claim. One is that Patriot missiles were originally intended as an anti-aircraft defense measure and therefore were equipped with proximity fuses to detonate the warhead if foreign objects were detected in the pre-set damage radius. Another factor is that the crude construction of the Scud missiles often led to disintegration of the missile body during high-speed descent, and fragments of the missiles including the warhead would be detected by the radar. Although unintended, the effect was to create a number of decoy targets, much as modern ICBMs employ during the terminal phase of the flight.

Figure 2.21. MIM-104 Patriot missile. Photo courtesy of the U.S. Army.

Figure 2.22. MIM-104 Patriot missile launcher. Photo courtesy of the U.S. Department of Defense.

During the second deployment in the region, Operation Iraqi Freedom, the Patriot system did deliver confirmed kills of the tactical ballistic missiles. Using the GEM-series upgrades to PAC-2 Patriot missiles and PAC-3s, Iraqi Al Samound-2 and Ababil-100 medium-range missiles were engaged, intercepted, and destroyed. In addition, the complex Patriot launch units were by this time sufficiently mobilized to provide forward protection of the air space in highly fluid battle situations.

The Patriot missiles, however, did fire on friendly aircraft. A British RAF Tornado GR4A was shot down with loss of two pilots after a number of ill-posed settings classified the RAF aircraft as an anti-radiation missile (ARM). On the Patriot side, the target classification algorithm was set too wide, taking the radar and emission signatures of an aircraft like Tornado to be designated as an ARM. An ARM targets systems like the Patriot system's ground radar, so that these targets are a high-priority, and the Patriot automatically engages the target without waiting for operator input. This automatic engagement algorithm can be deactivated, but the operators had not done so in spite of the fact that there were no known ARMs in the Iraqi arsenal. On the Tornado side, the RAF aircraft made its landing approach directly over the Patriot system's forward site, making it appear as an imminent threat. Last but not least, the Tornado's IFF is believed to have been turned off at the time, giving the Patriot system an automatic go-ahead with the intercept launch.

In an incident involving the U.S. Navy's F/A-18 Hornet, search radars from two separate Patriot batteries detected the aircraft and in both sites the Patriot target classification algorithm initially classified it as a tactical ballistic missile headed toward the Karbala Gap region where the U.S. Army contingent was operating. In one of the Patriot units, the operator's check of the target speed and altitude was inconsistent with the initial software assessment and the engagement protocol was manually halted. In the other, however, the manual check or override were unfortunately not made, resulting in a PAC-3 launch and a catastrophic impact a few moments later with the friendly aircraft. Again, an extenuating circumstance in this incident is that the responsible Patriot battery's radar had to be replaced earlier after a friendly AGM-88 HARM missile destroyed its own radar in a reversed case of mistaken identity. An Air Force F-16 pilot assumed that his aircraft was being illuminated by a hostile SAM radar, as alerted by an onboard radar warning receiver, and in response fired anti-radiation missile toward the Patriot radar. The replaced radar had not fully been integrated and tested with the PAC-3 software when the above incident involving F/A-18 Hornet occurred. With ballistic missiles incoming at high Mach speeds, the time to come to a snap decision was measured in seconds under highly tense battle situations. The potency and Mach 5-plus speed of Patriot missiles have thus proven that this is a viable defense against tactical ballistic missiles; however, both the target classification algorithm and operator judgment would have to be near perfect to avoid unfortunate incidents as above.

Figure 2.23. Stinger missiles can be fired from a gyro-stabilized air defense turret mounted on a modified heavy High Mobility Multipurpose Wheeled Vehicle (HMMWV, AKA Humvee). There are two launch tubes on the turret and up to eight Stinger missiles can be fired.

The FIM-92 Stinger is a compact, short-range anti-aircraft missile that is primarily launched from a shoulder-mounted tube, although the same missile has been adapted for firing from other platforms such as the HMMWV-mounted launcher (Fig. 2.23), AH-64 Apache, or OH-58D Kiowa Warrior helicopters. A Stinger system has a total weight of

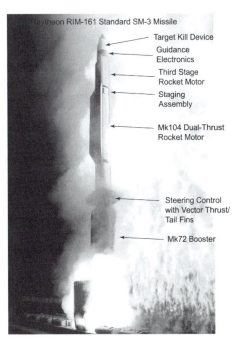

Figure 2.24 (a). Vertical launch of RIM-67 SM-2 missile. The rocket exhaust plume escapes upward from a separate vertical slot adjacent to the missile tube. Photo courtesy of the U.S. Navy.

Figure 2.24 (b). Main components in the SM-2 missile. Background photo courtesy of the U.S. Navy.

only 34.5 lbs with the 22-lb missile and consists of launch tube, missile, and a battery pack. The operator points the missile toward the target through a sight attached to the launch tube, and after IFF query is made to confirm the hostile identity the infrared sensor cooling is initiated. For short-range targets, the activated IR sensor may acquire the target prior to launch giving an audible indication (a growling noise), at which time the launch is made first with the gas generator to eject the missile out of the tube. The solid propellant motor engages a few yards out of the launch tube, to protect the firing crew from the effects of rocket plume and shocks. The missile itself is a 5-ft-long cylinder with a 2.75-in diameter and has rectangular forward pop-out wings and cruciform tailfins. The dual-thrust solid rocket motor generates speeds of Mach 2-plus and exceptional engagement altitude (over 10,000 ft) and range (3 miles) for its size.

The "Standard" missiles are a series of air defense systems to protect vulnerable surface ships developed for the U.S. Navy. The RIM-2 Terrier, RIM-8 Talos, and RIM-24 Tartar used by the navy in the 1960s were the precursors to the Standard missiles. The Standard RIM-66 replaces the Tartar for medium-range missions, while RIM-67 ER replaces the Terrier and Talos for extended range. Although intended as anti-aircraft and anti-missile missiles, both RIM-66 and RIM-67 (Fig. 2.24(a)) can be fired against surface ships using their semi-active radar, radar homing, or inertial/IR guidance. The definition of medium and extended range has evolved with the years. The RIM-66 missile has an impressive effective range of 40 km for the SM-1MR version and 70 km for the SM-2ER, while the RIM-67 SM-2MR version carries the warhead over a distance of 120 km and the SM-2ER "Block IV" 150 km. The diameters of both the RIM-66 and RIM-67 are identical at 0.34 m,

Figure 2.25. Launch of RIM-161 SM-3 missile. Photo courtesy of the U.S. Navy.

but RIM-67 has an added booster and thus has a length of 7.98 m for SM-2MR in comparison to a 4.72 m length for RIM-66 SM-2ER. Main components of the SM-2 missile are shown in Fig. 2.24b. The added propulsion power not only increases the range and altitude but also gives a much faster fly-out to meet the target. The SM-2ER Block IV incorporates some of the latest upgrades including vertical launch from protective tubes, integration with the Aegis fire-control computer, proximity fuse, and guidance to track high-speed, steep-dive, or sea-skimming missiles. These features are engineered to provide the naval surface ships with an effective anti-missile defense equivalent to the Patriot PAC-3 system. These Standard missiles are fitted to Ticonderoga-class and other cruisers and destroyers.

A variation of the SM-2ER Block IV with an added third stage bears the designation RIM-161 SM-3 (Fig. 2.25) is being considered for use in the NTW-TMBD (Navy Theater Wide-Theater Ballistics Missile Defense) program to achieve a ship-based theater-wide ballistic missile defense capability. The lightweight exo-atmospheric projectile (LEAP) is being developed to engage incoming ballistic missiles at altitudes up to 150 km within a range of 250 km. A small kill vehicle of 18 kg or less is mounted on the missile body along with an electro-optical/imaging sensor for warhead/decoy identification and vector-thrust control for rapid close-in on the target. As shown in the figure, there are three rocket motor stages, starting from the Mk72 booster, Mk104 dual-thrust second-stage, and advanced solid axial stage (ASAS). The primary sensor on the LEAP is a FLIR (forward looking infrared). An infrared image of a test target, the Aries ballistic missile, is shown in Fig. 2.26, as captured directly by the imaging sensor on SM-3 at an altitude of 500,000 ft.

GROUND-TARGET MISSILES

The ground-target missiles range from unguided anti-personnel barrage rockets fired from MLRS (multiple-launch rocket system), to target-specific missiles such as anti-ship (AShM), anti-tank (ATGM), and anti-radiation (ARM), to nuclear-tipped ICBMs. These missiles are typically interchangeable in their launch platform, with AGM (air-to-ground) missiles adaptable for surface launch and vice versa. With submarine taking multipurpose roles including attack support, some of these missiles can also be fired from shallow submerged depths.

A sizable arsenal of long-rang AShM can be carried by surface ships or submarines, and ship-launched helicopters or aircrafts extend the threat radius even further. To counter such threats long-range preemptive strike capabilities along with missile defense systems as described above are becoming absolute necessities in modern navies. Small corvettes at the 3500-ton range can carry multiple 100 km–range missiles capable of destroying much larger naval vessels, and submarines with 500-plus km–range missiles pose even greater risk for large naval task forces. Helicopters or aircraft with airborne radars can initiate or coordinate over-the-horizon attacks. Rarely would naval vessels exchange artillery rounds from visual range, but most of the attacks and counterattacks would be made in the radar space, giving the advantage to the side that possesses more advanced radars, attack weapons, anti-missile defense systems, and commander/crew to deploy them with quick and sound judgments.

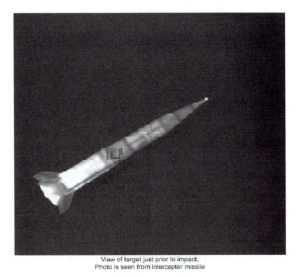

View of target just prior to impact.
Photo is seen from intercepter missile

Figure 2.26. An infrared image of a test target, an Aries ballistic missile, as captured directly on the imaging sensor on RIM-161 SM-3 missile at an altitude of 500,000 ft. Photo courtesy of the U.S. Navy.

The American-made Harpoon and French Exocet rank as the most widely distributed anti-ship missiles in the western block with an estimated 6000 sold to twenty-four customer nations for the former and 3300 to thirty-two nations for the latter. The AGM-84 Harpoon may be considered as a multi-use anti-ship cruise missile, because its primary power plant is an air-breathing Teledyne J402 Turbojet engine with 660 lbs of thrust. Solid propellant boosters are added on ship- and submarine-launch versions. After clearing the launch platform, the missile takes a low-altitude, sea-skimming, high subsonic trajectory toward the target as set by the radar altimeter. During the terminal phase, the active radar seeks and locks onto the target, at which time the missile will maneuver a sudden pull-up and attack from above with its hull-penetrating 488-lb warhead. The Harpoon has many variants including a modification to a stand-off land attack missile (SLAM) to engage high-value land targets as shown below.

AGM-84D: All-weather, over-the-horizon Harpoon missile with high survivability and effectiveness that can be fired from the aircraft like the U.S. Navy's P-3 Orion, surface ships using Mk 116 TARTAR launcher, or submarines through the torpedo tube launcher.

AGM-84D Harpoon Block 1D: Upgrade of AGM-84D with larger fuel tank and re-attack capability.

AGM-84E Harpoon/SLAM: Land-attack version of the Harpoon missile with the guidance replaced with GPS, inertial navigation, and infrared optical terminal guidance system. The payload is also replaced with the Tomahawk warhead for high-penetration capability.

SLAM-ER Block 1F: Provides long-range, high target penetration and control. The range is nearly double the prior versions, at 150-plus miles, and the titanium warhead increases the impact energy. The pilot interface with the missile guidance allows re-targeting or target switching.

The Russian anti-ship missiles tend to be large and fast, in line with their military doctrine of countering the western carrier-centered surface warships with an abundance of anti-ship cruise missiles. The Zvezda Kh-31 delivers 90 kg of warhead at a speed of over four and a half times the sonic velocity using a solid-rocket booster to get up to supersonic speeds first, and the ramjet engine then takes over to propel the missile to its cruise speed. The behemoth-class missile is the 4800-kg P-500 Bazal or SS-N-12 Sandbox in western designation (in comparison to 532 kg for AGM-84D Harpoon). This missile also uses a solid-rocket booster to reach its cruise altitude of approximately 4000 m, and then turns on its turbojet to cruise at a supersonic speed to the target vicinity within a radius of 250 km of the launch point. The radar seeker has a range of up to 90 km, and once the target is locked on the missile assumes a low-altitude (about 100 m) path for the terminal phase.

Anti-armor munitions can make use of high kinetic or chemical energy. Kinetic energy munitions like APFSDS (armor piercing, fin stabilized discarding sabot) rounds are fired from tank guns, and chemical energy warheads like HEAT (high explosive anti-tank), HESH (high explosive squash head), FRAG-HE (fragmenting high explosive), and SC (shaped charge) are used in both tank artillery rounds and ATGM. The kinetic energy penetrators use high mass at relatively low velocities, while shaped charge warheads generate low-mass, high velocity jets of 10 km/s using copper liner and 12 km/s with molybdenum liner to defeat the armor. Typical ATGM carry much more high explosive for the shaped charge or other warheads, and as an example, the AGM-114K Hellfire II is estimated to deliver sufficient penetration power to defeat all known tank armors. These missiles, due to their high energy capacity, are also used against concrete bunkers and hardened fortifications. The standard guidance method is semi-active laser where the target needs to be illuminated by the launch vehicle or a separate forward observation (FO)/combat observation lasing team (COLT), but the AGM-114L Longbow Hellfire has an active millimeter wave radar seeker to independently complete its terminal homing. These missiles deliver small-radius, concentrated energy to the target, so that the U.S. military has found it to be an effective option during urban warfare situations. There are several launch options for the Hellfire missile, the surest of which is to allow the missile optical sensor to acquire the target prior to launch in the "lock-on before launch (LOBL)" mode. This all but eliminates the risk of missile failing to find and acquire the reflected laser signature from the target during its flight but does require the launch vehicle to be in view of the target at close range and low altitudes. Lock-on after launch (LOAL) reduces the risk of launch vehicle exposure, but there is a finite chance that the missile may fail to acquire the target-derived laser signature and become unguided. LOAL-DIR mode sets a time delay before the missile will start to seek the target. LOAL-HI and LOAL-LO modes program the missile to clear 1000 ft or lower terrain features before attempting to find its target, so that the launch vehicle can remain hidden behind the terrain.

M-220 TOW (tube-launched, optically-tracked, wire-guided) missiles, shown in Figs. 2.27 and 2.28, are the anti-tank analog of the anti-aircraft Stinger missile, where the armor-penetrating warhead can be delivered from a compact launch tube. TOW missiles can be fired from a portable launch tube on a tripod, from HMMWV, from the Bradley Fighting Vehicle (BFV), or from helicopters and has a capability to penetrate through 30 in of armor within its effective range of 3 km. Steeply angled armors, reactive armors, and other constraints make the actual penetrable armor thickness much smaller, but still TOW has proven to be lethal for most armored vehicles. The TOW missile uses a simple yet effective guidance method, where the launch operator to keeps the target within the cross-hairs using a joystick to illuminate the target with an infrared beam. The missile itself has an infrared beacon at the tail to communicate its relative position from the line-of-sight between the target and the launcher as computed from the illuminating infrared beam. The corrective action to keep the missile in that line-of-sight is communicated to the missile via two fine-gauge steel wires that are being rapidly unwound from the launcher. The missile tail fins are then actuated by high-pressure helium to maintain the line-of-sight toward

Figure 2.27. TOW missile launcher with target sight and infrared sensors. Photo courtesy of the U.S. Army.

Figure 2.28. TOW missile tube on a tripod launcher. Photo courtesy of the U.S. Army.

Figure 2.29. HARM (high-speed anti-radiation missile) mounted on a Navy F/A-18 aircraft. Photo courtesy of the U.S. Navy.

the target until impact. The TOW missile has a nominal length of 1.5 m and a diameter of 150 mm, although they vary somewhat from version to version. After the missile clears the launch tube using a short-burn launch motor, the forward and tail fins pop open, and the flight motor fires up for 1.5 s before burning out. The missile is then essentially on a glide mode toward the target at a speed of 280 m/s for a maximum range of 4 km.

The AGM-88 HARM (high-speed anti-radiation missile) shown in Figs. 2.29 and 2.30 is another example of target-specific projectile that is typically launched from the air toward ground-based radar installations. It locks on to signals from the opposing search-and-track radars. In a typical air campaign, aircraft such as the F/A-18 and F-16 will attempt to pave the way for the waves of aircraft by knocking out the SAM-guidance radars. The seeker searches for radio frequency emission sources and based on the priority set by internal software and pilot input attacks high-priority radars using preformed steel (25,000 fragments in AGM-88B) or tungsten (12,845 fragments in AGM-88C) warheads to knock out the radar structure. Because radars do not respond to IFF queries and frequency spectra are similar between friendly and hostile emitters, ARMs in general do not have discriminating ability nor steer capability so that the human interface in the target acquisition and priority loop is more important than other missiles. In fact, as noted above a HARM missile was erroneously fired against a U.S. Patriot radar site during the Operation Iraqi Freedom disabling the system. The HARM missile can also be launched from A-6E and A-7 attack aircraft and EA-6B Prowler electronic countermeasure aircraft.

MISSILE PROPULSION

There are mainly two propulsion systems used in modern missiles. The first is the rocket engine, which in turn can be classified into solid or liquid propellant rockets. The other propulsion system is the gas-turbine engine and its variant. For air-to-ground assaults, guided or unguided bombs are also used relying on gravity to fall to the target.

The rockets are propelled by burning the propellant that is essentially explosive material. The rocket propellant generates a large volume of hot gas, which creates a high-pressure, high-temperature environment in the rocket combustion chamber. Contrary to popular belief, it is neither the hot exhaust from the rocket nozzle pushing against the outside air nor the pressure difference caused by the nozzle opening that generates thrust. It is the large mass of the exhaust gas accelerating out the nozzle that gives the rocket the forward momentum. This is called the "conservation of momentum," or Newton's second law. We can visualize it as an event where if a high-speed object such as a baseball is caught by the catcher he will feel a force pushing him backward. This force will be greater for larger masses and higher speeds, which are collectively known as the momentum (mass times the velocity). The exact converse also holds: If a device is able to eject a large mass at a large velocity, the system will be subject to a forward force. This is how both the rockets and gas-turbine gain momentum: They eject a large mass of exhaust gas at a high velocity

Figure 2.30. A HARM missile fired from an F-16: a view from the cockpit. The exhaust and multiple shock system trailing the missile are visible. Photo courtesy of the U.S. Air Force.

out the nozzle. The major difference between the rockets and gas-turbine is that rockets carry both the fuel and oxidizer needed to complete the propellant burning while the gas-turbine carries only the fuel and needs to ingest air. The ingested air also brings in backward momentum, so there is a limit to how fast gas-turbine-powered missiles can move.

There are two types of rocket propulsion systems: solid propellant and liquid propellant. Solid-propellant rocket motors tend to be less expensive and easy to maintain and as such are used in missiles with small to intermediate size. Therefore, for so-called tactical missiles such as the air-to-air or ground-to-air, solid propellants are primarily used as the rocket fuel. The solid propellants contain both the fuel and oxidizer components. These solid propellants go by names like HTPB or NEPE, which stand for hydroxyl-terminated polybutadien and nitrate-ester plasticizer. Fancy names, but they are pseudonyms for material that contains organic or hydrocarbon plasticizer as fuel and chemicals like nitrates or perchlorates as oxidizers. Table 2.4 lists some typical solid propellants used in tactical missiles. In spite of their explosive properties, under controlled conditions of surface-burning they only burn at about half an inch per second. So if the rocket packed a solid propellant in a 2-in-thick cylindrical shell, it will burn for about four seconds, and after that the rocket is just coasting but at a very high speed for a while. The hot gas from burning of these solid propellants reaches a temperature of 4000 to 6000 °F. With all the hot gas product from the propellants, the pressure inside the rocket combustion chambers (sometimes called rocket motors although there aren't any moving parts in solid propellant rockets) quickly reaches fifty times the atmospheric pressure or above. This high-pressure gas then rushes out through the rocket nozzle, thereby ejecting large momentum. That is how the thrust is generated in solid-propellant rockets.

Table 2.4. Solid Rocket Propellants Used in Tactical Missiles.

Propellant	Metal Content (percent by weight)	Density (lbs per cubic in)	Combustion Temperature (°F)	I_{sp} = Specific Impulse[1]	Burning Rate (in/s)
Double-base with ammonium perchlorate and aluminum	20 ~ 21	0.065	6500	260 ~ 265	0.78
Cross-linked double-base with ammonium perchlorate	19	0.067	6060	269	0.35
Polyvinyl chloride with ammonium perchlorate	21	0.064	5600	260 ~ 265	0.45
Polysulfide with ammonium perchlorate	3	0.062	5000	240 ~ 250	0.31
NEPE, nitrate-ester plasticizer	16	0.064	5800	260 ~ 263	0.55
HTPB, hydroxyl-terminated tetranitramine with ammonium perchlorate	14	0.064	5400 ~ 5600	260 ~ 265	0.32

[1]I_{sp} = specific impulse = the thrust force for one pound of propellant burned in one second.

In Table 2.4, the double-base propellants refer to a mix of nitrocellulose and nitroglyc-erin, which forms a gel when combined together. Different mixture ratios of nitrocellulose and nitroglycerine are used along with a number of plasticizers to improve mechanical properties and stabilizers to ensure durability during storage. Variants of the double-base propellants have names like Ballistite, Cordite, French S.D., and AFU but essentially represent the above variations and bear similar properties. Ammonium perchlorate is a potent oxidizer commonly used in solid rocket propellants with a chemical formula of NH_4ClO_2. The propellants listed in Table 2.4 include various binders (fuel component of the propellant that also acts as a form-shaping material) such as polyvynil chloride, poly-sulfide, NEPE, and HTPB combined with ammonium perchlorate. Other binders in solid rocket propellants are actually quite common materials such as polyester, synthetic rubber, polyethylene, polyurethane, and polybutadiene, basically anything that will burn and hold the propellant shape and properties. HTPB (hydroxyl-terminated polybutadiene) is the fuel component used for the space shuttle solid rocket boosters. Aluminum particles when embedded into these propellants not only burn and add energy, but also act as high-mass particles to add to the total momentum produced by the propellant.

Liquid-propellant rockets, while being more complex and therefore also more expen-sive, have a number of advantages. First, they have a much higher exhaust velocity. This means that for each pound of propellant more momentum and therefore thrust can be generated. Typically, solid-propellant rocket exhaust is in the range of 2000 to 2500 m/s, whereas for liquid-propellant the exhaust jet can reach speeds of 4400 m/s. In fact, the rocket exhaust divided by the gravitational acceleration (9.81 m/s^2) is a standard measure of the rocket's ability to generate thrust per given mass of propellant and is called the spe-cific impulse. So for solid-propellant rockets, the specific impulse is around 200 to 250, while for liquid-propellant rockets it can be as high as 450. The second advantage of the liquid-propellant rockets is that the fuel and oxidizer flow to the combustion chamber can be metered or shut off altogether and turned on again as desired. This gives a control of the rocket thrust where there is none for the solid-propellant rockets. Once the solid propel-lant is ignited, there is no stopping it. Even though many technologies have evolved to provide much greater thrust in modern rocket engines, the essential components remain

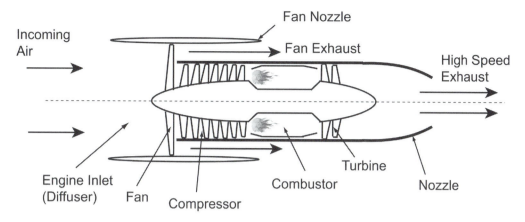

Figure 2.31. A schematic showing the main components of a turbofan engine.

the same in liquid-propellant rocket engines. They include storage for both fuel and oxidizer, the combustion chamber, and turbo- or other machinery to deliver the fuel and oxidizer to combustion chamber operating at high pressures up to 100 to 200 times the atmospheric pressure.

Gas-turbines are used in cruise missiles due to their large thrust-to-weight ratio and efficiency in terms of thrust per mass of fuel burned. The way they generate thrust is essentially the same as rockets: They eject high-momentum exhaust gas out through the nozzle to gain forward momentum. One major difference is that the gas-turbine engines need to ingest air to mix with fuel and burn and also to carry the energetic combustion product gas. The incoming air carries with it some negative momentum, so the jet momentum must exceed the incoming air momentum to provide positive thrust. This puts a limit on the maximum speed achievable through gas-turbine engines, whereas for rockets there is no theoretical limit on the top speed. For gas-turbine engines, the operation follows the sequence: The air comes in, gets compressed through a compressor, gets mixed with fuel and burnt in the combustor, runs through a turbine, and then accelerates down and out through the nozzle. This sequence is illustrated in Fig. 2.31. A turbofan engine has a fan section in addition to the main gas-turbine engine. The fan adds momentum to the incoming air and sends it out through the fan nozzle at higher momentum and thus is a device to gain thrust in an efficient manner. For gas-turbine engines for commercial airliners, the fan section tends to be large because the fuel efficiency is a much bigger consideration. For gas-turbine engines for military fighter aircraft, both the range (fuel efficiency) and high-speed operations are of concern so that they tend to have a smaller fan section. For cruise missiles, the fan section may be yet smaller or nonexistent depending on the operational speed and range of the missile. For supersonic cruise missiles, a ramjet engine—a variant of the gas-turbine engine—is used.

The main components of a gas-turbine engine are shown in Fig. 2.31. The compressor is connected to the turbine, so the compressor work is internally produced by the turbine. The energy released from the burning of the fuel with air in the combustor turns the turbine, which in turn turns the compressor and the fan. The remaining energy is converted to kinetic energy in the form of high-speed exhaust.

A ramjet engine is a simplified version of the gas-turbine engine, where the air compression is accomplished by the excessive momentum of the incoming supersonic stream. Supersonic flow of air becomes hot and highly pressurized when slowed down through the supersonic inlet. Such ram compression only occurs at supersonic speeds, so ramjet engines can only be operated at supersonic speeds. Since a cruise missile or any aircraft needs at some point to start from a standstill and go through subsonic speeds to attain supersonic speeds, ramjet-powered aircraft need an initial booster such as a solid rocket motor to accelerate to supersonic speeds before the ramjet can be operated. The ram compression then replaces the function of the complex and heavy compressor and turbine in conventional gas-turbine engines. Ramjet engines therefore can be considered a large combustor tube with the inlet and nozzle designed to maximize the ram compression and exhaust acceleration.

CRUISE MISSILES

Cruise missiles are intermediate- to long-range missiles that follow a programmed path for highly accurate delivery of conventional and nuclear armaments toward stationary or slow-moving targets (land targets or ships). They are flying objects in the sense that they have wings to provide lift during the flight, and the power plants used for cruise missiles tend to be variants of gas-turbine engines (e.g., turbofan or ramjet engines). The flight path is typically low altitude to avoid radar detection and intervention. Modern guidance technology discussed earlier in this chapter allows for precise targeting using a combination of GPS (global positioning system), TERCOM (terrain contour matching), and DSMAC (digital scene-matching area correlator). Depending on the cruise missile range and capabilities, cruise missiles carry a price tag ranging from $500,000 to $2,000,000. In theory, this high price per missile predicates that only high-priority targets should be designated for cruise missile missions. However, as recent events in the Iraq theater have shown, other constraints such as the large volume of targets and anti-aircraft defense around the targets can also dictate the use of cruise missiles.

A cruise missile is essentially an unmanned aircraft, and in that sense the German V-1, the buzz bomb, is the predecessor of all modern cruise missiles. The U.S. armed forces use several cruise missiles that can be launched from submarines, ships, or aircraft. A U.S. Tomahawk (BGM-109) cruise missile is shown in Fig. 2.32. Since the take-off is powered

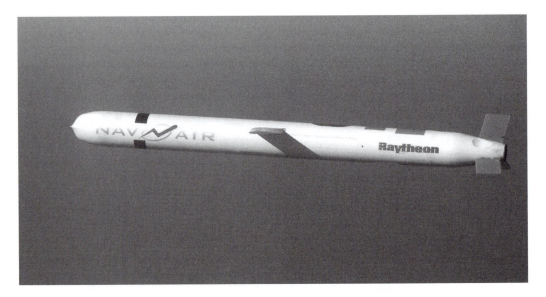

Figure 2.32. Tomahawk (BGM-109) cruise missile. Photo courtesy of the U.S. Department of Defense.

Figure 2.33. Harpoon anti-ship missile. Photo courtesy of the U.S. Department of Defense.

Table 2.5. Various Cruise Missiles Deployed by World's Major Armed Forces.

Type	Designation/Name	Country of Origin
Long-Range (Greater than 1000 miles), Subsonic	Kh-55, Granat	Russia
	Tammuz	Iraq
	BGM-109, Tomahawk (ship-launched)	United States
	AGM-86B, Tomahawk (air-launched)	United States
Medium-Range (500 ~ 1000 km), Subsonic	Storm Shadow	United Kingdom/France
	KEPD 350, Taurus	Germany
	Babur	Pakistan
Short-Range (100 ~ 500 km), Supersonic	P-500, Bazalt	Russia
	P-270, Moskit	Russia
	P-800, Oniks	Russia
	P-700, Granit	Russia
	PJ-10 BrahMos	India/Russia

by an auxiliary solid rocket booster, a cruise missile only needs a small wing to maintain its cruise lift along with control and stability tail fins. Modern versions of the Tomahawk missile include capabilities to pre-program up to fifteen different targets with video monitoring capability of the specific targets, so that the final target selection can be made by the weapons control officer in response to rapidly evolving battlefield situations.

The Tomahawk cruise missiles have a length of 20 ft 6 in at launch, and 18 ft 3 in after the launch booster has been jettisoned. As noted previously, a wing span of only 8 ft 9 in is sufficient to maintain the cruise flight. The turbofan power plant (Williams International F107-WR-402) propels the missile at a subsonic cruise speed of 550 mph.

Table 2.5 lists cruise missiles developed and deployed by the world's major armed forces.

REFERENCES

Clancy, Tom. *Fighter Wing: A Guided Tour of an Air Force Combat Wing.* New York: Berkeley Press, 1995.

Jensen, G.E., and D.W. Netzer (eds.). "Tactical Missile Propulsion," *Progress in Astronautics and Aeronautics*, Vol. 170. Reston, VA: American Institute of Aeronautics and Astronautics, 1996.

Laur, Col. Timothy M., and Steven L. Llanso. *Encyclopedia of Modern U.S. Military Weapons.* New York: Berkeley Books, 1995.

For more information on U.S. missiles, see the following Web pages: en.wikipedia.org/wiki/Missile_guidance, en.wikipedia.org/wiki/Air-to-air_missile/List_of_air-to-air_missiles, and www.globalsecurity.org/military/world/russia/missile.htm.

CHAPTER 3

HELICOPTER FORCE

HELICOPTERS USE ROTORS with variable pitch angle (inclination angle) to provide agile motion, including stationary hovers. With powerful gas-turbine engines to turn high-thrust rotors, a formidable arsenal can be carried with agile mobility by modern attack helicopters. The helicopters have proven their usefulness in many operations including troop and material transport, reconnaissance, medical and other evacuations, airborne command posts, naval anti-submarine missions, and minesweeping operations. As has been the case throughout the history of armed conflicts, however, innovations bring about counter-innovations. In spite of their strength against conventional opponents (e.g., those in hardened bunkers and mechanized vehicles), helicopters nowadays are becoming vulnerable to small projectile weapons such as shoulder-launched missiles or even rocket-propelled grenades fired from a close range. Helicopters' large cross-section, low operational altitude, and relatively low speed make them reachable targets by small projectiles fired from the ground. Nonetheless, few with any intention of survival would take on firepower of the magnitude carried by an attack helicopter like AH-64 Apache under normal battle situations.

The U.S. attack helicopter Apache, AH-64, shown in Fig. 3.1 symbolizes the firepower that can be wielded by military helicopters. AH-64 is powered by two main gas-turbine engines (two General Electric T700-GE-701 turboshaft engines) with 1696 horsepower output each plus an auxiliary power unit (APU). The main engines power the main rotors; the APU supplies electrical and mechanical power while the main engines are shut down on the ground. As shown in the photograph, the armaments that can be carried on an Apache helicopter include a machine gun (M230 30-mm chain gun with 1200 rounds), rocket launcher (Hydra 70 FFAR rockets), and a combination of missiles (AGM-114 Hellfire, AIM-92 Stinger, AIM-9 Sidewinder, TOW missiles, and AGM-122A Sidearm anti-radar missiles). In the Navy's Sea Apache version, AGM-84 Harpoon anti-ship missiles can be carried, as well as Penguin Mk2 Mod7 missiles. Other outboard equipment that can be carried includes the long-range fuel tank, an M130 chaff/flare dispenser, and the ALQ-144IRCM pulsed jammer.

Attack helicopters are most effective against ground targets such as hardened bunkers and armored vehicles. These helicopters can approach targets from low altitudes to avoid detection and strike from the air. This makes armored vehicles particularly vulnerable because their guns have limited elevations. In fact, during the Desert Storm Operation some 500 Iraqi tanks were destroyed by the Apache attack helicopters in the absence of any air cover for the Iraqis.

The Apache helicopter has an in-line cockpit arrangement with the gunner in the front and the pilot in the rear cockpit. Both are aided with a number of pieces of advanced electronic equipment. There is a sensor eyepiece that the gunner can look into with both

Figure 3.1. The U.S. Army's attack helicopter, the Apache AH-64. Main components visible on the exterior of the helicopter are shown. PNVS is pilot night vision system. TADS is the target acquisition and designation system. Photo courtesy of the U.S. Army.

eyes that is connected to the night vision and target acquisition displays. The sensor module for the TADS/PNVS (target acquisition/designation system and pilot's night vision sensor) is located at the nose of the helicopter. TADS is a combination of a direct-view device with wide-angle (18°) and magnified (4°) field-of-view optics, a TV camera, a laser tracker, and a laser rangefinder/designator. The entire system rotates on a turret with a

120° horizontal scan and +30° to −60° elevation range. The PNVS is a FLIR (forward-looking infrared) vision system, mounted on a separate turret. In addition, the gunner looks at a number of laser target tracking and control gauges in a central LCD display, along with flight data gauges (the gunner is also the co-pilot). The pilot's cockpit is similar to that of an aircraft, again augmented by video display. An integrated helmet and display sight system (IHADSS) allows the gunner to view the infrared night/adverse-weather displays through a monocular viewer connected to the helmet. Critical flight data are displayed on the monocle, such as air speed, altitude, and heading. In addition, the IHADSS tracks the gunner's head movements to align the machine gun and rocket launcher in the same direction. Other standard electronics include a UHF/VUF/AM/FM secure communication radio, an IFF with secure encoding, an IR jammer, and a radar jammer.

On the attack helicopter OH-68, Kiowa Warrior, the sensor pod is mounted in a rather large composite spherical dome above the rotors. Similar to the TADS/PNVS module on the Apache, the sensors are gyro-stabilized and include a laser rangefinder/designator, thermal imaging sensor, and video camera. This mast-mounted sensor pod has the advantage of all-around vision as well as minimum exposure of the helicopter body during observations. There was some resistance to such an arrangement due to excessive vibration and the weight of electro-optical sensors, which explains the configuration preferred by the Apache designers. However, with modern vibration isolation techniques and compact sensors, mast mounting is becoming more of a standard.

In modern aircraft, the heads-up display (HUD) allows the pilot the monitor the situation without having to look down on the control panel displays. In attack helicopters, this interface of the digital displays is taken one step further in so-called head-mounted displays (HMD). The IHADSS mentioned above combines the display functions with weapons control. The United States Army has been a pioneer in the use of HMDs in helicopters, and HMD technology was used in the AH-1S Cobras as early as 1970s. The U.S. Air Force is in the process of incorporating these systems in the F-15, F-16, and F-22 fighters, while the Navy version will be implemented in F/A-18s. IHADSS displays the views from the FLIR imaging system and also tracks the head movements of the wearer to direct the night vision cameras, guns, and rocket launchers.

The seats are armored and designed for crashworthiness to protect the occupant's vertebrae. Shock-absorbing material and structural design are embedded in the seats, minus the ejection rockets because this would not be possible due to the presence of the rotors in the ejection path. The crew compartment is shielded by a roll bar, armor, and blast/fragmentation shields, and a blast-resistant (not bullet-proof) material is used for the wind shield. There is an IR-suppressing cover for the exhaust of the main engine to minimize the infrared signature that many anti-aircraft missiles zero in on. The rotors are also designed to reduce noise. The gun turret at the bottom of the Apache helicopters is designed to avoid the crew in the event of a crash landing.

The Apache attack helicopters have a top speed of 227 mph, with a cruise speed of 165 mph. The diameter of the main rotor is 53 ft 8 in, and the height from the ground the tail rotor tip is 16 ft 10 in. The empty weight of an AH-64 is 10,624 lbs, but it can take off with a weight of over 20,000 lbs. The Apache helicopter was conceived to replace the UH-1 Cobra and a monstrous helicopter called AH-56A Cheyenne made by Lockheed. With recent modifications and upgrades, export versions of this helicopter can exceed $56 million. The firepower of AH-64 or its variants (AH-64D) has been purchased by Egypt, Greece, Israel, Japan, Kuwait, the Netherlands, Singapore, United Arab Emirates, and the United Kingdom, with several other nations scheduled to receive their shipment of the helicopter.

Apache helicopters have played key roles in numerous real battle situations. Although most of the glory usually has gone to the fighter-bomber pilots during the much televised attacks on Iraq, in both the 1991 Operation Desert Storm and the 2003 Operation Iraqi Freedom, it was a lead task force of nine Army AH-64 Apaches, one UH-60 Black Hawk, and four MH-53J Air Force Pave Low helicopters that cleared a narrow radar-free passage through the Iraqi air defenses during the Operation Desert Storm. A limited number of stealth fighters could be deployed against intense radar-illuminated regions, and the allied fighter-bombers had some radar jamming capabilities; however, the risk and probable losses were unacceptable if hundreds of aircraft had to fly through a fully functional air defense system dotted all over the land with radar and anti-aircraft missile installations. An opening in the air defense system was identified consisting of two Soviet-built radar installations separated by sixteen kilometers. If these two sites could be knocked out, then the aircraft could filter through the remaining space to initiate strikes against other anti-aircraft sites as well as key military and infrastructure targets.

The fourteen helicopters referred to as the Task Force Normandy were divided into two teams, and the operation commenced at 12:56 AM local time on January 17, 1991. The Apaches were given the task of carrying out the actual attacks, one Black Hawk served as a support helicopter, while the Air Force Pave Lows with their advanced navigation system guided the attack helicopters to the targets. The MH-53J has a more accurate navigation system using satellite global position system and terrain-avoidance radar. The mission objectives were to destroy the two radar installations to pave the way for a much larger air campaign. These helicopters were chosen for this key mission due to their ability to fly at low speeds and altitudes, outside the detection envelope of the early warning radars. The engagement plan was to knock out the site's communication and power equipment so that no alarm can be raised, and then neutralize the radar capabilities. To ensure success, two helicopters were assigned for a given sector to alternately make assaults on the targets and verify the results.

The mission profile called for reaching and attacking the targets by 2:38 AM, requiring close to one hour and forty minutes of flight in near total darkness. In spite of the advanced designs and electronics, flying in Apache helicopters is not a joyride. The cockpits are filled with displays and controls, and the pilot and the gunner both sit in cramped cockpit seats wearing a survival vest and a chest protector, plus the IHADSS helmet, in constant noise and vibration while all the preparations for the assault need to be physically and mentally made. The low-altitude and low-speed approach in the cover of darkness allowed the task force to reach its respective targets. At 6.5 kilometer from the target, the helicopter squadron adjusted the altitude to 150 feet from the ground, and soon after the onboard APR-39 radar warning receiver started beeping indicating that an active radar beam was illuminating the helicopters. However, the warning signal was simply due to the presence of high-power radars beaming upward into the empty nighttime sky, and the attack group approached the targets without being discovered. If anyone was alert enough within the Iraqi radar installations, he may have wondered about the source of this approaching roar of seven helicopters.

The first target was the command-and-control (C&C) vehicle parked in the vicinity of the actual radar site, and it is the C&C that communicates any of the radar warnings to the rest of the Iraqi military chain of command. To maintain the integrity of the entire battle plan, it was essential to cut off this communication channel with the first shot. Using the FLIR display integrated to the target acquisition/designation system (TADS), the gunner located the C&C van and placed it in the cross-hair of the TADS display. This kept the target illuminated by a laser so that the Hellfire missile could follow this bright spot on the target. TADS has capabilities to engage multiple weapons on the same target, and two Hellfire missiles primarily used for anti-tank attacks locked on to the C&C unit. As the gunner pressed on the fire button, the two missiles fired off its launch pods in sequence.

The display now counted the time to impact on the lower corner, but close to the zero count a gigantic explosion could be seen on the gunner's FLIR that also caused the laser lock to be lost because the radiation from the explosion overwhelmed the laser illumination. The first Hellfire thus sailed into the big fireball adjacent to the target. Fortunately, the fireball subsided rather quickly to allow the second Hellfire to maintain its course and hit the target. It turned out that the initial explosion that threw the first Hellfire missile off was the zealous work of the second attack helicopter whose target was the power generator in close proximity of the C&C van. With the C&C capability knocked out, the Apaches used the remaining Hellfire missiles on the radar itself, while spraying any hard objects and likely targets with Hydra 70-mm missiles and cannon fire after all the primary targets were engaged and confirmed destroyed.

The outcome at the other radar site was equally successful, with the entire attack phase being completed in less than five minutes, and all fourteen helicopters returned to the landing point. Long before the arrival, however, the Operation Desert Storm was already underway with aircraft streaming through the corridor established by the Apaches and support helicopters.

Not all helicopter operations have gone as planned. One of the more publicized helicopter operations gone awry has been discussed in several books and even been made into a Hollywood movie. The "Black Hawk Down" sequence of events, officially known as the "Battle of Mogadishu," occurred in 1993 within the rather turbulent surroundings of Somalia that pitted the UNOSOM II (United Nations Operations in Somalia) forces against the Somali militia fighters. UNOSOM II's intent was to bring about peace, law, and order by disarming and reconciling the opposing sectors in Somalia. The U.S. elite special operation teams from the Army Delta Force, the Navy SEALs, and Army Rangers were involved in a UNOSOM operation that called for capture and extraction of high-priority personnel targets of the Habr Gidr clan. The Habr Gidr clan was one of the feuding factions in Somalia headed by a Somali warlord, Mohamed Farrah Aidid, and was known for its well-armed and often violent militia force.

The plan was to use the MH-60 Black Hawk helicopters to send in the special operations troops, rendezvous with substantially larger teams of troops to go in by a ground convoy, and get out. However, the ground convoy was delayed by a series of road barricades consisting of rocks, burning tires, and so forth. In addition, an Army Ranger was seriously injured during a rope-down from a height of 70 feet. In the melee surrounding the mishap, a Black Hawk helicopter was shot down by a rocket-propelled grenade. In the densely populated city environments, the likelihood of direct hits from these RPGs being fired from close, well-hidden locations must have been very high. The ensuing confusion and breakdowns in linking with the reinforcements resulted in another MH-60 Black Hawk helicopter being shot down, and thirty-four UNOSOM troops being killed, including nineteen U.S. servicemen. Two of the killed were Delta Force snipers who volunteered to be inserted by a helicopter to the site of downed Black Hawk in the hope of rescuing the injured pilot and crewmen. The MH-60 Black Hawks with relatively light armor in comparison to, for example, the AH-64 Apache, were made vulnerable in the densely populated landing area and by long exposure to militia attacks due to a series of unforeseen mishaps.

HELICOPTER FLIGHT

In Chapter 1, we saw how different aerodynamic surfaces like the ailerons and vertical and horizontal stabilizers can control the flight of the so-called fixed-wing aircrafts. By contrast, rotary-wing aircrafts like helicopters use the tilt angle of the main rotor to alter

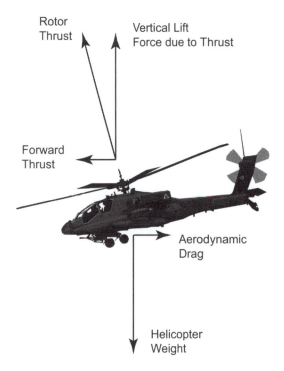

Rotor Thrust

Vertical Lift Force due to Thrust

Forward Thrust

Aerodynamic Drag

Helicopter Weight

Figure 3.2. The forces acting on a helicopter during flight.

their flight paths, as illustrated in Fig. 3.2. The rotating rotor produces thrust in the direction perpendicular to the plane of rotation. The vertical component of the rotor thrust is the lift that counteracts the weight of the helicopter. The horizontal component of the rotor thrust then propels the helicopter forward by overcoming the drag force, as shown in the figure. The rotor can also be tilted from one side to the other, steering the helicopter in that direction. Thus, in helicopters the rotor produces the lift and forward thrust as well as the side forces. By increasing the helicopter angle and the rotor angle, more rotor thrust can be aligned in the forward direction to increase the net thrust.

But we have a rotating axis for the rotor, and how the rotor plane of rotation is made to vary takes some engineering ingenuity. To see how this works, we can begin by looking at the rotor hub in Fig. 3.3. The rotor is connected to the rotor axis, which in turn is typically powered by the turboshaft engine. The rotors are also connected to the upper swash plate through the pitch link. The upper swash plate moves with the rotor while the lower swash plate is stationary. They remain in contact through bearings that allows the upper swash plate to move with respect to the lower swash plate. In a conventional helicopter cockpit, there are three control levers: collective-pitch lever, cyclic-pitch lever, and the tail rotor control pedals. The collective-pitch lever, or collective for short, is located to the left of the pilot's seat and simply moves the lower swash plate up and down through hydraulic and mechanical links. The movements of the lower swash plate will result in an identical motion of the upper swash plate, as shown in the figure, which in turn will change the pitch angle of the rotors. For example, when the pilot pulls up on the collective lever, there will be an upward movement of the swash plates that increases the rotor pitch. High rotor pitch generates higher lift forces with greater torque required to turn the rotors. For this reason, the collective control is connected to the engine throttle via a correlating unit. If the rotor pitch is increased by the collective requiring larger torque, the engine throttle is increased by a preset amount. The exact change in the engine torque can be fine-tuned using a twist-grip type engine rpm control at the end of the collective lever. To pull the helicopter off the ground, the pilot pulls up on the collective to increase lift as well as the engine power. As the rotor torque thus increases, the tendency for the helicopter to rotate in the opposite direction becomes stronger. To offset this tendency, the tail rotor is controlled by the pedal.

The cyclic control lever determines the tilt of the swash plates. Moving the cyclic forward, aft, left, or right causes an inclination of the swash plate. For example, for a helicopter motion to the right, we have the cyclic control pushed forward to cause a tilt in the swash plates. Now, when the rotor is in the left position its pitch angle will be increased while the opposite will happen as the rotor turns to the position on the right. At higher pitch angle, again larger lift is produced and vice versa. This creates an asymmetry in the rotor lift on the forward and aft sides of the rotor rotation, which tends to turn the rotor to a forward-inclined plane shown in the figure. The rotors have a range of motion in all three axes in so-called fully articulated

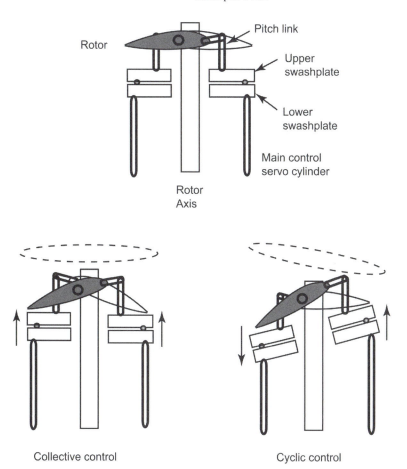

Figure 3.3. Components of a helicopter rotor hub and its control using collective and cyclic.

rotor hubs. The motion in the direction perpendicular to the plane of rotation is called "flap," and it is the flap angle change upward in the aft and downward in the forward side of the rotation that changes the tilt angle of the rotor rotation. The tilting of the rotor rotation plane turns the force vector and thus causes motion in that direction. Side motion follows the similar principle, enacted when the cyclic is pulled left or right. In a typical take-off, as the collective is pulled up the cyclic is pushed forward so that the helicopter gains speed as well as stand-off distance from the ground. The forward speed adds a wind velocity component across the rotors to increases the lift forces, and thus makes it much easier for the helicopter to lift off particularly under heavy load conditions. This standard maneuver is called "translational lift."

A partial view of a helicopter rotor hub is shown in Fig. 3.4, where the large cylindrical object at the center is the rotor shaft. Two of the control cylinders are also visible. The top part of the rotor hub is shown where the rotor blades are

Figure 3.4. A partial view of the rotor hub of the Air Force HH-60G Pave Hawk helicopter. Photo courtesy of the U.S. Air Force.

Figure 3.5. The relative velocity between the air speed and the rotor speed.

attached along with other mechanical components like the flapping hinge, drag hinge, and lag dampers in a fully articulated hub. We saw above that the pitch of the rotors can be cyclically controlled about the rotor hinge. The flapping hinge allows the rotor to move up and down to tilt the rotation plane of the rotors, as controlled by the cyclic. In addition to tilting the plane of rotor rotation, the flapping compensates for the differential lift generated by forward- and backward-moving rotors. As shown in Fig. 3.5, if we look at a counterclockwise rotor rotation from the top, the right half of the rotor will see a greater velocity because it is moving against the air. For example, for a helicopter moving at 120 mph with a rotor tip speed of 400 mph, the right rotor tip will be traveling at 520 mph while the left rotor is actually moving backward at 280 mph. For a given blade pitch angle, the lift is proportional to the square of this relative air velocity, so that the right half of the rotor will generate a much greater lift than the left. This will result in unbalanced lift as well as unbalanced torque on the rotor axis and the helicopter airframe. Allowing the rotor to lift up at higher lift conditions alleviates this torque. Thus, it is the centripetal acceleration of the rotor and the lift force that will set the rotor elevation angle, since the rotors are free to move up and down in the flap direction. Without rotation, the rotors will tend to droop down under gravity, and there are lower stops for the flap angle to prevent the rotors from completely leaning down. For marine helicopters, there are also upper stops to prevent high wind from knocking the blades upward. In addition to the pitch and the flap degrees of freedom, the rotors are also allowed to rotate in limited amounts in the drag direction, which is in the direction of the rotor motion. As the lift is varied by the pitch angle, so is the drag on the blades, which will cause fluctuations of the force in the drag direction. To alleviate mechanical stress associated with this fluctuation in drag, the drag hinge is used to allow small back and forth rotation. The drag hinge is also useful in folding the blades in the horizontal plane, to line up all the blades in one direction so that the helicopters may fit into small hangar spaces. Some of the mechanical linkages to connect the rotor hub to the main rotors are shown in Figs. 3.6 and 3.7.

Fully articulated hubs are already mechanically quite complex, much more so than aerodynamic surfaces on fixed-wing aircraft, simply because they involve multiple, conjugate rotations and translations. For this reason, high-lift aerodynamic devices such as flaps (commonly used in fixed-wing aircrafts) or boundary-layer control are not readily implemented on helicopter rotors although any increase in lift would enhance helicopter performance. Flaps are retractable surfaces at the trailing edge of wings used to increase the wing surface area and also the allowable angle of attack deployed during take-off and landing of fixed-wing aircrafts. Another high-lift approach called boundary-layer control uses compressed air blown through tiny slits or holes on the wing or the rotor to again allow high angles of attack. Another unique aspect of helicopter operation is the level of

Figure 3.6. Rotors attached to the rotor hub. Background photo courtesy of the U.S. Air Force.

vibration arising from the rotation of rotors that are typically imbalanced in the load conditions (lift and drag). For both civilian and military helicopter flights, excessive vibration is to be avoided for passenger comfort for the former and minimum crew/equipment fatigue and combat efficiency for in the latter. Even with the gyro and digital stabilization in the targeting systems, it helps to have stable optical axes for aiming one's weapons. There have been several innovative vibration isolation schemes, such as "Noda-Matic" and liquid inertia vibration eliminator (LIVE). In the Noda-Matic, the fuselage is hung on the rotor hub and gear assembly on beams

Figure 3.7. Rotor hub on the SH-60F Seahawk helicopter showing various hinges. Photo courtesy of the U.S. Navy.

or linkages that are allowed to move in limited amounts, and this movement is damped by tuned masses to cancel as much as possible the vibration frequencies. In the LIVE type of devices, the link between the fuselage and the propulsion train consists of piston damper against heavy liquids like mercury contained in a cylinder. This acts like a shock absorber, with elastomeric material liners inside of the cylinder further dampening the vibrations.

The helicopter controls include the collective pitch control lever, cyclic control stick, and the directional control pedals. The collective is typically located on the left side of the pilot's seat, while the cyclic control is in front of the pilot as are the control pedals on the floor. As the collective is raised the overall pitch of the rotor increases requiring higher engine torque, and this in turn increases the overall tendency of the helicopter to rotate in the opposite direction of the rotor rotation. For example, for a counterclockwise rotor rotation as seen by the pilot, there will be a tendency for the helicopter to rotate in the clockwise direction since the helicopter is not anchored to the ground but rather is suspended in the air. To counter this torque, a gradually increasing amount of anti-torque needs to be applied by the tail rotor which is controlled by the directional pedals. Thus, as the collective is raised, the pilot pushes down on the left pedal and with decreasing pitch the right pedal. The directional control pedals alter the pitch of the tail rotors, with the left pedal increasing the pitch and the right decreasing it. These motions are of course coupled also to the cyclic that changes the direction of the helicopter movement. These three-dimensional motions are a complex process, in addition to the control nuances for different helicopters that need to be familiarized by the pilot. In modern military aircraft, such classic direct controls are hard to find where multiply redundant digital fly-by-wire has taken its place to maximize the aircraft agility and control. In modern attack submarines, the traditional control rudder and hydroplane, each separately manned, has been replaced by digital control sticks. Such digital control in helicopters is sometimes called ADOCS (advanced digital/optical control system) and will perhaps someday remove many of the complexities and nuances of flying helicopters with classical controls.

The rotors can be arranged in several different configurations as shown in Fig. 3.8. The most common one is perhaps the lift rotor/tail rotor combination, as we saw in an earlier photo for the Apache AH-64 helicopters. Two rotors can be used either in side-by-side or tandem configurations as shown in the figure. The tandem configuration is represented by the Boeing Vertol Chinook helicopter used for transport. Two rotors can also be operated in intermeshed planes of rotation, which obviously requires mechanical timing of the rotors as the two planes of rotation intersect. Twin coaxial rotors have also been used.

The twin-rotor configurations do not include the tail rotor as in the single rotor helicopters. For single rotor rotation, the helicopter main body is free to rotate as is the rotor, so the tail rotor is used to apply a counter-torque. As the main rotor torque increases, so does the torque for the helicopter main body and stronger counter-torques is needs to be provided by the tail rotor. The pedal action that controls the tail rotor thus needs to be adjusted to keep the helicopter yaw angle straight. A different design called NOTAR does not use a tail rotor but instead sends fan-pressurized air through slot(s) in the tail section to offset the torque. In the NOTAR system, some of the air is ejected at the tail, like a jet, while the remainder is sent through slots along the tail boom to control the air flow so that the tail boom creates lift in the anti-torque direction. For twin rotors, running the rotors in opposite directions negates the tendency for the airframe to rotate in the opposite direction as the rotor.

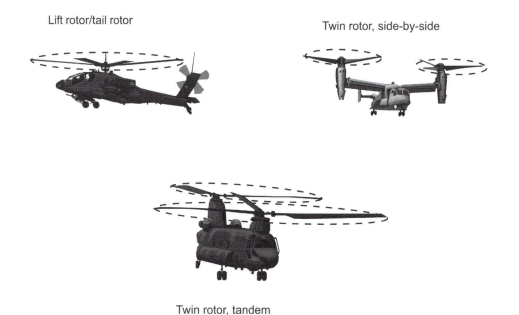

Figure 3.8. Different rotor configurations.

As in most military fixed-wing aircrafts, modern helicopters are powered by gas-turbine engines (e.g., the General Electric T-700 turboshaft engine shown in Fig. 3.9). In contrast to jet engines, which derive most of the power from the high velocity and therefore high momentum of the exhaust jet, gas-turbine engines for helicopters convert most of the power into torque or shaft power. This is accomplished by having multistage turbines convert the thermal energy produced by combustion of fuel and air into mechanical energy. For

Figure 3.9. The General Electric T-700 turboshaft engine used on the UH-60 Black Hawk helicopters. Photo courtesy of the U.S. Navy.

this reason, the gas turbines used for helicopter power are called turboshaft engines. Gas-turbines in general are known for their reliability, high sustained power, large power-to-weight ratio, and use of jet fuels that tend to be less volatile than gasoline. Typical turboshaft engines used in helicopters generate several thousands of shaft horsepower with the power-er-to-weight ratio of five or above in terms of shaft horsepower and pounds for the engine weight. So an engine generating 2000 shaft horsepower may weigh only about 500 pounds. Gas-turbine engines ingest large amounts of air and push them through various components like the compressor, combustor, and turbines, most of which are sensitive to the presence of particles. Since military helicopters are subject to use in harsh environments involving dust, sand, or foreign objects, it is of key importance to filter out these particles or objects before they enter the main engine. Filters, magnetic particle traps, and curved flow passages are used to prevent these particles from damaging the engine components that operate at high rotational speeds and temperature. In modern turboshaft engines, the most of the particles 3 microns and above are prevented from going into the engine to prolong the life of the engine components.

The main engine powers both the main rotor and the tail rotor, if any. For the Apache helicopters shown in an earlier photograph, there are two turboshaft engines connected through two gearboxes to the main rotor.

HELICOPTER ARMAMENT

The integrated helmet and display sight system (IHADSS) in modern helicopters allows the gunner to view and direct the fire toward the targets, and the gun itself is swivel-mounted for a wide-angle coverage and carries a big punch with each 30-mm diameter cannon shell fired. Those are 1.18-in diameter cannon bullets with a muzzle velocity of 2600ft/s being fired by the Hughes M230 "Chain Gun" at a rate of up to 750 rounds per minute. A photograph shows the M230 cannon. Other guns used on helicopters carry even bigger destructive capabilities, like the GE 225 mounted in the chin turret of AH-1 Cobra helicopters (predecessor of AH-64 Apache) with a muzzle velocity of 4400 ft/s at up to 2000 rounds per minute. The use of guns in helicopters of course had a much more modest beginning.

Rifle-caliber machine guns were mounted on a gimbaled mount to be controlled manually or in the doorways as on the UH-1 "Huey." The door-mounted guns could be effective in covering ground troops, clearing the landing zones, suppressing the opposition fire, and basically spraying bullets over anything that seemed like threats. The fixed guns controlled by pilot or the gunner required the helicopter to be aligned in the direction of fire. Against stationary targets, the fixed guns have become accurate with vibration damping and better helicopter pitch and yaw controls. The fundamental hover or low-speed flight capabilities of helicopters make fixed guns an effective weapon against stationary targets. Although not as advanced as sight-controlled, swiveled chain guns, fixed guns are easy to install and maintain. However, a large number of helicopters employ at least some degree of freedom in aiming by installing the guns on turrets with a slew (horizontal sweep) and some pitch capabilities. The helicopter gun turret manufactured by Lucas Aerospace, for example, has a mechanized sweep at 80°/sec with a pitch control of −4 to +6°.

The ultimate in the gun mount is the swivel mount found on the Apache helicopters, with a 220° powered sweep and +11 to −60° elevation. As noted above, the aiming can be slaved to the IHADSS or controlled manually. Due to the recoil and ammunition weight of high-powered guns, the guns tend to be located on the chin of the helicopters preferably close to the center of gravity. Any offset from the centerline will tend to swing the helicopter around due to recoil, and a location far from the centerline shifts the overall helicopter weight balance as the ammunition is used up. For example, 1200 rounds of XM789 shells can weigh over 2000 pounds.

The Hughes M230 Chain Gun shown in Fig. 3.10 has a total weight of 56 kg, and has a length of 1.64 m. On Apache helicopters, typically 1200 rounds are carried with different options for rounds. For example, M789 high-explosive dual purpose (HEDP) shells are used for anti-armor, while M799 high-explosive incendiary (HEI) shells are reserved for anti-material and anti-personnel. The rounds fired by M230 have a maximum range of 4000 m and an effective lethal (for armor and material) range of 1500 m. Several other guns made by the Hughes Corporations are available for helicopter mounts: EX34 (7.63 mm caliber), Heligun (7.63 mm) with two barrels, Mk11 Mod 5 (20 mm), and M129 grenade launcher.

Other U.S. manufacturers of helicopter guns include Browning and General Electric. Two of the notable guns by the General Electric are GE XM214 and GE M134 (Fig. 3.11), with electrically rotated barrels. The five- or six-barrel configuration allows a much higher rate of fire, up to 10,000 rounds per minute for the XM214 "Microgun" and 4000 for the M134 "Minigun," with the latter shown in the figure. There is nothing "micro" or "mini" about the destructive powers of these rapid-fire weapons, but they are named to reflect the fact that they are scaled-down version of the GE M61 Vulcan cannons that fired 20-mm shells. In comparison, the GE M134 Minigun uses 7.62-mm caliber rounds and 5.56-mm

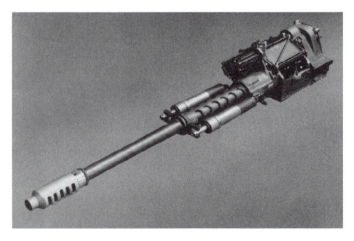

Figure 3.10. The Hughes M230 Chain Gun used on Apache AH-64 helicopters. Photo courtesy of the U.S. Department of Defense.

Figure 3.11. A GE M134 Minigun.

rounds for the GE XM214 Microgun. These rotating barrel machines use electric motor to power the barrel rotation. They were specifically developed for helicopter and light aircraft, as the motion of these aircraft require sweeping the target area with a rapid firing rate to maintain the hit density. However, these guns are used by all branches of military, and due to its impressive image have also been shown in numerous Hollywood action films (in spite of the fact that XM214 along with the gun, ammunition, and power supply for the rotary motor would weigh way too much for handheld action as shown in several movies, not to mention the tremendous recoil which would spin the gunner around). Since most helicopters carry several thousand rounds of ammunition, setting the firing rate at maximum will quickly deplete the ammo. The firing rate can be adjusted from several hundred to the maximum 10,000 rounds per minute for the XM214, with 10,000 rounds per minute corresponding to 166 shots per second. In addition, single bursts of 30 to 1000 rounds can be set. Similarly, the XM214 Microgun firing rate can be adjusted from 400 to 4000 rpm. XM214 has five barrels that are rotated by a 0.8-hp electric motor.

The next ubiquitous armament on attack helicopters is the rocket launcher, holding multiple rockets in open-ended tubes. Rockets differ from missiles in that they are unguided projectiles that follow their initial launch path. Similar to missiles, the thrust is provided by solid-propellant charges. Frequently, two booster stages are used, first for the high-thrust launch and the second stage to sustain the rocket line of flight. Folded fins open up on launch in so-called folding-fin aerial rockets (FFAR). At launch, the spin rate of 10 rev/s is generated. The fins provide the spin to the rockets to stabilize its attitude angle, and therefore also aerodynamics. Without spin stabilization, the rockets become sensitive to aerodynamic and other external perturbations and may tumble off their directed paths. This effect is familiar to anyone who has thrown a football. A football thrown with insufficient or incorrect spin wobbles out of its axis, and at the high speeds involved in rocket flights any wobble will quickly increase the drag and tumble the projectile off its path. Depending on the mission and targets, the rocket booster can be fitted with different warheads.

The Hydra 70 rocket system, for example, is a classic unguided missile system with many warhead variations. The Hydra system with its nominal 70-mm diameter rockets is used on the AH-64A Apache and AH-64D Apache Longbow helicopters in nineteen-tube launchers (see Fig. 3.1) and also on the OH-58D Kiowa Warrior and the AH-1F updated version of Cobra in seven-tube launchers. The Hydra 70 is a complete system including the lightweight launchers (LWSs), rocket motor, and various warheads. The M260 LWL is the seven-tube launcher, while the M261 is the nineteen-tube version on Apache helicopters. The rocket motor is designated MK66 with several modified versions. The MK66 consists of an aluminum alloy housing with a rocket nozzle and spring-loaded fins. Once ignited, the MK66 generates a thrust of 1335 pounds. Different modifications to the MK66 were mostly necessitated by false ignition from electromagnetic radiation (radio and other signals). The electrical circuit for remote ignition thus was fitted with radio frequency filters. The current modification (MOD4) version of the MK66 is believed to extremely stable and impervious to even external electrical sparks other than that directly given by the fire control. The MK66 booster has a weight of just under fourteen pounds, and its propellant has a burn time of just over one second. The booster propels the rocket from a speed of 148 ft/s at launch to 2425 ft/s at burnout, which is again just one second after ignition. This corresponds to an acceleration of 70 to 100 G. As with most propellants, the booster is designed to remain stable over a large range of temperatures: −65 °F to 165 °F for storage and −50 °F to 150 °F for operation.

As noted above, different type of warheads can be fitted to the MK66 rocket motor. The M151 HE (high-explosive), for example, is an anti-personnel warhead with a 10-lb high explosive charge. Although difficult to visualize its impact, these warheads are designed to maximize lethality on reaching the target. The 10-lb charge may not seem like much, but attached to the charge are numerous pointed cast iron fragmentation projectiles that will fan out in all directions on explosion. The lethality range is estimated at 50-m radius of the impact point. The M229 HE warhead is an expanded version of the M151 HE with a 17-lb explosive charge instead and higher mass for the fragmentation charge as well. The M156 White Phosphorous warhead almost appears benign by comparison. It contains 2.2 pounds of white phosphorous for smoke generation (target marking) and incendiary functions. The M255A1 Flechette warhead is used for air-to-air and air-to-ground anti-armor (light armor) and anti-personnel attacks. Flechette is the French word for darts, and on detonation the warhead breaks up into 1179 pointed, hardened steel flechettes that follow the given trajectory but with a predesigned, repeatable dispersion (similar to a shotgun charge). There are three or more tracer darts contained in the M255A1 for tracking purposes. The M261 high-explosive multipurpose submunition (MPSM) has multiple uses as the designation MPSM suggests. It can be used against light armor, vehicles, bunkers, and personnel. The warhead contains nine M73 sub-munitions and one expulsion charge. On detonation, the each of the submunition charges explodes into 195 high-velocity fragments that fan out at 5000 ft/s. The M257 Illumination warhead has a controlled fuse delay, and its magnesium sodium nitrate burns for 100 seconds as the warhead descends at 15 ft/s. Other warheads include the M264 Red Phosphorous (RP) smoke, M267 Practice rounds, and M278 IR Flare for infrared vision and target acquisition for up to three minutes.

Various air-to-air and air-to-ground missiles are also effectively used by helicopters. A simple TOW (tube-launched optical tracked wire-guided) missile requires the pilot or the gunner to follow the missile path and transmit any corrections via a rapidly dispensing wire from the missile. For nighttime operations, infrared vision systems can be integrated for

TOW launches. For tracking, the pilot or the gunner simply keeps the target in the cross-hair of the tracking telescope, and the corrective signals are generated by the computer and relayed via the wire to the missile fin control. The Hellfire missile is a laser-tracked anti-tank missile (Fig. 3.12) carried on U.S. attack helicopters including Kiowa Warriors and Apaches. In place of the cumbersome wire, laser illumination is used on Hellfire missiles. A laser beam with a specific wavelength is pointed at the target by the operator, and the laser sensor at the nose of the missile picks off the reflection from the target and points the missile toward the direction of the maximum reflection. The sensor section includes a glass canopy at the noise, a signal preamplifier, a telescope, and the laser sensor itself. The signal is again sent to the control unit which again activates the fins to guide the missile toward the target.

For naval operations, an example of the anti-ship missile launched from helicopter is the British BAe Sea Skua missile with a semi-active radar homing head, shown in Fig. 3.13. Sea Skua is an effective short-range missile (10 nautical miles or 18.5 km) when the target is radar-illuminated by the launch helicopter. Sea Skua is a so-called sea-skimming missile to fly below the radar scan angles. On launch, the missile will follow a low altitude path and during the final approach drops to a terminal sea-skimming altitude using the onboard altimeter. Penguin-series missiles like the Mk2 for

Figure 3.12. A Hellfire anti-tank missile is shown mounted on the right side of the Bell OH-58 Kiowa Warrior. The sensor pod at the top of the mast allows the helicopter to acquire the target at low heights without exposing the main helicopter body. Photo courtesy of the U.S. Army.

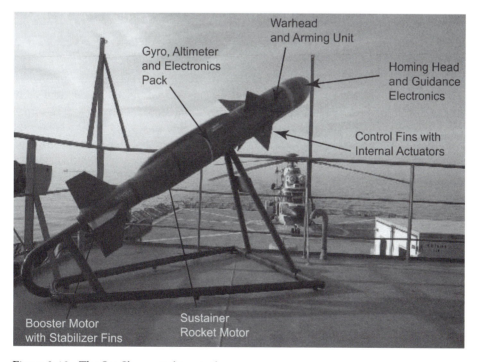

Figure 3.13. The Sea Skua anti-ship missile.

helicopter launch are fire-and-forget missiles with active radar guidance, with a range of 14.5 nautical miles (27 km). Similar to the Sea Skua, the rocket motor consists of the booster for launch and acceleration and the sustainer for course maintenance. Mk2 missiles can be programmed for dog-leg approach using the active guidance radar and onboard controls. A dog-leg path is another way of avoiding detection, and the missile may fly behind a natural barrier (e.g., a small island) and then make a sudden turn toward the target ship.

The AGM-84 Harpoon is an anti-ship cruise missile, with all-weather, long-range capabilities. Following the current U.S. military philosophy of developing multi-branch weapon systems, Harpoon missiles can be launched from fixed-wing aircraft, helicopters, land-based launchers, and naval vessels including submarines. The range varies on the AGM-84 models, but can be as high as 120 nautical miles for the AGM-84D and 150 nautical miles for the AGM-84H/K. Similar to cruise missiles, Harpoons, with a price tag of $720,000 per shot, are powered by a turbojet engine (Teledyne J402 with 660 pounds of thrust), but have optional solid propellant booster for land and submarine-launched versions. 488 pounds of high-explosive warhead arm the missile.

Torpedoes and depth charges also make up the anti-submarine armament arsenal in naval helicopters. The Mk46 is a standard lightweight ASW torpedo. Mk46 is powered by reciprocating (piston) engine with solid or liquid monopropellant fuel. Monopropellant—one of a class of fuels that do not require external supply of air or oxygen—is used in small rocket boosters and also in this case to drive the reciprocating engine under water. Although considered lightweight by torpedo standards, the Mk46 has a diameter of 12.75 in and length of 102.36 in. The estimated range of the Mk46 is 10,000 yd, and it is guided to the target using active or passive sonar. The warhead is a 100-lb shape-charged high explosive designed to penetrate the thickest submarine hulls. Depth charges are one of the oldest weapons against submarines going back to the World War II era. The fuse can be set off using a preset time delay or preset water depth, with the latter being actuated by the water pressure to release a mechanical or electrical detonation device.

MILITARY HELICOPTERS

The Bell 205 or UH-1 Huey, originally named Iroquois, is a venerable multipurpose helicopter, extensively used in the Vietnam War. The UH-1 entered service in 1955, and though mostly replaced by the UH-60 Black Hawk in the United States it still remains in service in many military services around the world. The Hueys were used as a part of new military strategy to bring in troops by these helicopters to remote areas of operation and pull them back at the end of the mission. The later version of UH-1H carried fourteen armed troops, while its variants functioned as the air-to-ground fire support, medevac, search and rescue, and cargo transport.

Due to its long service in many different countries, a large variety of armaments has been used on UH-1 helicopters:

AS-12 attack missile
Avibra Helicopter Armament System (7.62-mm gun and rocket launcher)
BAe Sea Skua anti-ship missile
Bofors Bantam anti-tank missile
Brandt 68-22 rocket launcher and 68-mm rockets
Browning 12.7-mm M3 heavy machine gun
Cardoen PJ-1 depth charge
Cardoen PJ-1 manually dropped bomb

Emerson Flexible Turret System with Minigun

FFV Uni-Pod 0127 with 12.7-mm gun

Hydra rockets with nineteen-tube launcher.

Mathogo anti-tank missile (Argentina)

M129 40-mm grenade launcher

M21 MAMEE armament system (7.62-mm M134 Minigun with 3000 rounds and M158 rocket launcher with seven rockets)

M5 ball turret with M75 40-mm grenade launcher

Martin Pescador supersonic missile

Mk44 AS torpedoe

Oerlikon KBA 25-mm cannon

SNORA 81-mm rockets and launcher

SNIA BPD HL-12-70 or HL-7-80 rocket launcher

XM-31 20-mm cannon

A photograph of the Huey helicopter during its deployment in the Vietnam War is shown in Fig. 3.14. The gas-turbine is mounted directly below and aft of the main rotor (the exhaust can be seen aft of the engine mount). The oil and fuel tank access is close the engine compartment, and the transmission is located at the bottom of the rotor shaft. The pilot and co-pilot sit side-by-side. The tail rotor is connected to the main engine by two gear boxes, and as noted above the increase in the main rotor torque is compensated by generating more tail rotor counter-torque. There are two articulated rotors that had a length of 48 ft and a 21-inch chord. To balance the rotors, there was a stabilizer bar with two heavy balls on the tips at a right angle to the rotors. The engine typically used was the

Figure 3.14. The UH-1 Huey helicopter during an operation in the Vietnam War. Photo courtesy of the U.S. Department of Defense.

Avco Lycoming T-53 turboshaft engine with up to 1400 hp power output in later versions. UH-1 had a maximum cruise speed of 127 mph, hovering ceiling of 4000 feet, and a range of 318 miles. The hovering ceiling depends on the density, which decreases with altitude and air temperature. At lower density, the lift is insufficient to provide an upward force equal to the weight of the helicopter at zero velocities (hover). However, so-called translational lift allows the helicopter to operate at higher altitudes as the relative velocity between the rotor and air is increased to enhance the thrust when the helicopter is moving. In fact, under heavily loaded conditions helicopters use translational lift by bringing the helicopter to a forward motion before rising through the air.

The unique terrain and situation in Vietnam led to the development of the "Airmobile Program" by the U.S. Army, and later the Air Cavalry with a breed of enlisted helicopter pilots. The impassable jungles and mountainous terrain proved to be an effective sanctuary for the unconventional North Vietnamese troops, and to engage them the United States experimented with the Piasecki H-21 helicopters to airlift paratroopers to the suspected regions. These fighting units were sent in to the operational areas in the morning, and then ferried back in the evening in what became known as the "Picnic Lunch" excursions. This strategy was soon highly organized with a large fleet of Bell UH-1 Huey helicopters with powerful gas-turbine engines. The Huey was the first turbine-powered helicopter to be employed by the U.S. military. Because the primary function of the Huey was to transport troops to and back from operational areas, losses from small-arms fire became a serious issue and soon 0.3-in machine guns and 2.75-in rocket launchers were installed. This evolved into fully dedicated gunships based on UH-1B and UH-1C, where M60 machine guns were mounted on each door along with seven-tube XM158 2.75-in (70-mm) rocket launcher. The human and material cost of the war was shared by those who flew Huey helicopters during the Vietnam War, with 2500 of these aircraft lost and 2202 pilots killed in action. The Hueys were deployed under extremely difficult battle conditions—hot landing zones, troop extraction, or medical evacuation in active battle zones, not to mention excessive flying hours without much sleep or rest at times.

The UH-60 Black Hawk (Army) or the Air Force counterpart, the MH-60G Pave Hawk, is currently the main utility helicopter of the U.S. armed forces (Fig. 3.15). The Black Hawk and its variants are made by Sikorsky and carry out multiple functions as did their predecessor, the UH-1 Huey. Two General Electric T700-series turboshaft engines power the four-blade rotor with 1940 hp (T-700-GE-701C). To improve the strength of the rotor assembly, the rotor hub is forged from a single titanium block, and elastomeric bearings between the swash plates, as well as self-tuning vibration dampers. The rotor blades themselves are made from titanium tubular spars (frames), with the volume material of graphite with glassfiber/epoxy skin. The performance is substantially enhanced over the UH-1, with a top speed of 222 mph (cruise speed is 167 mph) and a hover altitude of 10,400 ft (service ceiling of 19,000 ft). With internal fuel, the Black Hawk helicopters can cover 373 miles or stay in the air for two hours and eighteen minutes.

Although there are dedicated attack helicopters in the U.S. military arsenal, the Black Hawk can carry a respectable array of armaments. The General Electric Black Hawk Weapon System includes two 7.62-mm Miniguns or two GECAL 0.50 Gatling guns. External pylons called the external stores support system (ESSS) can be used to mount up to 10,000 pounds of gear, from external fuel tanks that increase the range to 1380 miles, sixteen Hellfire missiles, and M56 mine dispensers to a nineteen-tube Hydra rocket launcher with FFAR (folding-fin aerial rockets). HOT missiles, TOW missiles, and an assortment of other armaments have also been used in the tank-killer version of the Black Hawk. HOT (Haut subsonique optiquement teleguide, or high subsonic optical guided) is an anti-tank missile made by Euromissile and, similar to TOW, uses wire guidance.

Figure 3.15. A tandem formation of UH-60 Black Hawk helicopters. The M60 7.62-mm machine guns are shown in the rest positions. The two engine cowlings to the sides of the main rotors are also prominent. Photo courtesy of the U.S. Department of Defense.

As noted above, the UH-60 is used by all branches of the military and also the civilian sector, as the Army's Black Hawk, Navy's Sea Hawk (Fig. 3.16), Air Force's Pave Hawk, and The U.S. Coast Guard's Jayhawk. Naval use includes mine and missile deployments. Most military versions have bulletproof seats and side panels, shock-absorbing landing gear and seats, self-sealing fuel tanks, and redundant electrical and hydraulics. The shock-absorbing seats, or crashworthy seats, have an impact attenuation device wherein soft stainless steel tubes are crushed on impact to absorb the force of the crash. The seats also have wraparound armors made of boron carbide or other lightweight yet protective material. Armor panels made of Kevlar panels or ceramics also are used in strategic locations, and the windshield itself can be made of blast-resistant materials.

Now replaced by the fearsome AH-64 for the U.S. Army, the Bell 209 AH-1 Cobra has a unique design with a narrow frontal area, fitting the name "Cobra." A schematic of the AH-1 is shown in Fig. 3.18. Since the Department of Defense contracted with Bell Helicopters in 1966, more than 1000 of the AH-1 and variants have been delivered. Cobras have many of the modern features of attack helicopters, including FLIR, HUD (heads-up display), Doppler navigation, and laser targeting. These helicopters thus have all-weather and night attack capabilities. Different versions have been used by the U.S. Army (Cobra, Huey Cobra, Super Cobra, King Cobra) in the past and are currently in use by the U.S. Navy (Sea Cobra, AH-1J) and the Marine Corps (AH-1T). The standard armaments included TOW missiles, two 2.75 in. Hydra rocket launchers, and 20-mm guns. The Marines have used these helicopters since the Vietnam War for armed escorts of helicopters such

Figure 3.16. The MH-60R Sea Hawk, the Navy version of the UH-60 helicopter. Photo courtesy of the U.S. Navy.

Figure 3.17. Cockpit of the Air Force Pave Hawk. Photo courtesy of the U.S. Air Force.

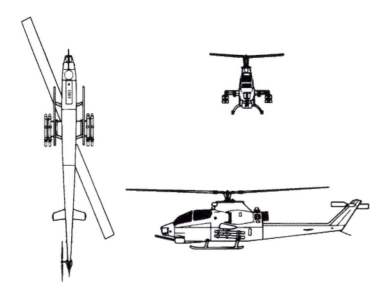

Figure 3.18. Schematics of the Bell 209 AH-1 Cobra helicopter. Image courtesy of the U.S. Army.

as Hueys, landing zone fire suppression, and aerial ambush. As can be guessed from the narrow width of the helicopter, the gunner and the pilot rode in tandem similar to the Apache helicopter. A single Lycoming or Pratt & Whitney engine was used, although in some of the later versions two General Electric T-700 engines have been installed on the same airframe. The single-engine versions had a climb rate of 1925 ft/min and a maximum attainable speed of 195 mph (cruising speed of 175 mph). An example of the current version, the AH-1W Super Cobra, is shown in Fig. 3.19. In the classical frame, modernized sensors and armaments make the navalized AH-1W an effective vehicle for amphibious assaults and close-in fire support for the Marines. A number of critical missions coordinated with the landing force can be launched from helicopter-able warships, such as landing zone fire suppression, anti-tank/anti-armor fire, armed reconnaissance, and cargo/personnel escorts. Being a dedicated attack helicopter, the AH-1W carries substantial armament: eight TOW/Hellfire missiles, two 2.75-inch rocket tubes, and a 20-mm three-barrel M197 gun with 750 rounds. Protective armor shields the cockpit from small-arms fire, while advanced composite materials in the rotors and the tail boom are designed to withstand damage from heavy-gauge cannon hits from up to 23-mm rounds.

While the naval versions of the Black Hawk and other helicopters exist, the Sikorsky CH-53E Super Stallion (see Figs. 3.20 and 3.21) perhaps exemplifies the super-heavy naval helicopters. Super Stallion is a heavy-duty, multipurpose helicopter with a take-off weight of 73,500 pounds, making it one of the largest helicopters in the world. Although based on the RH-53 Sea Stallion, the Super Stallion has a much larger capacity powered by three 4380-hp turboshaft engines. Along with seven rotor blades with extended length, the Super Stallion has roughly double the lift capability of its precursor, the Sea Stallion. The lift capability was designed in because one of the intended duties of the helicopter was recovery of downed aircraft. Up to fifty-four fully equipped troops can ride in RH-53, making it a troop deployment vehicle of choice by the Marine Corp as well. Some of the self-defense armaments on the Super Stallion include the Browning MG3 0.5-in machine gun, MLMS Stinger missiles, and AIM-9L Sidewinders, along with a chaff and flare dispenser.

Figure 3.19. The AH-1W Super Cobra used for amphibious assaults and expeditionary close support. Notice the narrow cross-section of the leading helicopter already in the air. Photo courtesy of the U.S. Navy.

Figure 3.20. The CH-53E Super Stallion. Photo courtesy of the U.S. Navy.

Figure 3.21. Cockpit of the Super Stallion helicopter. Photo courtesy of the U.S. Navy.

Figure 3.22. An MH-53E Sea Dragon retrieving an AN/AQS-14A side-looking sonar.

The MH-53 Sea Dragon is shown in Fig. 3.22, dragging a sled-like hydrofoil antimagnetic vehicle with an Mk 104 acoustic minesweeping gear. The MH-53E is based on the Sea Stallion airframe and is the U.S. Navy's largest helicopter with bigger fuel and load capacity. Sea Dragons are used for air-to-air refueling of other helicopters, internal/external cargo transport, or any other mission requiring heavy loads. The Sea Dragon, if used for the latter purposes, can transport either fifty-five fully armed troops or a 16-ton payload over 50 nautical miles (nm) or a 10-ton payload over 500 nm.

A unique twin-rotor design is found on the V-22 Osprey (Fig. 3.24) used by various branches of the military including the special forces. Osprey is a so-called tilt-rotor aircraft with vertical take-off and landing (VTOL) capabilities, with the rotor being tilted to upright position during take-off, landing, or hover. The alignment of the rotors with the aircraft motion allows higher speed and better fuel efficiency, thus combining the virtues of helicopter and airplane. As the first full-production tilt-rotor aircraft, the V-22s endured a long, over-the-budget development history, with entrance to the service in 2005. The complexities in the tilt-rotor aircraft emerged during the development period. Many of the aircraft and engine operation parameters are controlled by sensors and an onboard computer that sends commands to the control surfaces and the engine. Uncommanded engine acceleration occurred due to a glitch in the hardware wiring to the digital engine control, which caused the aircraft to take off during engine idle. The stability of the aircraft is also sensitive to the computer commands, and a faulty chip or software could cause the aircraft to lose control, which of course had to be eradicated during development. Some of the hardware corrections included leakage from the gearbox that could cause engine fire and malfunction. Compressor flow conditions were at times unstable which also had to be engineered back to design operations. Compressor blades operate at the fluid dynamic level much like an airfoil, with the motion of the blade creating a pressure difference across the compressor stage. If the incident flow magnitude or the angle is mismatched with the blade orientation, a compressor surge or stall (like airplanes stall at high angles of attack) can occur, leading to loss of engine power. The flow speed, angle, and uniformity therefore must be ensured using a combination of the modifications in the engine inlet and compressor inlet guide vanes.

The photograph in Fig. 3.24 shows the Osprey during take-off. The V-22 is a multipurpose aircraft with the Marines using it for troop and material transport to assault areas, the Air Force for long-range special operations in the CV-22 version, and the Navy for search and rescue and logistic transports in the HV-22 version. The Osprey is a much larger aircraft than previous helicopters described and can carry up to thirty-two troops or 10,000 pounds of cargo plus the two pilots. It has a wing span of 46 feet plus rotors of 38 feet in diameter. The tilt-rotor design allows higher speed than conventional rotorcrafts (316 mph), and also longer range (1011 miles).

The Boeing CH-47 Chinook is a classic helicopter, much like the UH-1 Huey, going back to the Vietnam War ear, except Chinook still remains in service as a large-capacity, heavy-lift helicopter. The tandem, counter-rotating blades are torque-balanced without the need for side-force rotors. Various turboshaft engines have been used on the CH-47, with up to 4500-hp output each (Lycoming L-712). As shown in Fig. 3.25, the Chinook is

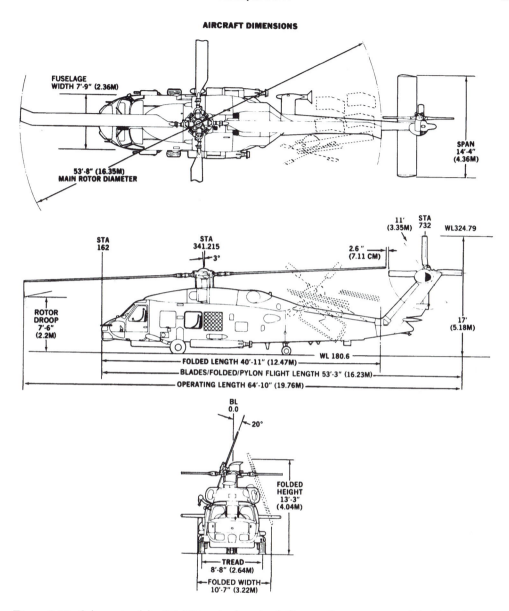

Figure 3.23. Schematic of the SH-60B anti-submarine helicopter. Image courtesy of the U.S. Navy.

essentially a transport vehicle with a large loading ramp that opens up the cargo compartment from the rear.

A counter-rotating twin-rotor configuration can also be found in a Russian helicopter, Kamov Ka-27. On the Ka-27, the two rotors are stacked on top of one another. Again, due to the opposite torques provided by the counter-rotating rotors no side-force tail rotor is needed. Instead, fixed tail stabilizers are installed at a compact geometry, suitable for shipboard use. One of the reasons for the length of single-rotor helicopters is to provide a long moment arm for the tail rotors, so that the excess power is not expended on the tail rotor. The stack design does complicate the rotor control, with two swash plates running on the same axis line. The Kamov Ka-27 and its precursor Ka-25 are naval helicopters, and their

Figure 3.24. U.S. Air Force CV-22 Osprey during take-off. The light refraction from the hot engine exhaust is visible. Photo courtesy of the U.S. Air Force.

Figure 3.25. The Boeing CH-47 Chinook helicopter. Photo courtesy of the U.S. Army.

uses include anti-submarine attacks using conventional and nuclear depth charges. Anti-submarine torpedoes, both standard and wire-guided, are also carried. In addition to the radar, Ka-27 can drop a sonobuoy to monitor underwater activities. A modern Kamov helicopter, the Ka-50 Black Shark, serves as the Russian Air Force's main anti-tank attack helicopter. Although there is a two-seater version of the Ka-50, the baseline design is the classic co-axial counter-rotating double-rotor with a single crew, both aspects of which are unique in an attack helicopter. It is primarily manufactured by the Russian Kamov design bureau; however, in an interesting twist of military technology transfer Israeli Air Industries also produces a modified tandem two-seat version of the Ka-50 designated as the Ka-50-2 Erdogan.

The philosophy of the Ka-50 design emerged from the Russian experience in the Afghanistan conflict. The mission profile called for a low-level flight to the target area and a climb up for target acquisition and missile launch which in principle can be handled by a single crew. The single-crew arrangement allows for the entire aircraft to be smaller, lighter, and therefore more agile and efficient. The absence of the tail rotor also renders higher maneuverability for the Black Shark. The twin-rotor design means that thrust can be generated with smaller-diameter rotors, which delivers an advantage of higher air speed. The maximum air speed of helicopters is limited by the velocity difference between the relative air speed toward the rotor and the rotor speed, as shown in the figure below. Because of the opposite directions of the relative air speed toward the helicopter and the speed of the rotor on the far side in counterclockwise rotations, the velocities actually add up to a higher value. For the rotor, the highest speed is found at the rotor tip, because for solid body rotation at a given rpm the linear velocity is proportional to the radius. Therefore, the relative velocity between the air and the rotor speed can exceed the speed of sound long before the helicopter reaches that sonic barrier. For the rotor blade designed to operate in the subsonic (less than the speed of sound), significant problems occur when the relative velocity approaches sonic speed with loss in lift and big increases in the drag. This is a fundamental limitation of the propeller-driven aircraft, but more severe for helicopters for the above reason. Thus, shorter-radius rotors are advantageous in achieving higher speeds in helicopters.

The Ka-50 carries up to twelve laser-guided Vikhr anti-tank missiles that have an impressive range of 10 km. The target acquisition and missile controls are advanced, with target sharing between helicopters, and target data can also be fed by an advance ground scout. A 30-mm Shipunov 2A42 cannon is mounted almost rigidly with relatively small azimuth or elevation range, but the maneuverability of the aircraft makes up for the lack of aiming control on the cannon. Other armaments include Vympel R-73 missiles, S-8 rockets pods, S-13 rocket pods, and up to four 1100-lb bombs.

Another series of Russian helicopters, made by the Mil Moscow Helicopter Plant, follow Mi- designations. The Mil helicopter plant was founded by a fellow named Mikhail Lentyevich Mil and started as Mil Experimental Design Bureau in 1948. A series of military and civilian helicopter designs emerged from Mil that included attack helicopters Mi-24, Mi-25, and Mi-28. In the Mi-28 helicopters, five-blade rotor design is used with two Isotov turboshaft engines with power output up to 2200 horsepower each. The two engines are mounted on the side close the rotor base, similar to the Apache design. The gunner and pilots sit in tandem in stepped cockpits. The empty weight of the Mi-28 is estimated at 15,000 pounds and thus is heavier than an empty Apache, but the gross weight is similar at 20,060 pounds. Maximum speed is estimated at 230 mph with a mission radius of 149 miles. Armaments on the Mi-28 can vary from SA-14 air-to-air missiles modified for helicopter use in a dual-tube launcher, to a quad launcher for AT-6 (anti-tank) Spiral Mod missiles, a UV-32-57 rocket launcher, an updated 30-mm cannon, and FAB-250 bombs. The predecessor to Mi-28 was the Mi-24, with a size and speed characteristics of Russian designs. Bulk and speed over maneuverability appears to have been the philosophy of Russian military engineering. Two Isotov TV-3-117–class turboshaft engines with 2200 horsepower each lifted the Mi-24 with a maximum takeoff weight of 24,250 pounds. The Mi-24 had a cruising speed of 180 mph, in comparison to, for example, 135 mph for the Bell UH-1. Mi-24 versions from A to G have been manufactured. Although durable and well-armored, Mi-24's size (52 ft length by 21 ft height) along with lack of maneuverability emerged as its shortcomings during the Afghanistan engagements by the Russians. They were large, exposed targets against shoulder-launched missiles and even rocket-propelled grenades fired from short distances. Some Mi-24 helicopters are also known to have crashed during high-G maneuvers, which inevitably seems to occur during battle situations, when the rotors broke off under high stress and tore into the fuselage.

In Europe, aerospace industry is consolidated in a four-nation consortium called the European Aeronautics Defence and Space (EADS), with the subsidiary Eurocopter producing helicopters and Airbus manufacturing military and civilian fixed-wing aircrafts. A major attack helicopter made helicopter is the "Tiger," introduced in 1991 and used by various European military branches. Tiger bears a resemblance to the Russian Mi-28, with tandem, stepped cockpits and two outboard engines. Tiger helicopters are used for multi-role attack and armed reconnaissance purposes by the German, Spanish, and French armies. Various engine and weapons combinations have been installed in different versions (e.g., Tiger ARH for armed reconnaissance with upgraded MTR 390 engines, Strix laser target designator, Hellfire missiles and M299 smart launchers, HAD version for combat support armed with Rafael-Spike missiles and Mistral AAM, HAC version for anti-tank attacks). Like its counterparts from the United States and Russia, Tiger helicopters come with advanced electronics and armaments. The TADS/PNVS (target acquisition/designation system and pilot's night vision sensor) module includes the Osiris vision system mounted at the top of the rotor mast and nose-mounted laser rangefinder and FLIR with a wide-angle view. The basic armaments are a 30-mm AM-30781 cannon, two twenty-two-tube 68-mm rocket launchers, and four Mistral AAMs.

The light weight of the helicopter owes to the advanced materials used in the airframe, such as the Kevlar and carbon laminate frames, panels made with Nomex honeycomb, and the skin again made with Kevlar and carbon composites. The rotor blade material is high-strength fiber composite. Kevlar is a synthetic fibrous compound produced by DuPont. Its light weight and extreme strength make it a highly desirable material for military and aerospace applications. Some of the protective shields in helicopters are made with Kevlar, as are some of the major airframe components in helicopters as noted above.

HIGH-STRENGTH MATERIALS FOR MODERN HELICOPTERS

Kevlar, mentioned above, is produced by synthesizing two chemical compounds in strong acids, which form chemical structures with multiple inter-chain bonds between benzene rings surround by oxygen, hydrogen, and nitrogen atoms. Its strength-to-weight ratio is about five times that of steel. Kevlar has other advantageous properties such as resistance to degradation, to extreme temperatures, and of course to extreme external forces. Composite materials are, as the name suggests, a combination of two or more materials that results in improved material properties. Reinforced concrete with metal skeletons and concrete fills can be considered as an example of composite materials, although for aerospace applications lighter, higher-strength combinations are used. In composite materials, the matrix and reinforcement materials are combined to produce lightweight, high-strength components. In carbon composites (sometimes referred to as carbon fiber reinforced composite materials), for example, carbon fiber filament serves as the reinforcement while plastic material serves as the matrix that adds form for the final shape. The plastic matrix material can vary from epoxy, to polyester, vinyl ester, and others. The carbon composites exhibit high strength, low weight, an ability to tailor the composite layers (of matrix and reinforcements), high stiffness, and resistance to corrosion and fatigue. Composite materials, however, have a tendency to crack under severe loads, and that limits their use in critical structural components yet. The production requires layering of carbon filament sheets, sometimes manually, and then curing the resin material, which is expensive and time consuming, leading to the high cost of the material and limited use.

The fiber or the reinforcement material provide the strength and stiffness but by themselves are brittle in the sense that over-stretching these materials leads to failures, in contrast to metals which undergo strain or elongations before failure. This is the reason the matrix or plastic materials are combined with fibers that are layered in multiple directions. If the fiber material is carbon, then the material is called carbon composites. Another cheaper fiber material that is used more ubiquitously is the glass fibers, which are representative of fiber materials in that they exhibit stiffness and high strength in the longitudinal direction but are subject to breaking when pressed in the normal direction. Composites made with glass fibers are naturally called "fiberglass," used in boats, bathtubs, sports equipment, and many other daily applications. Other fiber materials are Kevlar, graphite, boron, and so forth.

The matrix material functions are holding the fibers in the proper position, transferring the loads between the fibers, and providing strength between the fiber layers. The matrix material is also selected for resistance to heat, chemicals, and moisture depending on the applications. Matrix materials are essentially plastics such as polyester, vinyl ester, epoxies, polymides, phenolics, and others. As with most plastics, matrix materials noted above will be in liquid or liquid-like states at high temperatures, and this allows for easy shaping of the composite components but also sets the limit on allowable temperature range during use.

Once the fiber and matrix material is selected, then they can be fabricated into various helicopter or other components. The fibers typically are supplied in woven fabric forms, much like clothing materials. Some woven fiber fabrics are even pre-impregnated with the matrix resin materials in what are known in the industry as "prepregs." To form the final shape, the prepregs or fabric plus the resins are layered on a pre-form die and typically placed in a curing chamber called an autoclave. The autoclave applies electrical heat to melt the resin material so that they will follow the pattern in the pre-form die, and also high-pressure gas presses the composite layers against the die for faithful reconstruction of the shape.

A BRIEF HISTORY OF HELICOPTER FLIGHT

The level of technology embedded in modern helicopters is in sharp contrast to the modest beginning of the early helicopter developments. The success of the fixed-wing aircraft is marked with distinct achievements, most notably the first controlled flight by the Wright brothers in 1903. There were some fundamental difficulties with successful helicopter flights in roughly the same periods. First, the power required for a vertical flight, as is characteristic of helicopters, is much higher than that for airplanes. The reason is that the vertical lift is provided by the fixed wings in airplanes, which increases as the velocity squared. Thus, if the engine generates sufficient power to overcome the horizontal aerodynamic drag, then eventually the airplane speed will increase to a level necessary to produce high enough lift force. For vertical flight, the engine must produce the lift equal to or greater than the helicopter weight, which invariably is much larger than the aerodynamic drag. If a larger engine is used, of course that simply adds to the overall helicopter weight defeating the effort to overcome the weight problem to begin with. Second, rotating wings on helicopters produce torque, or a tendency to spin the rotorcraft, and methods to counter this torque took some time to mature. Another challenge was neutralizing the different lift generated on the two halves of the rotors. The rotor blade moving into the direction of the flight sees a higher relative velocity than the blade on the other side which is moving in the opposite direction during a circular rotation. This difference in the relative velocity results in different lift making the overall rotor lift unbalanced, and therefore the helicopter is intrinsically unstable. In addition, large rotor blades rotating at high speeds invariably led to vibrations threatening the integrity of light construction of early helicopters.

After miscellaneous attempts mostly by European and American inventors and engineers from 1907 to 1930, rotorcraft flights with human control started becoming successful in the 1930s. An Italian, Corradino d'Ascanio, constructed a coaxial, counter-rotating two-rotor helicopter, overcoming the torque problem. A crude pitch control of the rotors was accomplished by tabs attached to the trailing edge of the rotors that were controlled by cables and pulleys. It was a collective control, with all of the pitches changing by the same amount, and additional small rotors were used for roll and yaw controls. An American design by Maitland Bleeker used a similar mechanism called "stabovators." The d'Ascanio coaxial two-rotor design was also used by French aviation pioneers Louis Breguet (whose name is borne on some of the French Breguet Aviation and later "Avions Marcel Dassault-Breguet Aviation" aircraft) and Rene Dorand, who introduced the use of swash plates so that the pitch could be cyclically controlled for pitch and roll movements. Their design achieved a range of twenty-seven miles and an endurance of sixty-two minutes. Helicopter development accelerated due to the industrial and military prowess of Nazi Germany in the 1940s. Focke-Wulf Company and Weir Company produced a series of capable helicopters during the early 1940s, with the Weir W-5 coaxial helicopter achieving a top speed of 75 mph. Another design by German engineer Antoine Flettner used an intermeshing rotor configuration known as the "synchropter" due to the synchronization of the two rotors to avoid rotor collision. A Russian émigré to United States, Igor Sikorsky, pushed along the helicopter developments in the United States during this period. Sikorsky remains a major helicopter manufacturer, with a number of notable military helicopters: the Sikorsky RH-53 Sea Stallion, CH-53E Super Stallion, UH-60A Black Hawk, and SH-60F Seahawk, along with many others in its continuous history.

Soon production of helicopters was being accomplished in both the military and civilian sectors, with other manufacturers like Bell Helicopters, Kaman Aerospace, Boeing (originally Vertol) Helicopters, Hughes Aerospace, and McDonnell Douglas Helicopters finding their share of the market in the United States. Now, it is estimated that there are close to 50,000 helicopters worldwide, and military versions serve as essential vehicles for military transport, battlefield command and control, reconnaissance, assault, and naval operations in the military sector. Civilian use is no less important with wide uses in air ambulance, search and rescue, agricultural spraying, fire fighting, crime fighting, and corporate transports.

NAVAL HELICOPTER OPERATIONS

Although not as publicized as the over-land uses, helicopters perform important functions during naval operations as well, including anti-submarine warfare (ASW), anti-ship warfare, missile and artillery targeting, amphibious assault and transport, search and rescue, minesweeping, airborne reconnaissance, and early warning and transport of troops/materials. Helicopters have the distinct advantage of the vertical take-off and landing, and thus airborne missions can be launched in helicopter-launch surface ships that are much smaller than full aircraft carriers. Amphibious naval vessels, for example, can be built and operated at much lower cost and give versatile landing capabilities with helicopters providing close-in air support.

Helicopters are well suited for operations like anti-submarine warfare, due to hover and vertical landing capabilities, so that they can deploy submerged, wire-linked sonar and sweep an area at low speeds and can take off and land on small naval vessels. Anti-submarine warfare, however, involves large areas, and they tend to involve a task force of fixed-wing aircraft and naval vessels as well as helicopters. The ASW starts from the detection and positive identification of the opposing submarine. Radars, magnetic detectors, and sonar are the principle methods for detection. Conventional radars can only register signals from surfaced submarines and are of limited use with modern submarines, particularly nuclear-powered ones, having long durations of underwater operations. The magnetic detectors look for anomaly in the earth's magnetic fields and are thus called MAD, for magnetic anomaly detectors. Submarines are relatively large, metal objects that distort the normal magnetic field by small, but measurable amounts (typically 1 part out of 10,000). In addition, the earth's magnetic field itself is not uniform, and detailed mapping of the baseline magnetic field exerted by the earth is one important segment of the vast amounts of oceanographic data amassed by the United States and other navies. MAD modules are functional when placed as close to the ocean surface, and for that reason they are typically dragged by the helicopter at reduced speeds. Also, MAD has a limited range because it measures the columnar magnetic field change from the ocean surface to the bottom. MAD sensors involve nuclear magnetic resonance (NMR), the same method used for medical imaging. NMR is a process in which the energy of electromagnetic waves at radio frequencies is absorbed by the atomic nuclei at the spin resonant frequencies under a preset magnetic field. Any alterations in the magnetic field, in this case due to the presence of a submarine that alters the earth's magnetic field, subdues the resonance effect, which can be detected by the change in the amount of radio wave energy absorbed. This NMR sensor is housed in a fiberglass casing that looks like a bomb with a conical opening at the end and hung from the helicopter at a height as close to the ocean surface as possible. Some stand-off distance is required as the helicopter itself may cause fluctuations in the magnetic field. In some advanced MAD sensors, the helicopter's magnetic influence is shielded or digitally compensated so that MAD probe can be operated without having to leave the helicopter.

Sonar is a powerful sensor in incompressible fluids like the water in the ocean. Although sound propagates in air, the speed of sound is 344 m/s at 21 °C and sound energy tends to get attenuated over some distance. In contrast, the speed of sound in water is approximately 1500 m/s, depending on the temperature and salinity. The attenuation in air is typically around 50 dB/km, while in water it is below 0.1 dB/km which varies somewhat depending the sound frequency. So the range of sound detection at least 500 times greater in water, and even higher if one accounts for some particular effects like deep channel propagation. Like the radars, both passive and active sonar can be used, with the latter generating a pulsed sound wave and "listening" to all the reflected signals including those possible from submarines. For helicopter ASW, sonobuoys can be dropped on the surface, or dunking sonar can be dragged with a wire link back up to the chopper. More powerful ship-based sonar can be linked to helicopter weapon systems for guiding anti-submarine armaments. A photograph shows a U.S. Navy MH-53E Sea Dragon retrieving an AN/AQS-14A side-looking sonar. Sonobuoys are oblong tubes that release the hydrophone assembly to a preset depth. The hydrophone assembly consists of a super-sensitive microphone listening in the audible range of 10 to 24 kHz and beyond and transmitting the acoustic signals through a cable to the VHF antenna that is floating on the surface. Because dunking sonar is retrievable, they tend to be more sophisticated and sensitive with array of hydrophones and also echo (ping) sounders.

A utility helicopter in the naval operations is the H-60 Seahawk series, equivalent to the Army's UH-60 Black Hawk. The naval helicopters are typically given the designation SH-60, with other versions such as HH indicating search and rescue, MH for multimission, and CH for transport. A schematic of the SH-60B is shown below. The ASW SH-60 carries a bigger load, weighing over 20,000 pounds fully loaded. The Navy versions also come with rotor brake and electric power folding of the main rotors, both due to limited space on naval vessels and possible high wind conditions. Some of the anti-submarine and anti-ship weapons and sensors carried by the SH-60 are the Penguin Mk-2 Mod anti-ship missile, the BAe Sea Skua anti-ship missile, the Mk 36 mine, the Mk 53 depth bomb, the Mk 46 anti-submarine torpedo, the Mk50 advanced lightweight torpedo, the AGM-84 Harpoon cruise missile, the ASQ-81 MAD towed module, the Bendix AQS-13F dipping sonar sensor, and the Spartan dwarf DIFAR sonobuoys. ASW capabilities are also installed on the Sikorsky SH-3 Sea King, introduced in 1961 but still in active service with modernized sensors and ASW weapons. The Sea King carries a crew of two pilots plus two ASW operators for the various sonobuoys and Mk 46/44 torpedoes. A B-57 nuclear depth charge can also be deployed from the Sea King helicopter.

REFERENCES

Bradin, James W. *From Hot Air to Hellfire, The History of Army Attack Aviation*. New York: Presidio, 1994.

Gunson, Bill, and Mike Spick. *Modern Fighting Helicopters*. Baltimore, MD: Salamander Books, 1986.

Leishman, J.G. *Principles of Helicopter Aerodynamics* New York: Cambridge University Press, 2000.

CHAPTER
4

STEALTH, INTELLIGENCE, AND SURVEILLANCE TECHNOLOGY

THE IMPORTANCE OF intelligence and the need to protect against intelligence (counterintelligence) have always been well noted in the minds of successful military leaders. Written in sixth century BCE, the "Art of War" by a Chinese scholar of military affairs named Sun Tzu contains several succinct but meaningful quotations such as "All warfare is based on deception," and "If you know both yourself and your enemy, you will come out of one hundred battles with one hundred victories." The history of war and its generals is filled with statements following the same approach to intelligence. "No war can be conducted successfully without early and good intelligence" (Duke of Marlborough). "The necessity of procuring good intelligence is apparent and need not be further argued" (George Washington). Alexander the Great relied on the locals throughout his campaign into the Middle East and Asia to learn of the size of the population, strategic routes, defensible terrains, sources of water and food, and strength of the opposing armies. His approach to making sure that the intelligence data he was getting was accurate was simple and straightforward. For useful and correct information, he rewarded the informant with gold and other riches, of which he had plentiful. For those with false information, he ordered them killed.

With technological advances in stealth and surveillance, the methods with which intelligence is obtained and hidden have changed, but some of the principles of military intelligence remain the same. The intelligence still can be acquired through human or signal intelligence, delivered to the user, validated and interpreted, and finally implemented in the battle plan. In spite of the emphasis on technological intelligence, which is the signal intelligence to be discussed in this chapter, the human factor in intelligence should not be overlooked. No amount of visual or signal information can delve into the knowledge and intricacies of human minds, nor can it exceed the capabilities of human observation and judgments based on signal information. Technology is an instrument, and that instrument needs to be used with good judgment and purpose by humans. Although technology is studied and appreciated in this book, and humans create and benefit from technology, central military functions will always evolve around well-trained, dedicated people aided by technological gadgets.

The Gulf War during 1990 to 1991, or Operation Desert Storm, may be considered as an example of a successful synthesis of technology with overall war strategy. Data based on satellite and aerial images provided target identifications, and the air campaign knocked out much of the opponent's command and control infrastructure, rendering the army more or less blind to the actions of the coalition forces. Operation Desert Storm is considered to be the first modern information war where space-borne surveillance, global communication networks, and system-level synthesis and dissemination of the battlefield data gave the coalition force commanders unprecedented clarity of the situation down to the field command levels. The coordinated initial air strikes are particularly noteworthy because many of the attacks were carried out under the cover of darkness and through the use of F-117 stealth aircraft (Fig. 4.1).

The initial objectives during the air campaign were to (1) establish a total air supremacy for the subsequent air and ground campaigns; (2) disable the Iraqi military leadership capabilities by destroying key command facilities; (3) eliminate the threat of the nuclear, biological, and chemical weapons; and (4) neutralize the Iraqi army offensive capabilities by knocking out a majority of their military hardware. Objective (1) could only be achieved first by knocking out the Iraqi air defense system consisting of some 7000 radar-guided anti-aircraft missiles, 9000 infrared surface-to-air missiles, and up to 7000 anti-aircraft guns. Much of the initial attack on the air defense was carried out by the F-117 stealth aircraft, aided by ship-launched Tomahawk missiles. The F-117 was at that time a relatively new addition to the U.S. Air Force, and its futuristic design is not just for looks but deflects most of the probe radar beams scanning the sky. We will return to the aircraft stealth technology later in this chapter.

The high-tech precision guided bombings were extensively televised around the world, in spite of the fact that a significant percentage of the bombing during the entire campaign was of the conventional kind delivered by B-52 bombers. Along with the fleet of F-117A bombers making surgical strikes, some 200 Tomahawk missiles were fired toward key targets. The accuracy of the Tomahawk missiles in reaching faraway targets with pinpoint accuracy is the result of advanced technology along with much prior human intelligence. In planning the TLAM (Tomahawk Land Attack Missiles) missions, an elite team of

Figure 4.1. F-117 Stealth aircraft. Photo courtesy of the U.S. Air Force.

specialists from the U.S. Central Command, the Navy, Pentagon, and Raytheon (manufacturer of TLAMs) worked to carefully draw a list of high-priority targets based on satellite and other intelligence data. The target coordinates now needed to be converted to exact path commands for the Tomahawk missiles, because they use a combination of inertial guidance, global position system, TERCOM (terrain contour matching), and DSMAC (digital scene matching and correlation) to carry out the mission under all weather, night/day conditions. Tomahawk missiles launched from ships or submarines have an initial flight path over water, then they approach the so-called first pre-planned waypoint (FWP) to enter their flight phase over land. An onboard contour sensor from that point scans the land terrain below, matches it with the stored data to track a path toward the target. As the missile nears the target, the guidance typically switches to DSMAC for refined accuracy. Thus, a successful TLAM mission is a culmination of guidance technology and satellite and other airborne intelligence data on enemy targets and terrain and on the air defense systems.

The next major U.S. military engagements with Iraq beginning in 2003 drew massive attention and analyses, not so much on the military operation to advance to Baghdad but more on the pre-war intelligence that served as the justification for the invasion. The political and diplomatic maneuvers toward war with Iraq were based on intelligence or the presentation of intelligence on Iraqi possession of weapons of mass destruction and on harboring the elements of the terrorist group, Al-Qaeda. The presentation of intelligence on these issues and how it convinced the U.S. political leadership and a sufficiently large fraction of the public into waging a major war is a long, twisted story, perhaps outside the scope of this book. It suffices to say that these claims were more or less proven to be inaccurate at best; some speculate they were even compromised by a preconceived notion or agenda by an isolated group of war proponents. It serves as a historical lesson that the political leadership must exercise judgment and establish an absolute mandate based on sound intelligence and interpretations thereof before committing an entire nation and portions of the world to a major financial, military, and human endeavor. Bad intelligence is self-destructive and obviously is worse than no intelligence at all.

Even the Persian Gulf War of 1991 to dislodge Saddam Hussein from Kuwait had an element of intelligence failure in that advance warnings of Iraq's intent were improperly interpreted or ignored. A sequence of preventive diplomatic maneuvers would have gone a long way in avoiding a later, financially costly campaign to militarily resolve the situation. An interesting aspect of U.S. intelligence in this series of encounters with the Iraqi army is that it has had the best resources in the world to gather military data and was well aware of the fact that the Iraqi army at the time was the fourth largest in the world with 5000 tanks and 7000 armored infantry vehicles along with more battlefield helicopters than the Royal Air Force. During the Cold War and even up to 1993, much of the U.S. intelligence capability was focused on Russia and the Eastern Bloc nations, amassing data on bombing targets and military assets of encyclopedic proportions. Perhaps, this time period can be considered as a transition in which U.S. intelligence started to deal with more diverse threats around the world including regimes with unpredictable intentions. It also points to the fact that mere accumulation of intelligence data leaves open the chance for misinterpretations, and the sheer volume of unprocessed data can overwhelm the user without proper filtering and synthesis of information. Iraq and its leadership certainly had a combined psyche that was not entirely familiar to the United States and other western intelligence communities.

Technology has given unprecedented advantages to armies that possess it in highly mechanized warfare including the potential use of nuclear weaponry. A large amount of the technological resources have been invested to develop capabilities in conventional and nuclear weapons and defenses. The history, however, is laden with unconventional guerilla and insurgent warfare, because conflicts between unequal powers tend to persist in clandestine, isolated, and sometimes fanatical forms. Desperate situations tend to bring out desperate actions. The ubiquity of unconventional warfare is simply due to the relative ease and low capital needed to wage it. Known instances of insurgent warfare in ancient times are plentiful, including the Jewish "sicarrii's" who resorted to stabbing Roman legionaries and their families in the narrow back streets of Jerusalem and elsewhere. Lenin and the Bolsheviks started their uprising as a loose group of partisan soldiers who eventually revolutionized the Russian and the world political landscape. Unconventional warfare has persisted into recent history, from the North Vietnamese Viet Cong to the Irish Republican Army, the Palestine Liberation Organization, and now Al-Qaeda. This is a type of warfare where technology has less impact unless a completely new genre of intelligence technology can be developed and applied to penetrate these highly decentralized and demechanized organizations.

SPY SATELLITES

The advantage of having an aerial vehicle or a satellite in orbit to monitor what is on the ground has long been realized by military planners. Since 1955, the United States has allocated significant resources to develop and use reconnaissance satellites for the purpose of determining the enemy war-making capabilities and intents. During the early years of spy satellites, a rather cumbersome method was used that involved loading films on to the satellites and recovering them once the missions were completed over the target territory. Nowadays, digital cameras are commonplace and spy satellites use high-resolution CCD (charge-coupled device) digital imaging systems to acquire and transmit images in encoded formats. Through advances in imaging devices, optics, and image analyses, it is believed that modern high-resolution imaging satellites achieve a spatial resolution of 10 cm (approximately 4 in) or better, although the satellites have an inherent temporal resolution problem. That is, satellites are limited by how often they can fly over the target areas, which can be several hours or several days depending on their altitudes and trajectories. Details of design and resolution capabilities of modern reconnaissance satellites are classified, and also the image analysis methods are probably the most sophisticated ones available. It can however be assumed that reconnaissance satellites consist of the super-high-resolution imaging devices with advanced optics, solar cells to power the electronics, secure encoded downlink communication modules, and orbit and attitude control boosters, along with stealth devices. A less-than-informative photograph of a spy satellite under construction is shown in Fig. 4.2.

Figure 4.2. A U.S. reconnaissance satellite, Lacrosse, under construction. Photo from the public domain of the U.S. National Reconnaissance Office.

It may be compared with an early spy satellite, the Corona KH-4B, a schematic of which is shown in Fig. 4.3. The early Corona satellites had a film canister installed in a recovery vehicle, which jettisoned after the mission and returned to earth's surface for recovery. A photograph taken by the Corona KH-4B in Fig. 4.4 shows the coarse but discernable features in the imaged area.

The United States and most military powers in the world operate a fleet of reconnaissance satellites. The United States is known to be the dominant user of these devices and has several separate agencies to gather and analyze data through these means.

The United States Navy, for example, has the so-called ELINT (electronic intelligence) program that used the GRAB (galactic radiation and background) satellite in 1960, followed by "Poppy" satellites and later Naval Ocean Surveillance System (NOSS). However, the most notable of the U.S. space-borne reconnaissance programs is the "Keyhole (KH)" series of satellites. The Corona satellite shown in the figure was one of the progenitors of this series. The early KH satellites were codenamed "Coronas" and lasted from 1959 to 1972. Early versions, KH-1 through -3, were the first imaging satellites operated by the United States and had film canisters for ground recovery. The optics had a focal length of 0.6 m and spatial resolution of 7.5 m. Later versions of the Corona had a resolution down to 1.8 m but still used film recovery. A parallel program called SAMOS (Satellite and Missile Observation System) was abandoned after technical difficulties in radio relay of the images produced low-quality reconnaissance data. However, SAMOS cameras were later adopted by NASA's Lunar Orbiter program. The SAMOS camera was equipped with two lenses, one for large-area scans and another for high-resolution imaging; 70-mm-width Kodak films with grain resolutions of 450 mm were used. The arrangement was to develop the exposed films on board using a Kodak process called "Bimat." A layer soaked with developer solutions was pressed against the film for 3.5 minutes, and later the layer was removed, similar to what happens in Polaroid cameras. To transmit the film data to earth, a crude (by today's standards) projection method was used where a light beam 5 μ in diameter was scanned across the film surface, and the resulting transmitted light through the developed film negative was detected using a photomultiplier tube. The sequential signals from the photomultiplier tube then furnished the image data in electrical form to be transmitted to the earth via radio waves. Although innovative in some ways, the number of analog steps taken on board, not to mention the relatively large bank of photomultiplier tubes to convert the image to electrical format, resulted in image qualities not suitable for reconnaissance purposes as noted above. Some computer-based techniques were developed to remove the noise in the images but were successful only to a limited level.

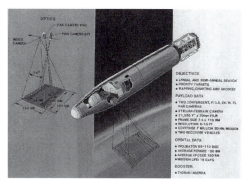

Figure 4.3. An early U.S. spy satellite, Corona KH-4b. Photo from the public domain of the U.S. National Reconnaissance Office.

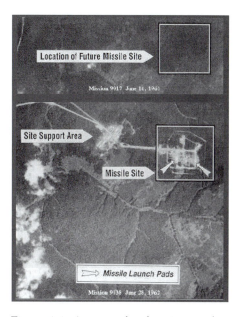

Figure 4.4. An example of an image taken from the Corona KH-4, with a spatial resolution of 7.5 m. The above image is low-resolution area scan of the target area. Photo courtesy of the U.S. National Reconnaissance Office.

The last of the film-loaded satellites, KH-9 (codenamed "Big Bird"), had a resolution of 0.3 m and used five separate reentry vehicles. However, if most of the U.S. predecessor spy satellites were incremental improvements over the designs similar to Corona KH-4B, the Big Bird made a quantum leap in terms of resolution and image quality. The Air Force funded a program to develop a satellite equipped with a 2-m reflective mirror to give a resolution of 0.3 m from an altitude of 500 km and above. The optical system operates as a Newtonian reflective telescope, where the 2-m reflective mirror collects the light, and the focused light is imaged by the camera. The total weight of this system was 18,000 lbs (about five times the weight of the preceding designs), with a 50 ft length and 10 ft diameter. This satellite also had a monopropellant (hydrazine) thruster for orbit maneuvers including de-orbiting at the end of the mission. The Big Bird satellites were taken into orbit using Titan III D boosters. Again, because KH-9s were expendable, a series of these satellites needed to be launched to maintain the surveillance capabilities, mostly on Soviet ICBM build-up and deployments during this time period. Table 4.1 is a partial list of the data on film-loading KH satellites used up to 1972.

After 1976, digital imaging devices became available for use in these satellites. The KH-11 was the first U.S. reconnaissance satellite using digital imaging and also was equipped with mirror optics of 2.3 m in diameter. It is believed that the KH-11 is similar in design and dimensions with that of the Hubble Space Telescope that was used for astronomical investigations. The Hubble Space Telescope simply turned its optics toward the sky rather than the ground. The initial use of the KH-11 was in 1976, whereas the Hubble telescope was launched in 1990, so there is a gap of fourteen years before the military technology trickled into the civilian community. The KH-11's operational altitude was 212 miles or 341 kilometers, in comparison to 101 miles (162 km) for the preceding Big Birds (KH-9). In addition to the improved optics provided by TRW Corporation, the use of digital imaging device (charge-coupled device cameras, see below) was at that time revolutionary. If film loading and development were cumbersome for tourists or daily use, these factors made reconnaissance satellites useless after all the films were used up, in addition to making the entire operation extremely expensive in terms of having to constantly launch new satellites and run recovery missions for the film canisters. Digital imaging allowed the spy satellites to remain operational until other components such as orbit control booster propellants were expended, extending the lifetime of these satellites to several years as opposed to several months for prior satellites. In addition, recovery of the data was no longer a time-consuming affair because the digitized image data could be downloaded directly to the ground or via an intermediate satellite. As described below, digitized images can be processed and analyzed using computers and this allows the data mining to be highly automated and efficient. However, due to the limitations in the CCD pixel density the spatial resolution of KH-11 images was only 6 feet! Nowadays, pixel density of 5 to 10 million pixels is commonplace; however, at this time fabrication methods were not developed to provide pixel resolutions anywhere close to conventional films. For this reason, KH-11's were primarily used for area coverage, and KH-9's were still needed in instances where high-resolution images were required.

The next step up to KH-12 "Ikon" finally brought the digital imaging resolution down to 6 inches. This was achieved during the 1980s, so it can be extrapolated that the current resolving power of U.S. reconnaissance satellites is possibly higher. Ikon operated by transmitting the images to the earth in real time, and a fleet of four or more satellites around the earth provided nearly continuous surveillance of major strategic areas on earth. By this time, the space shuttle was also available to service the satellites, making their service life even longer. In spite of the important functions performed by these spy satellites, the development of these devices to the current level of technology was not always devoid of setbacks. As noted above, the first set of satellites equipped with digital image devices produced images with lower spatial resolution than film counterparts, and also cost overruns and occasional launch problems brought critics to the forefront of continuing arguments between military and civilian spenders. For example, during a launch of the KH-11 via the Titan 34 D rocket one of the liquid-propellant engines shut down, resulting in insufficient boost to bring the satellite into orbit. The cost of this mishap: $150 million.

Table 4.1. KH Corona Satellite Data Up to KH-6 (adopted from "Eye in the Sky").

	KH-1 CORONA	KH-2 CORONA	KH-3 CORONA	KH-4 CORONA	KH-4A CORONA	KH-4B CORONA	KH-5 ARGON	KH-6 LANYARD
Period of Operation	1959–1960	1960–1961	1961–1962	1962–1963	1963–1969	1967–1972	1962–1964	1963
Lifetime	1 day	2–3 days	1–4 days	6–7 days	4–15 days	18 days	N/A	N/A
Perigee [nm]	103.5	136.0	117.0	114.0	N/A	N/A	N/A	N/A
Apogee [nm]	441.0	380.0	136.0	224.0	N/A	N/A	N/A	N/A
Number of Missions	10	10	6	26	52	17	12	3
Camera Model	C	C'	C"	MURAL	J-1	J-3	N/A	N/A
Camera Type	Mono/ panoramic	Mono/ panoramic	Mono/ panoramic	Stereo/ panoramic	Stereo/ panoramic	Stereo/ panoramic	Frame	Panoramic
Scan Angle	70	70	70	70	70	70	N/A	22
Lens	Tessar f/5	Tessar f/5	Petzval f/3.5	Petzval f/3.5	Petzval f/3.5	Petzval f/3.5	N/A	N/A
Focal Length [in]	24	24	24	24	24	24	3	66
Optical Resolution (lines/mm)	340	340	N/A	480	480	480	N/A	340
Spatial Resolution [ft]	40	25	12	10	9	6	460	4–6
Film Type	1213	1221	4404	4404	3404	3404	N/A	3404
Film Width [in]	2.10	2.10	2.25	2.25	2.25	2.25	5	5

Also, the Challenger disaster limited the U.S. satellite launch capabilities, and for surveillance of strategic weapons a continuous coverage of the key sites is considered essential to maintain an accurate count and tracking of ICBMs.

The advancement in the KH-series resulted in the KH-13, for which little information is yet available. It is conjectured that KH-13 has multi-spectral capabilities (that is, sensitivity in visible and other wavelength bands such as infrared or possibly radar) along with embedded stealth technology to avoid detection. The optical mirror diameter could be as large as 4 m to give a spatial resolution down to 4 cm to discern minute objects on the ground. In addition to the most updated imaging technology, KH-13 is believed to have stealth capability to cloak its observational maneuvers.

Many of the other military powers in the world maintain programs in airborne and space-based surveillance. The former Soviet Union also actively monitored the United States and NATO nuclear and conventional armament capabilities, using satellites such as Zenit, Cosmos, Almaz, and Yantar. Similar to the United States, Soviet use of satellites for military purposes began in the 1950s. In fact, an officer in the military rocket research institute named Mikhail Tikhonravov had the vision of using the rocket technology to send artificial satellites up in earth orbits for ground observations. However, he was demoted when he submitted an unsolicited proposal for further development of this idea to the high commands. Only with the support of influential high-ranking officials was this work allowed to proceed, which resulted in authorization for a photo-reconnaissance satellite in 1957 for the Soviet Union. A prototype, OD-1, was conceived that was similar in design to the U.S. counterpart, Corona, with a self-contained camera for later capsule recovery of the film. During this time, the priority for reconnaissance satellites was not very high in the Soviet military, with the work on lunar and other space probes receiving more attention in part due to their propaganda values. With the ICBM arsenals rapidly growing in the United States and the Soviet Union, both countries were pressed to determine the ICBM production and deployment counts of one another. After much work to develop new technologies, the Zenit-2 was completed by the early 1960s. Zenit-2, unlike the prototype OD-1, turned out to be a rather large satellite of 4740 kg, with a length of 5 meters and a diameter of 2.43 meters. This higher weight required larger boosters for Zenit satellites, with R-7/8A92 and R-7/11A57 boosters being used for their launches in the 1960s. For the early Corona satellites, smaller Thor-Agena A or Thor–Agena D boosters were sufficient. The Soviet engineers opted for designing pressurized chambers for the camera equipment, as opposed to developing vacuum seal technologies, which contributed to increases in the overall weight. Zenit-2 was equipped with four cameras: three 1000-mm focal length SA-20 cameras and one 200-mm SA-10 camera, where the latter was used for wide-view, low-resolution imaging for location reference purposes. The images from the high-resolution cameras taken simultaneously then could be precisely referenced. The total development and testing of the Zenit-2 took nearly two years, from November 1961 to October 1963, and paved the way for later Zenit and other Soviet reconnaissance satellites such as Cosmos.

Early versions of Cosmos, a series of Soviet reconnaissance satellites, were launched in the 1960s equipped with cameras and conventional films to be recovered on the ground after several days of satellite operation in orbit. The Soviets did not have easy access to the ocean or the technology for mid-air recovery. Also, the frigid and low-visibility conditions prevailing in much of the Soviet territory precluded reliable recovery. The Soviet satellite missions during this period were therefore limited to warm-weather seasons. By the mid-1960s, Soviets regularly launched a cluster of high- and low-resolution satellites to altitudes of about 128 miles (205 km) that functioned for eight days or more. It was during this time that the United States responded to the Soviet satellite reconnaissance activities by monitoring the trajectories of these satellites and alerting the ground bases housing sensitive military equipment to perform anti- or counter-reconnaissance measures and by concealing or misleading the armament deployment during the satellite passes. One of the drawbacks of the Cosmos satellites was their relatively short operational lifetime in comparison to their U.S. counterparts. One estimate has it that the Soviets needed to launch ten times as many satellites to have a capability equivalent to the contemporary U.S. spy satellites of the period. An effort made to overcome this drawback was a series of manned space missions, better publicized as the "Soyuz" missions referring to the spacecraft that transported the cosmonauts to the "Salyut" space stations.

Almaz was a manned space station used mostly for military purposes under the guise of the civilian "Salyut" orbital space stations. Three Almaz orbiting stations were launched from 1971 to 1978, and due to the excessive cost of launching and maintaining them the former Soviet Union also reverted to using reconnaissance satellites after 1978. Soyuz is well known in the western world due to its prolonged use in conjunction with the Salyut stations. The Soyuz spacecraft consisted of the service module containing the rocket engines and fuel tanks and the two large solar panels for electrical power. The command module was bell-shaped and was used to bring the cosmonauts back to the earth. So the design is quite similar to the Apollo command and service modules during the same era. The major difference between the Soviet and the American space program, of course, was that Soviets maintained long-term missions in the space station while the Americans were focused on sending men to the moon successfully. The Soyuz spacecraft itself has been used for reconnaissance purposes, with the films moved to the command module prior to the reentry and brought back to earth. By mid-1980s, the Soviet Soyuz was using radio transmission to send image data.

Yantar is a series of modern Russian reconnaissance satellites with multi-wavelength capabilities, much like the current U.S. counterparts. The data link was provided by Potok relay satellites. One major function of these satellites was monitoring of the western ICBM deployment status for early warning. As the Soviet economy faltered and those of the western alliance thrived with key technologies rapidly being developed, the optical and imaging device technology usually lagged behind the Soviet launch capabilities. However, most of these technical bugs were removed, and by the mid-1980s the Soviet Union also operated a fleet of modern reconnaissance satellites. Yantar satellites also used the Soyuz launch rockets and typically operated in the 180 to 280 km range with a mission lifetime up to 259 days.

China's proximity to the Soviet Union and a constant global standoff with the United States highly necessitated independent reconnaissance and space programs. Unfortunately for the United States, and fortunately for China, a prominent aerospace engineer named Dr. Chien Hsueh-Sen who worked with Dr. Theodore von Karman at the Caltech Jet Propulsion Laboratory, became a victim of McCarthyism during the 1950s. He returned to China in 1955, led the Chinese space program that initially used the Soviet rocket launchers, and made modifications and improvements to suit the Chinese needs to counter the U.S. ICBM and other threats (and probably enjoyed every minute of it). By the early 1970s, the Chinese started using their ICBM launchers to place rather large reconnaissance satellites into orbit. The "China 3" satellite that went into orbit in 1975 is believed to carry a television camera and weighed 7718 pounds. A series of "China" satellites followed. The modern Fanhui Shi Weising (FSW) series of satellites starting in the 1990s are estimated to have modern reconnaissance capabilities, and given the economic and technological growth of this nation the Chinese monitoring capabilities are expect to keep pace with those of their western counterparts.

NATO nations all have or had maintained satellites programs for military purposes, including the French Helios series, German SAR-Lupe satellites, and British Zircon missions (cancelled in 1987). Other high-resolution satellites around the world include India's Technology Experiment Satellite, Iran's Sinah-1, Israel's Ofeq, Japan's Information Gathering Satellite, and South Korea's "Arirang" series.

The digital cameras used in most imaging devices, including the ones on reconnaissance satellites, used charge-couple devices. CCDs were first developed as memory-storage devices by American scientists Willard Boyle and George E. Smith at AT&T Bell Laboratory in 1969. CCDs are essentially devices that can hold the electrical charge at a given location and transfer it in a sequence as a voltage output. For example, if a linear array of CCDs had an electrical charge sequence of 1, 0, 0, 1, 1, 0, 1 . . . , then that sequence can be downloaded and read as a voltage signal. Engineers quickly realized that CCDs could be coupled to silicon-based light sensors (photodiodes) to make imaging devices. The light sensors induce an electrical charge at a location on the CCD that can later be read out in sequence to form the distribution of light on the CCD chip, or essentially re-create the image in an electrical or digital format. This approach of digitizing the image and bypassing the film exposure and development has now completely reshaped imaging technology, ranging from fax machines to digital cameras, video cameras, and scanners. For reconnaissance purposes, this of course meant that the film-loading satellites were now obsolete, and highly cost-effective imaging satellites could be maintained in orbit and their data downloaded through a communications link.

Digital image properties can be characterized by the pixel resolution, the intensity distribution, and the framing rate. Pixel resolution means the number of pixels on the imaging chip. 1024×1024 pixels would give a total of close to 1 million pixels, or 1 "megapixels." High pixel densities are common in civilian digital cameras, of which there are quite a few nowadays into 10 megapixels and higher. The final spatial resolution of the imaging system depends on both the optics and the pixel density. The intensity is the brightness of the light signal registered on the imaging chip, and this in turn is digitized using an intensity scale from 1 to $2^8 = 256$, $2^{10} = 1024$, etc, where the superscript "8" or "10" is the number of bits used in the intensity scale. Thus, a 10-bit digitization means that the imaging device can discern up to $2^{10} = 1024$ levels of "gray" or brightness. The higher the bit number, the finer differences in the brightness can be discerned by the camera. Finally, the framing rate is the speed at which images can be acquired. It takes a finite amount of time to read out the pixel data in CCD arrays and reset the pixel voltages, and therefore the framing rate is inversely proportional to the pixel density. However, 1000 frames per second speeds are easily achieved in modern digital cameras with several millions of pixels or more, and for highly custom-designed surveillance cameras none of the above camera characteristics presents a technical hurdle in achieving the necessary performance. The same devices can be made operational outside the visible wavelength range. Although visible wavelengths are useful because most optical and imaging devices have been developed to operate in this range, one problem is that without sunlight not much is visible in this limited wavelength range. However, objects still emit "light" or radiation in the infrared in the absence of external illuminations. Infrared imaging devices can therefore be useful under low-light conditions, provided that the target objects are at an appreciable temperature above the surroundings so that their infrared signatures contrast against the surroundings. Another use of the infrared imaging is for night vision, as discussed below.

Once the digital images are acquired and stored in essentially number formats, they can be processed and analyzed by computers for image enhancements and shape recognition. If the light conditions resulted in weak, the image brightness can be artificially increased by adding to or the multiplying the pixel intensity values. Another result of low light conditions is low-contrast (small difference between light and dark) images, which again can be corrected by stretching the intensity distributions in the image. Some of these basic functions can be performed on PCs using relative simple programming tools. Of course, the image analysis computers at the national scales use the most sophisticated programs and analysis methods available. Complex patterns, target geometrical shapes, or specific type of motions can be prescribed into the analysis programs to seek these patterns or shapes among millions of images. Some of the noise or resolution limits can even be overcome by applying image enhancement techniques, which essentially are mathematical approaches to fill in the missing details based on the surrounding pixel data. For military and scientific purposes, image processing and analysis is a highly developed field.

As noted above, some of the spy satellites employ multi-wavelength detectors to acquire images in the visible, infrared, or other wavelength ranges. Thus, the use of the satellites is certainly not limited to the visible wavelengths. In fact, many scientific and observational satellites use a large fraction in the electromagnetic spectrum to acquire the desired data. For example, LANDSAT satellites widely used for monitoring earth resources and land conditions employ seven detection bands: Band 1 (blue-green, 0.45–0.52 μm); Band 2 (green, 0.52–0.60 μm); Band 3 (red, 0.63–0.69 μm); Band 4 (near infrared, 0.76–0.90 μm); Band 5 (mid-infrared, 1.55–1.75 μm); Band 6 (thermal infrared, 10.40–12.50 μm); and Band 7 (mid-infrared, 2.08–2.35 μm). The reason for using multiple bands or other electromagnetic wave bands is simply that different information is contained in the respective wavelength bands; also the propagation characteristics through the atmosphere are also different. Since LANDSAT is used for land use analysis, different colors reflected from different surfaces (ground, tree, urban areas, etc.) register different signals in each band. Infrared signatures carry information concerning the surface temperature, moisture content, or other parameters that can be extracted from the infrared bands. Depending on the target parameters, detectors operating in the various parts of the electromagnetic wave spectrum can be installed on satellites. This branch of the intelligence is referred to the "electronic intelligence" for the U.S. military and dates back to World War II. ELINT operations can be ground-based, airborne, or performed via satellites. Other components of the intelligence follow a similar acronym pattern: HUMINT for human intelligence, COMINT for communication intelligence, SIGINT for signals intelligence, and IMINT for image intelligence. Using radar signal detectors, for example, ELINT operations map out the enemy surface-to-air missile guidance radars, command and control centers, or other major hardware exhibiting outgoing radar signals. In addition to the location mapping, ELINT systems characterize the radar signals for jamming purposes.

The U.S. Navy's "White Cloud" is a satellite-based ELINT system that tracks the location and movements of a very large number of military naval vessels. White Cloud operates by recognizing the electromagnetic signals (communications, navigation, radars, weapons control, radars, etc.) emitted by foreign naval vessels and triangulating their position from a fleet of satellites designed to pick up these signals. It is used to chart foreign naval vessel deployment and movements and also to prioritize and program for possible attack on these targets. To improve accuracy, a group of four satellites is used in synchronization. This satellite formation maintains a relative distance of 30 to 240 km, and due to high altitudes (approximately 1100 km) and an inclination of over 60 degrees a satellite group can monitor a zone with a radius of over 3000 km. The White Cloud program deploys sufficient satellites so that the region between the 40 to 60 degrees latitude can be monitored over thirty times a day. The ELINT data feed is used in conjunction with imaging satellite and other data to map out potential targets well beyond the horizon of operating naval vessels using long-range armaments such as ship-to-ship or cruise missiles. Also, due to their high altitude the ELINT satellites have a long operational lifetime—typically six to eight years. Titan IV boosters (shown in Fig. 4.5) are the main launch system used to place these satellites in high orbits.

Figure 4.5. Launch of a Titan IV-B rocket booster, used to send military satellites into orbits. Photo courtesy of the U.S. Air Force.

NUCLEAR EARLY WARNING SYSTEM

In addition to the global surveillance and intelligence, the United States and Russia also maintain a network of ground-based and satellite-based observational platforms to detect possible launch or launch maneuvers for strategic nuclear weapons. More information on this topic is given in Chapter 5 (Space Warfare). Due to the high speeds attained by ICBMs and SLBMs, the amount of time available to respond to a nuclear attack is in terms of minutes (typically twenty-five minutes for ICBMs and fifteen minutes for SLBMs). This makes it imperative that any potential missile launch events are immediately detected, identified, and communicated to the top levels. As nuclear weaponry is in constant danger of being proliferated, the requirements become more severe and expansive to monitor the world for potential use of nuclear weapons, particularly through avenues other than the traditional delivery methods discussed above. The U.S. Strategic Command (STRATCOM) operates a global monitoring system for nuclear early warning. A system of radars and satellites along with satellite image data for deployment maneuvers are networked to accomplish this mission.

The early warning system can trace origin to the 1950s when the United States sought to build up its air defense against the growth of the Soviet Union's bomber capabilities. A network of radars called the Distant Early Warning (DEW) was constructed in Canada. Again, even at this early stage the radar sites were linked to a command center which in turn communicated with surface-to-air missile sites and interceptor bases. The DEW was designed for early warning against bomber attacks and therefore was made obsolete by the advent of the ICBMs. Because the Siberian region of the Soviet Union, for example, was very close to the United States, the threat of ICBM attack was real and potentially immediate. Work began on the Ballistic Missile Early Warning System, with radar stations in Thule (Greenland), Clear (Alaska), and Fylingdales Moor (England). However, the ground-based radars could not see beyond the horizon as the radars rely on electromagnetic beams traveling to the target and the reflected signal returning to the radar site. The distance from the radar sites and potential launch locations in the USSR meant that only about fifteen minutes of warning time would be given assuming that the missiles were caught by the radar sweeps and correctly identified, which was not a certainty at that time. Thus, the necessity for space-borne early warning satellites was again brought up.

The Midas (Missile Defense Alarm System) satellites were developed to overcome the limitations of the ground-based radars. Again, a system of satellites, up to eight, was called for to provide large-area, near-continuous coverage. Onboard rocket engines on these satellites maintained the orbital positions. With this group of satellites in place, the launches in most parts of the Soviet Union could be detected based on the thermal emission with a probability of 80 percent or higher. Without the infrared imaging camera, not available during the early phase of the Midas, the "Aegina" satellites used in the Midas relied on the strong thermal emission of the ICBM boosters that became prominent soon after launch. The sensors and the communication link, along with the satellite orbital control rockets, resulted in a 3246-lb module. Midas evolved into later programs for nuclear early warning such as BMEWS (ballistic missile defense early warning system) and IMEWS (integrated missile early warning system). Currently, the defense support program (DSP) is operated by the United States Air Force to provide reconnaissance data for missile early warning including strategic nuclear and conventional missile activities. For example, DSP capabilities were used during Desert Storm operations to detect launches of Iraqi Scud missiles. Modern DSP satellites are placed in high-altitude geosynchronous orbits and are equipped with infrared sensors coupled with telescope optics. Fig. 4.6 shows an artist's depiction of a modern DSP satellite used for missile early warning. The modern DSP satellites operate at orbit altitudes of close to 35,000 km and weigh in excess of 5000 lbs (2380 kg) at a cost of $400 million per satellite. The diameter of the satellite with all of the components extended is 6.7 m.

The integrated strategic early warning system consists of the (1) DSP (defense support program) satellites, as noted above; (2) BMEWS (ballistic missile early warning system) radars; (3) Pave Paws for early warning of sea-launched ballistic missiles; (4) PARCS (perimeter acquisition radar attach characterization system) radar; (5) Cobra Dane phased array radar; and (6) conventional radars. Details of some of the above radars can be found in a later discussion on that subject in this chapter.

Figure 4.6. U-2 "Dragon Lady." Photo courtesy of the U.S. Air Force.

SATELLITES AND ORBITAL MECHANICS

In the previous discussions of military satellites, orbital aspects were inevitably included. The operation of placing satellites in earth orbits and beyond requires appropriate rocket boosters and orbit considerations. The heavier the payload and the higher the target altitude, the more powerful the rocket boosters would be required to be. However, the term "powerful" in rocketry has several aspects. It is not enough to simply burn more propellants to generate sufficient thrust. The maximum velocity attainable by a rocket, and therefore the maximum altitude, depends on the ratio of the initial and final mass and also on the rocket exhaust velocity. The initial mass includes the payload, propellants, and structural mass of the rocket, and the final mass usually is the payload mass itself. The rocket exhaust velocity itself depends on many parameters, such as the molecular weight of the propellant, rocket combustion chamber pressure and temperature, and the nozzle design. For example, the lower the molecular weight of the propellant, the larger the exhaust velocity that can be generated. This is the reason for the choice of liquid hydrogen for space shuttle main engines. A large exhaust velocity accomplishes two things: One is that it generates a large amount of momentum out the nozzle that translates into large thrust force, and two, it gets rid of the propellant mass quickly so that the rocket becomes lighter and easier to accelerate. To improve on the mass ratio aspect, staging is often used, which simply involves getting rid of unneeded mass. Jettisoning of the lower stages is staging, as are the liquid propellant tanks and solid rocket boosters being separated from the space shuttle after their functions are completed during the boost phase.

Consideration of the required kinetic energy to overcome the potential energy of the earth or other gravitation field provides escape velocity. For earth surface launch, a velocity of 11,179 m/s (25,012 mph) would be needed to provide sufficient kinetic energy to escape the pull of the earth's gravity. In the moon's weaker gravitational field (a little less than one-sixth of the earth's), the escape velocity is 2366.22 m/s or 5325.75 mph. However, this is not to mean that a spacecraft must acquire this velocity for outer space travel. Escape velocity is simply an initial velocity with sufficient kinetic energy to overcome the gravitation field. A spacecraft in principle can go anywhere provided that it can generate more thrust force than the gravitational force, and of course the latter decreases rather rapidly with increasing distance from the earth. For earth launch in the eastern direction, the earth rotation adds 914 mph to the rocket speed.

Depending on the north-south direction of the rocket motion, the final orbit around the earth will be different. The angle of the orbit with respect to the equator is called the inclination angle. Since earth's rotation plane intersects the equator, satellites with a zero inclination orbit essentially see the same latitude regions close to the equator during their passes over the earth. If the inclination angle is 90 degrees, it is called a polar orbit, and a satellite in a polar orbit will see the entire earth as the earth rotates beneath it. To cover the entire Soviet Union during the Cold War, a majority of the U.S. reconnaissance satellites were sent into orbits with 80 to 100° inclination angles in contrast to the 65 to 81° for the Soviet satellites. Other useful orbits are sun-synchronous orbits (SSO) and geosynchronous orbit (GEO). GEO involves sending satellites with a zero inclination angle into relatively high altitudes where the speed of the satellites coincides with that of the earth rotation so that the satellites appear to be fixed over the same location. To achieve GEO, the spacecraft is sent to an elliptical orbit with an apogee of 35,785 km (22,236 miles) and then orbit adjustments are made to circularize the orbit. SSO involves placing the satellites in an orbit again with the same rotational speed as that of the earth except the inclination angle is not zero. This will result in the satellite path that sweeps different points on earth at exactly the same local time regardless of the location. The utility of SSO is for observational methods that depend on solar illumination. If the satellite passes over the location at the same local time, then the sun's angle will be the same at all locations.

The orbital speed is directly related to the altitude. This can be visualized as the momentum that is required to maintain an object circling around with a string holding it in. The object will keep that circular motion as long as it is rotating fast enough to keep the string taut. For shorter string, the speed needs to be faster and vice versa. To get into a little mechanics, an object rotating at speed of v at a radius of r is subject to a centripetal acceleration of v^2/r. Centripetal acceleration is the component of velocity that keeps the object in a circular motion, and in earth's gravitational field the centripetal acceleration is given by the gravitational acceleration $g = GM/r^2$. Here, G is gravitational constant of 6.670×10^{-11} m^3/s^2kg and M is the mass of the earth (5.974×10^{24} kg). Equating v^2/r with GM/r^2 and then solving for v, we get v equal to the square root of GM/r. Noting that r represents the distance from the center of earth so that at altitude of 5000 miles gives r = 5000 miles + (earth radius) = 8960 miles. We can run some numbers from this formula. At an altitude of 5000 miles, the orbital speed is approximately GM/8960, or 11,765 mph whereas at a 22,236-mile altitude the speed is 6880 mph with a period of 24 hours, therefore resulting in a geosynchronous orbit. The period is obtained by using the radius of 22,236 + (earth radius) = 26,196 miles. 2π times this radius gives the circumference of this orbit, and the circumference divided by the orbital speed of 6880 mph gives 24 hours and thus GEO. In orbital mechanics, the apogee refers to the highest altitude and thus lowest speed in an elliptical orbit where as the perigee is the lowest altitude and highest orbital speed.

A satellite launch using a Titan IV rocket for a 100 nautical mile (1 nautical mile is about 1.15 mile) altitude low-earth orbit placement will typically undergo the following mission sequence:

t = –5 sec, initiate the inertial guidance system.
t = –2 sec, stage I ignition signal given.
t = 0.0, lift-off.
t = 9.0, roll to flight azimuth.
t = 19 sec, end stage I roll maneuver.
t = 20.0 sec, start pitch rate 1.

t = 25.0 sec, drive angle of attack to zero (pitch rate 2).

t = 30.0 sec, begin zero lift.

t = 110.0 sec, end zero lift, start pitch rate 3.

t = 135.0 sec, start pitch rate 4.

t = 156.9 sec, end of state I steady-state burn.

t = 157.7 sec, stage I separation (80 nautical miles downrange, altitude 35 nautical miles, velocity 8865 ft/s).

t = 161.0 sec, begin linear sine steering.

t = 210.9 sec, payload fairing separation (140 nautical miles downrange, altitude 64 nautical miles, velocity 11,123 ft/s).

t = 332.8 sec, stage II shutdown (450 nautical miles downrange, altitude 102 nautical miles, velocity 25,524 ft/s).

t = 378.0 sec, converge to commanded attitude, begin velocity trim.

t = 406.0 sec, end velocity trim.

t = 434.0 sec, start maneuver to payload separation.

t = 519.0 sec, payload separation (1200 nautical miles downrange, altitude 100 nautical miles, velocity 25,677 ft/s).

Space shuttles are also used for placement of satellites, both military and civilian. There is a standard sequence for space shuttle missions.

Ignition and lift-off (t = 0 hour, 0 minutes).

Roll and initiate pitch.

Solid rocket booster separation (t = 0 hour, 2 minutes).

Main engine cutoff and external tank separation (t = 0 hours, 8 minutes).

Orbit insertion and circularization (t = 0 hours, 45 minutes).

Orbiter orientation and verification.

Open cargo bay doors, deploy antenna (t = 1 hours, 0 minutes).

Orbiter checkout over tracking station (t = 1 hours, 18 minutes).

Orbiter checkout over tracking station (t = 2 hours, 53 minutes).

Orbiter maneuvers, cargo deplyments (t = 3 hours, 0 minutes).

SPY PLANES

The vantage afforded by height was known to men long before the advent of satellites. The French used manned balloons for reconnaissance and symbolic purposes in 1794. Winged aircraft were used for this purpose in the early 1900s and during World War I, although in the latter the reconnaissance missions have been known to degenerate into airborne pistol duels, giving birth to the aerial dogfights between opposing aircrafts. However, the aircraft that perhaps best symbolizes airborne reconnaissance is the U.S. U-2 "Dragon Lady" (shown in Fig. 4.6). The Dragon Lady, made by Lockheed, entered service in 1955 and is still in service carrying a variety of detection equipment ranging from a multi-spectral imaging camera to electro-optic, infrared, and radar sensors. The main attribute of the U-2 is versatility, at the expense of risking piloted missions over enemy territory. The aircraft can be sent to target locations, make multiple passes, and deploy appropriate sensors at arbitrary times. In that sense, aircraft perform surveillance functions as opposed to reconnaissance. Although the terms "surveillance" and "reconnaissance" are used interchangeably, in military terminology surveillance means sustained observation of the events and layouts of a fixed location while reconnaissance is associated with making limited passes over the target location as in satellite reconnaissance.

The U-2 aircraft as shown in Fig. 4.6 has a high aspect ratio and straight wings that provide glider-like performance at the expense of speeds. The wing design allows for large lift and low drag, and the aircraft weight is kept to a minimum so that flight duration and range are maximized. The wing area is 1000 square feet, with an empty aircraft weight of 14,900 lb (at take-off with fuel and equipment, the U-2 can weigh up to 41,000 lb). The U-2 has a maximum speed of 510 mph, less than the cruise speed of 567 mph for a commercial Boeing 747, but has a range of 11,000 miles or 7.5 hours of flight time without refueling. The U-2 is designed to operate at high altitudes up to 80,000 feet for sustained periods of time high above any enemy threats, although the latter aspect has been compromised at least once in a much publicized "U-2 Crisis" in which the aircraft was shot down over Soviet territory in 1960. However, under normal conditions U-2 operates at an altitude of 70,000 feet, beyond the reach of most Soviet aircraft, missiles, or radars. The combination of the light weight, high altitude, and large aspect ratio wing makes the U-2 aircraft difficult to fly, with a small envelope of stable flight. An estimated thirty-plus U-2 aircraft are operated by the U.S. Air Force, and they have played important roles recently during the conflicts in Iraq and Afghanistan and over Bosnia and Kosovo in support of NATO forces. The U-2 can carry a multitude of photographic, electronic, radar, infrared, and air sampling sensors that can be configured for a given mission. A number of electro-optic sensors (digital imaging cameras) of various resolution and field of view are typically simultaneously operated for referencing and identifications. ASARS-2 synthetic aperture radar (SAR) is capable of gathering detailed ground terrains and objects under night/day, all-weather conditions. This SAR uses two V-shaped arrays that scan the ground on each side of the aircraft within a range of over 100 miles. As opposed to simple two-dimensional pictures generated by the electro-optical sensors, SAR data are used to build three-dimensional synthetic images of the world below for far superior identification of objects (on the ground and in the air) and situational awareness. In addition, multiple moving targets can be identified and posed in the synthetic background image. A signal intelligence suite called "Senior Glass" contains extremely sensitive antennas that monitor the radio and other communications. The intelligence data obtained from the sensors can be sent in real time via satellite-borne uplink routes. For their high-altitude capabilities, the U-2 aircrafts are also used in the ER-2 version by the NASA to carry sensors to monitor earth resources, atmospheric dynamics and chemistry, ocean dynamics, and upper-atmosphere physics.

If the U-2 Dragon Lady is the efficient workhorse that has served useful functions for over fifty years, then the SR-71 Blackbird is the blazing racehorse version of a spy plane. Its futuristic design and high speed (Mach 3) have made this aircraft the flagship for exhibiting U.S. aerospace technological advances. In fact, many if not most of the design and components to go on the SR-71 represented important advances in high Mach number flight technology. In contrast to the subsonic U-2, the Blackbird was powered with Pratt & Whitney J-58 afterburning turbojets with a combined thrust of 65,000 pounds along with a wing-body design to send this aircraft moving at a maximum speed of Mach 3.2 (possibly greater). This corresponds to 2200 mph at the aircraft service altitude of 80,000 feet (24 km or 15 miles). To put this kind of speed in perspective, the SR-71 would require only sixty-four minutes to go from New York City to London in comparison to the Concorde flight time of three hours and twenty-three minutes and the Boeing 747's six hours and fifteen minutes. Of course, we have to account for the fact the commercial airliners probably would not accelerate the passengers at the level of the SR-71, thus taking longer to achieve the maximum flight speeds. For some time, the Blackbird was the world's most advanced aircraft, breaking the records for the highest speed and altitude for its class. The Blackbird's unclassified maximum speed is 2193 mph and its maximum altitude 85,070 feet. The high speed and altitude of the SR-71 made the aircraft impervious to enemy threats. It could simply accelerate or move into a higher altitude to avoid contact with incoming missiles or aircraft. The SR-71 design also included a flattened profile (as shown in the photograph and schematic in Figs. 4.7 and 4.8) to minimize the radar profile and aerodynamic drag. This is the one of the first attempts at aircraft radar stealth technology. However, due to the uncovered engine exhausts and the vertical stabilizer, the SR-71 actually ended up with a large radar profile, and civilian radars could track bright spot on the screen for hundreds of miles. In spite of its impressive performance and looks, the Blackbird

Figure 4.7. The SR-71 Blackbird strategic reconnaissance aircraft. Photos courtesy of the U.S. Air Force.

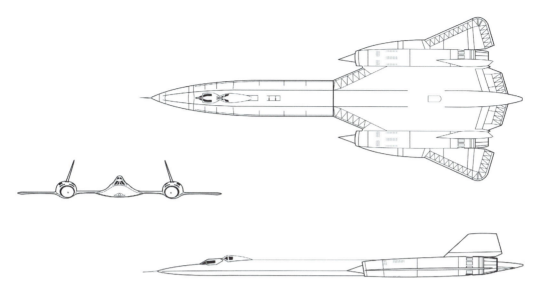

Figure 4.8. Schematic of the SR-71 Blackbird. Graphic courtesy of the NASA Dryden Flight Research Center.

was formally retired in 1998 mostly due to budgetary reasons, with its functions to be covered by the U-2, spy satellites, and unmanned aerial vehicles under development.

The aircraft body is made of titanium alloy for light weight and strength. The black paint over the aircraft body is for visual camouflage as well as thermal dissipation. The high Mach number of the aircraft brought to the test some of the advances in thermal control and air intake designs. At low or zero speeds, the air molecules just contain thermal energy corresponding to its temperature. At high speeds however, the extreme speed of these molecules add kinetic energy to the overall thermal energy of the air. Thus, any object moving at high Mach numbers with air impinging on its surface will be heated to very high temperatures. One simple example is the meteor or any objects entering the atmosphere. The gravitational pull accelerates the objects to hypersonic speeds, and the heat generated through collisions with air molecules disintegrates most of the objects, also resulting in bright glows. A consideration of the energy due to the relative motion between the aircraft and air gives the temperature increase as a function of the Mach number squared. So at an altitude of 80,000 feet, the outside temperature may be -62° F and the pressure less than 3 percent of the atmospheric pressure. However, an aircraft traveling at Mach 3 will see a temperature of 653° F at the point where all of the kinetic energy has gone into raising the temperature. In reality, since the air mostly flows around the aircraft the temperature on the surface of the SR-71 ranges from 462 to 622° F, depending on the exact location. Because of the protrusion of the windshield this area saw some of the highest temperatures on the aircraft surface. The high temperature experienced by the aircraft led to several challenging but interesting technological solutions. To account for the thermal expansion, the aircraft frame was designed for excess spacing between the joints and fittings at the sea-level static temperature, so much so that the fuel leaked through the wing tanks on the ground. A proper fitting was achieved only after the aircraft achieved high Mach number speeds. The usual rubber lining used to seal the fuel compartments would not have lasted very long and therefore was absent in the design. With fuel being consumed and drained from the tank, the remaining space was filled with inert nitrogen to prevent any air leakage into the tank thus creating an ignitable mixture. The high speed of air impinging on the windshield also heats up the cockpit, which needs to be cooled using an air conditioner that dumps excess heat onto the fuel. Other heat dissipating schemes were embedded on to the SR-71. The black paint had a higher irradiative emissivity than bare metal skins by about a factor of three. At high temperatures the surface glowed dark blue, radiating away some of the surface heat. The wing surface also was machined with small longitudinal corrugations, so that thermal expansions do not warp any of the constituent panels.

The high speed also necessitates a control device to lower the engine intake velocity. A shock cone visible at the inlet of the turbojet engine creates a shock well ahead of the engine. The air flow slows down somewhat while its temperature and pressure again go up. The shock cone travels back and forth along the direction of the engine axis to optimize this deceleration process at various flight Mach numbers. Subsequent shocks that develop at the annular region between the shock cone and the engine shroud bring the air speed further down so that the main part of the engine sees a subsonic air speed. The speed of the incident air also allowed air into the Pratt & Whitney J-58 afterburning turbojets without running the air through the compressor-combustor-turbine of the engine (the core part of the gas-turbine engine). Due to high Mach numbers, the ram compression elevated the pressure to a substantial level so that only fuel needed to be injected in the afterburner section. This operation is called the ramjet propulsion, and the Blackbird engine inlet design allowed for hybrid operation to go to ramjet mode at high Mach numbers and normal turbojet operation at low and intermediate Mach numbers. As noted above, at Mach 3 the outside temperature of –62° F can be raised to 653° F due to the ram effect, while the pressure will go up thirty-six times—this surpasses the pressure increase that gas-turbine compressor can generate. However, control of the shock pattern by moving the shock cone back and forth led to a quirk in flying the SR-71. The shock cone movement was not fast enough to adjust to the increasing speed of the Blackbird, and if the inlet condition was mismatched the engine basically shut down due to a number of events that can occur if the inlet pressure is not matched with engine operating conditions (e.g., compressor stall, engine flame-out). With two engines, one engine shutting down meant a sudden spin moment to violently turn the aircraft. This situation was corrected by the vertical fins turning to provide an opposite moment while the other engine was deliberately shut down. Once the normal aircraft angle was recovered, the both engines were relit to resume the flight.

The sensors carried by the Blackbird evolved with digital electronic technology. Originally, relatively simple tracking and surveillance cameras were mounted that operated in the visible and also in the infrared for nighttime vision with moderate resolution capabilities. High resolution cameras that were used on Blackbird later included a stereo-imaging camera called "Operational Objective Camera (OCC)," which allowed a precise three-dimensional reconstruction of the terrain and objects under the aircraft. Prior to decommissioning of the Blackbird, an imaging device called "Technical Objective Camera (TEOC)" was used that had a swivel of +/– 45 degrees from the centerline and a spatial resolution of six inches from the Blackbird's operational altitude of 80,000 feet. With two TEOC cameras usually carried by the SR-71, high-resolution images of the ground objects were brought back for analyses, although the satellite imaging capabilities soon caught up with the level of performance. Side-looking radars (SLR) and synthetic aperture radar systems (SARS) were also one of the primary surveillance tools carried on the SR-71. The principles and use of the radars are described later in this chapter. In addition, electronic intelligence (ELINT) sensor pods were used on the Blackbird missions, with the sensor programmed to pick up particular signals of interest.

Although the Blackbird was retired while the U-2 Dragon Lady remains in service as of 2007, the design of the SR-71 Blackbird was conceived as a replacement of the U-2 Dragon

Lady in anticipation of the U-2s becoming highly vulnerable to the developing Soviet air defense technology. The Lockheed design called at that time A-12 won over the U.S. Navy's proposed design of using a pure ramjet aircraft to be elevated to operational altitude on a balloon and then propelled to supersonic speeds with rocket boosters at which time the ramjet would fire up. The A-12 design with a hybrid engine mounted on a modified XF-104 (an experimental aircraft designed for supersonic speeds) airframe developed into the SR-71. As with many aerospace systems, the development of the hybrid engine capable providing enough thrust for the A-12 became the technological bottleneck, and initial test flights of the SR-71 precursors had to be conducted using weaker J-75 engines giving a maximum speed of Mach 2 as opposed to Mach 3.2 with the thrust generated by the Pratt & Whitney J-58 engines. Even without the high thrust of the J-58 engines, the new design provided some initial excitement during the first test flights with wild flight instabilities experienced in all three axes and somehow flown out of by the test pilots. With the J-58 engine finally fitted to the Blackbird, other new issues emerged, such as the cockpit overheating due to the ram effect. Some of the pilots complained of not being able to hold on to the hot control stick and the cockpit area becoming overheated. In spite of these trials, the A-12 design evolved and was designated SR-71 and flew over 3500 missions, with 53,490 total flight hours. Moreover, through collaboration with NASA much scientific and engineering knowledge in high-speed aircraft aerodynamics, structure, control, and propulsion was accumulated for use in other military and civilian aircraft developments.

UNMANNED AERIAL VEHICLES FOR SURVEILLANCE

As the name suggests, unmanned aerial vehicles (UAVs) fly under remote control or follow pre-programmed paths using onboard or externally linked navigation systems. Because human pilots are not on board, UAVs do not need cockpit and pilot support equipment and thus can be made more compact. It can undertake high-risk missions and can be produced at lower cost and therefore allowed to be expendable. Thus far, most of the UAV use is military due to high cost and its narrow range of functions. Reconnaissance, surveillance, and small-scale attacks can be carried by UAVs. In fact, cruise missiles can be considered as a type of UAV since it delivers munitions under its own propulsion and navigation, and it is conceivable that larger, more complex bombing missions may be carried out by UAVs in the future because more of the navigation and targeting now rely on machine vision (digital cameras) and onboard computers. Already, the U.S. military possesses and deploys a number of UAVs (see Table 4.2).

The BATMAV (shown in Fig. 4.9) stands for battlefield air targeting micro air vehicles and gives an appearance of a small, remote-controlled model airplane, except it carries a price tag of about $49,000 as of 2006. As the name suggests, it is used for situational awareness in the battlefield and target acquisition and directions through the use of a high-resolution camera with nighttime vision capabilities. It has a collapsible airframe for easy storage and transport and runs on an electric motor with rechargeable lithium ion batteries (so it could serve as a toy airplane except again for the price tag). The internal global position and inertial navigation allows autonomous, programmable flights, but it can also be piloted using a handheld remote control unit. The wing span is only 42 cm (16.5 in) with a length of 29 cm (11.5 in) and a weight of 6.5 kilograms (14.4 lbs). BATMAVs twin-blade propeller can propel this micro vehicle to a speed of 40 mph.

In Table 4.1, the medium altitude and long endurance (MALE) categorization refers to UAVs with a altitude of up to 30,000 ft and a range over 200 km, while high altitude, long

Table 4.2. Examples of the U.S. Military's UAVs.

Name	Military Branch	Characteristics
BATMAV	Air Force, Marine Corps	
Gnat 750	Air Force	Low altitude, long endurance.
MQ-1 Predator	Air Force, Marine Corps, Army	Medium altitude, long endurance (MALE).
RQ-4 Global Hawk	Air Force	High altitude, long endurance (HALE).
RQ-3 DarkStar	Air Force	High altitude, long endurance, low visibility (so-called Tier III UAV, but program terminated).
RQ-11B Raven B	Marine Corps	Low altitude, long endurance.
RQ-2 Pioneer	Marine Corps	Medium altitude, long endurance (MALE).
RQ-7A/B Shadow 200	Army	Short range, tactical UAV.
RQ-5A/MQ-5A/B Hunter	Army	Medium range, tactical UAV.

endurance (HALE) means service altitude of over 30,000 ft and range beyond 200 km. For altitude up to 18,000 ft and a range up to about 160 km, the UAVs are considered "tactical."

The MQ-1 Predator shown in Fig. 4.10 is a MALE UAV, with a weight of 1020 kilograms (2250 pounds) at take-off. A small Rotax four-cylinder reciprocating engine propels the Predator to a speed of up to 135 mph with a range of 454 miles. MQ-1 can perform reconnaissance, targeting, and interdiction functions, with the last being accomplished by two laser-guided AGM-114 Hellfire missiles. Although they are not on board, MQ-1 is a remotely piloted aircraft requiring a crew of one pilot and two sensor operators. However, the MQ-1 was designed as a theater reconnaissance system with a base unit consisting of four MQ-1s, a ground control station, and a satellite link. The sphere under the nose of the aircraft houses the color and infrared camera with variable apertures for day/night piloting. The ground-based pilot receives the real-time views either directly or through satellite link and guides the aircraft. The MQ-1 also carries a multi-spectral targeting system for observations and also for deploying the onboard AGM missiles. The payload of 450 pounds allows a variety of electro-optical sensors to be carried by the MQ-1.

Figure 4.9. U.S. Air Force Battlefield Air Targeting Micro Air Vehicle (BATMAV). Photo courtesy of the U.S. Air Force.

Figure 4.10. MQ-1 Predator, an unmanned surveillance aircraft. Photo courtesy of the U.S. Air Force.

The RQ-4 Global Hawk is a HALE-type UAV, and as can be seen in Fig. 4.11 is a much larger aircraft. Its straight-wing design is reminiscent of the U-2 Dragon Lady reconnaissance aircraft, except of course RQ-4 is pilot-less. The wing span is 116 feet with a length of 44.4 feet, so its wing span is almost three times the length, providing glider-like range and endurance (forty-two hours). It can fly at altitudes up to 65,000 feet and its estimated cruise speed is 404 mph. The power plant is an Allison Rolls-Royce turbo-fan engine rated at 31,400 Newton (7050 pounds). The dimensions and cost ($35 million each) of the Global Hawk places this aircraft in a different category, with large coverage and auto-pilot capabilities. The landing and take-off is controlled by a ground-based unit called the "launch and recovery element (LCE)." High-precision GPS is used during take-off and landings, where the precise altitude and speed data are used to control the aircraft's aerodynamic surfaces and engine. During the flight phase, an inertial navigation augments the GPS to follow pre-programmed paths. In some instances, the Global Hawk is known to have flown along civilian air space, so there is an outside chance that this aircraft may have been seen cruising along pilot-less in the vicinity of civilian aircraft.

The surveillance package is referred to as the "Integrated Sensor Suite (ISS)" and consists of a SAR, an electro-optical sensor, and an infrared sensor operating in either wide-area search or high-resolution imaging mode. The SAR unit, for example, can view an area 37 km wide with a six-meter resolution in the search mode, or zoom in to a 10 square kilometer area with a 1.8-meter resolution. More information on the synthetic aperture radar and other sensor systems is discussed later in this chapter.

Figure 4.11. RQ-4 Global Hawk. Photo courtesy of U.S. Air Force.

AIRBORNE EARLY WARNING SYSTEMS

Airborne early warning systems have a notable lineage in military history and technology evolution. Observation of the opponent army's size, movement, and composition has always led to critical information needed to make correct battlefield decisions. As noted prevoiusly, the French are known to have first deployed an airborne device for this purpose in 1794 during the Battle of Fleurus against the Austrians. A tethered balloon was used to send an observer to extreme heights, who then sent signals via flags and messages down the tether line. The American Civil War also saw some instances of the use of tethered balloons by both the Confederate and Union armies. With the winged aircraft coming of age in the early 1900s, its use was first seen as an observational platform. The United States Army, for example, established an aeronautical division of the Signal Corps in 1907, and by 1917 the Army had a staff of seventeen trained pilots to man its own aircraft.

The airborne capabilities rapidly developed during the trench battles in World War I, where to detect the opponent activities far beyond the trench lines aircraft were sent to check troop strengths and deployment. Routine incursions into the opponent's air space brought back useful information that could be used to plan counter-moves and defensive maneuvers. Strategies to harass these flights across the trenches were soon developed, with aircraft being flown up to ward off the offending parties. However, because the aircraft could not be located at the right place at the right time, being able to respond with aircraft sorties was quite limited. It was a matter of knowing where and when the enemy aircraft would make their incursions, and thus a form of early warning was needed. Two early warning schemes were devised. The first method involved having aircraft constantly patrol the space over the friendly territory, which turned out to be quite wasteful because the pilots and airplanes both wore down in the relatively primitive state of the technology.

The second scheme was to use a line of logistically located ground observation points to communicate the location and direction of the opposing aircraft flying across the battle lines. The key word here is the communication, or lack thereof. Due to lack of a reliable communication network (the telephone lines of the time could not handle communication traffic of more than a handful of simultaneous calls), the latter scheme also could not be made effective.

In 1930, prior to World War II , a key development occurred in what is now called radar technology. During World War II, the radars were used as a part of the air defense and also for naval observations, but not on an airborne platform. Placing radars on airplanes is analogous to placing observers at high altitudes using balloons and aircraft, except of course radars have a much larger range. The need to have a larger observational range was deeply impressed on the military minds during World War II, particularly on the U.S. Navy, which saw the criticality of knowing the Japanese aircraft movement toward its carrier battle groups. Under a project codenamed "Cadillac," the Navy started with a small aircraft platform to carry radars. The Grumman Avenger could be launched from either land base or navy carrier, and was designated as the combat information center (CIC) aircraft. The radar development itself was aided by the MIT Radiation Laboratory, and on the CIC aircraft S-band (2 to 4 GHz) search radars were first used. The data gathered by the CIC aircraft was relayed via VHF (very high frequency) radio signals to the shipboard displays. Use of carrier-based aircraft for CIC purposes continued up to 1960s with the Grumman Guardian, Douglas Skyraider, Grumman Tracer, and Grumman Hawkeye. In parallel, to overcome the limitations of small radars on small aircraft, a program called "Project Cadillac II" proceeded to make use of larger radars installed on Boeing B-17G Flying Fortresses. In contrast to a single pilot on the Grumman Avenger, the B-17G could now carry observation crews to direct fighter traffic to the targets discovered by the onboard radar system.

In 1949, a Lockheed aircraft called the Constellation, originally a forty-seat passenger aircraft designed and manufactured at the request of Trans World Airlines and Howard Hughes, was fitted with then–state-of-the-art radars and was given the designation WV-1. The WV-1 carried an S-band surveillance radar as well as an X-band height-finding radar to pinpoint target locations. The Air Force soon adopted the WV-series aircraft as its own early warning aircraft, but with a designation of EC-121 Warning Star. The larger aircraft not only allows bigger radars and more equipment and personnel to be carried on board, but also its higher altitude permits larger range of detection. For example, the maximum range of detection for radar on a 100-foot tower may be 51 nautical miles for a target at an altitude of 1000 feet, whereas this range increases to 162 miles for the same radar placed on an aircraft flying at 10,000 feet and to 428 miles if placed at an altitude of 60,000 feet.

The EC-121 was used quite extensively during the conflicts in Southeast Asia, including forays deep into North Vietnam. Although the radars at this time had difficulty in discerning objects on the ground due to the large radar reflection off the ground texture itself, the EC-121 still provided valuable service in the opposing MiG alerts and guiding friendly aircraft for intercepts and other missions. Close to this period, the concept for the next-generation airborne early warning system materialized into so-called AWACS, or airborne early warning and control systems. In 1970, a Boeing 707-320 was adopted as the mother aircraft on which a Westinghouse Doppler radar along with an IFF (identification friend or foe)/SIF (selective identification feature) interrogator was installed inside a rotating rotodome. The prominent round rotodome itself was mounted on top of the fuselage in the aft section of the aircraft. This bears the designation E-3 Sentry AWACS shown in Fig. 4.12. The E-3 Sentry requires an operational crew of about twenty personnel

Figure 4.12. The E-3 Sentry Airborne Early Warning and Control System (AWACS) aircraft. Photo courtesy of the U.S. Air Force.

for flight operations (for piloting and navigating the aircraft), technical operation (for maintenance and repair of onboard equipment), surveillance operation, and weapons control. The latter two groups maintain vigilance over the battle space, to detect enemy aircraft or missile appearances far beyond what small radars on fighter or bomber aircraft can see and thus perform a critical function of guarding the friendly aircraft against ambush-type missile or aircraft attacks.

Fig. 4.13 shows a general layout of the E-3 aircraft. The radome (1) contains the main surveillance antenna, IFF antenna, and ancillary antenna equipment. In the operations room (3) a data processor functional group is located along with computer operator consoles. Bailout and jettison mechanisms are also placed in this section. The electronics bay (4) houses communication, essential flight avionics, bailout chutes, DC power supply, and power distribution equipment. In the utility section, a special-purpose console may be placed along with miscellaneous radar maintenance equipment. Radar receiver, signal processor, communication, navigation, and identification electronics are also usually installed in this section. In the power supply bay lie the radar transmitters and auxiliary power units.

An acronym, JSTARS, is sometimes used synonymously with AWACS. JSTARS stands for joint surveillance target attack radar system, and if AWACS surveys the air space then the function of JSTARS is to scan the ground targets and threats. Thus, the same airborne platform can be used for JSTARS with appropriate replacements of the sensor equipment. The data from airborne JSTARS is linked to mobile common ground stations (CGS) that usually remain in close proximity to the corps commander's headquarters. The JSTARS furnish the commanders with the location and movement of vehicles and detailed terrain maps. The synthetic aperture radars have sufficient resolutions to identify the type of the

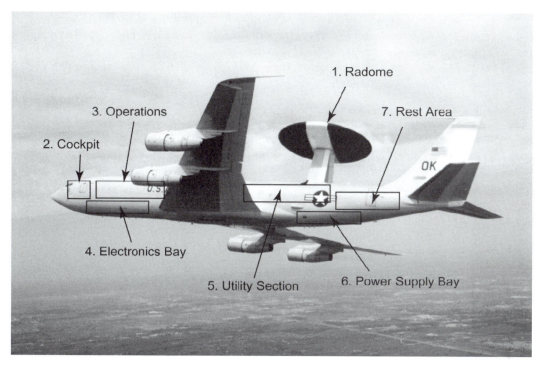

Figure 4.13. A general layout of the E-3 Sentry aircraft. The original photo courtesy of the U.S. Air Force.

Figure 4.14. EA-6B Prowler used in the Electronic Attack Squadrons of the U.S. Navy. Photo courtesy of the U.S. Navy.

vehicle and therefore friendly or foe identification capabilities. With JSTARS, essentially all the movements and locations of friendly and enemy vehicles are mapped in real time within an area of several hundred kilometers.

The above principles of operation for AWACS or JSTARS are carried out by a set of sophisticated, integrated electronics:

1. Antenna and Rotodome Equipment (this is the radar sensor unit).
   - One 8 m (26 feet) × 1.3 m (4.5 feet) antenna consisting of twenty-eight slotted waveguide radiators that provide narrow, focused beams.
   - Twenty-eight reciprocal beam steering phase shifters.
2. Phase Control Electronics.
   - Beam angle control circuits.
   - One high-power channel for transmission, seven coaxial RF channels.
   - Microwave receiver.
3. Transmit Group.
   - Transmit low-power amplifier.
   - Transmit angle control.
   - Two high-power Klystron amplifiers with two pulsers and grid pulser circuits.
   - Pressurized high-voltage supply units, with 90 kV transformer, filter and regulator.
   - Protection sensors for power distribution and control.
4. Radar Control and Maintenance Panel.
   - Spectrum analyzers.
   - Multiple data display units.
   - Fast Fourier transform displays.
5. Surveillance and Radar Computer.
   - 24-bit precision with 5 MHz data rate capable of performing 23 billion operations per second.
   - 534 real pipelined arithmetic unit gate arrays operating at 20 MHz.

The future AWACS and JSTARS will be required to provide resolutions for yet smaller targets, greater range, and better height accuracy along with improved tracking. In addition, capabilities will be added for identification and tracking of slow-moving targets, helicopters, and high-speed missiles with diverse frequency scanning.

A Boeing 707-300 aircraft is the platform that carries either AWACS or JSTARS electronics, with major modifications to accommodate the surveillance, communication, and defensive countermeasure equipment. The Boeing 707-300 (with military designations of E-8, EC-135, or E-3 Sentry depending on the use) is powered by four Pratt & Whitney TF33-102C turbofan engines with 19,200 lbs (82,000 N) of thrust each. The maximum take-off weight is 336,000 lbs, and the aircraft is operated by a flight crew of four and twenty or so Air Force and Army personnel. The Boeing 707-300 is capable of remaining in flight for up to nine hours, but with refueling its endurance can be extended almost indefinitely. With advances in electronics equipment and to replace the aging Boeing 707-300, a new fleet of AWACS and JSTARS on the Boeing 767-400E airframe is planned for the future. The United States along with NATO states operate long-range early warning aircraft such as AWACS and JSTARS. The air forces of Russia, France, India, Saudi Arabia, Greece, and Japan also possess AWACS aircraft, either of their own design or an export version from the United States. The Australian and South Korean militaries are also anticipated to acquire the U.S. export version of AWACS based on the Boeing 737-700 airframe.

Figure 4.15. Phased-array radar (APG-75) on the nose radome of F/A-18 aircraft. Photo courtesy of the U.S. Department of Defense.

RADARS AND OTHER SENSORS

A number of elements are now considered in electronic intelligence and warfare. These are radars, IFF, radio, electronic support measures, infrared sensors, and electronic counter-measures for self-protection. Radars (radio detection and ranging) are powerful devices due to their all-weather, day and night capabilities. In addition to long-range target detection, radars provide functions for flight operations and weather and terrain monitoring. Thus, radars are capable of surveillance, target tracking, height measurements (of targets

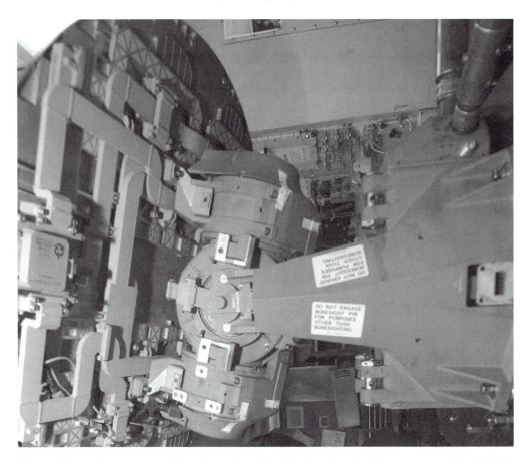

Figure 4.16. A close-up view of the radar used in fighter-bomber aircrafts. Photo courtesy of the U.S. Air Force.

and terrains), and target identification/classification. The electromagnetic frequency that can be used for radars ranges from UHF (ultra high frequency, about 400 MHz) to the so-called K_a (35 GHz) bands, and selection of the frequency for a particular radar use depends on the target type, land/sea/weather environment, and other mission objectives. For maximum resolution of target geometry and dimensions, the high-frequency K_a band is useful, with any higher frequency being avoided due to atmospheric attenuation (i.e., limited range). Usually, frequencies between 400 MHz (UHF) and 4 GHz (S band) are used form long-range surveillance. The lower UHF frequencies have the advantage of both low cost and improved detection of low radar cross-section targets such as missiles and stealth aircraft, while high frequency radars provide better angular and height resolutions. Table 4.3 lists the different radar bands and their primary uses.

In a similar manner to sun light that is reflected or scattered from solid surfaces and particles, all electromagnetic waves including those in the radar frequency are reflected from surfaces. The amount and the manner in which the radar waves are reflected depend on the surface material, surface finish, and shape. Since most aircraft, ships, and other military vehicles are made of metals or carbon fibers, radar reflection is usually significant unless a great deal of effort is made to make the surface resistant to radar detection using stealth technology. The frequency of the radar wave also dictates the characteristics of the

Table 4.3. Radar Bands (adopted from http://en.wikipedia.org/wiki/Radar)

Band	Frequency	Wavelength	Primary Use
HF	3–30 MHz	10–100 m	Over-the-horizon radars
P	<300 MHz	>1 m	Early radar systems
VHF	50–330 MHz	0.9–6 m	Very long-range radars, ground penetrating radars
UHF	300–1000 GHz	0.3–1 m	Ballistic missile early warning radars
L	1–2 GHz	15–30 cm	Long-range air traffic control and surveillance
S	2–4 GHz	7.5–15 cm	Terminal air traffic control
C	4–8 GHz	3.75–7.5 cm	Satellite tracking
X	8–12 GHz	2.5–3.75 cm	Missile guidance, marine radars, weather radars
K_u	12–18 GHz	1.67–2.5 cm	Satellite altimetry, high-resolution mapping
K	18–27 GHz	1.11–1.67 cm	Meteorological radars, speed guns
K_a	27–40 GHz	0.75–1.11. cm	Airport surveillance, short-range mapping, traffic control radars
mm	40–300 GHz	7.5–1 mm	
Q	40–60 GHz	5–7.5 mm	Military communications
V	50–75 GHz	4–6 mm	
E	60–90 GHz	3.33–6 mm	
W	75–110 GHz	2.7–4 mm	High-resolution meteorological radars

return signals as well as their propagation in the atmosphere. As noted previously, high frequency and therefore short-wavelength waves are useful for discerning the shape of the target in high-resolution radars, but these waves are easily absorbed by the atmosphere and therefore their energy quickly diminishes over a distance. Military radars use a range of radar frequencies in various configurations to achieve the mission objectives.

The use of the radar spans across all branches of the military and serves many important functions. Installed in a fighter/interceptor aircraft, the radar gives the capabilities for search, threat assessments, and weapons management including fire control. The fire control aspect is achieved by the radar generating the data needed for calculation of the optimum engagement angle, range, and speed for the armament. The search mode needs to cover a large volume of information involving range and angular coverage and thus may give the operator a situational awareness but not the details of the target signals. The track mode, on the other hand, uses a narrow "pencil" of radar waves at optimum frequencies to

Figure 4.17. An artistic rendition of the modern missile early warning reconnaissance satellite. Image courtesy of the U.S. Air Force.

Figure 4.18. The synthetic aperture radar used in the BMEWS (Ballistic missile early warning system) site in Thule Air Base, Greenland. Photo courtesy of the U.S. Air Force.

Figure 4.19. A typical radar display showing the surface scan in a polar coordinate (circumferential angle). Photo courtesy of the U.S. Navy.

Figure 4.20. Multiple radar displays in battle management stations. Photo courtesy of the U.S. Navy.

Figure 4.21. AN-TPS-75 air surveillance radar. Photo courtesy of the U.S. Air Force.

identify the number and type of threats discovered in the scan mode. The high resolution of the radar interrogation in this mode gives the detailed range and speed using the Doppler shift. Most modern military radars allow track-while-scan so that both the overall battlefield situation as well as the detailed threat tracking can be accomplished simultaneously. Although IFF is first deployed discern the detected objects, more precise determination of the target is possible by analyzing the reflected radar echo. In some advanced systems with high resolution, a two-dimensional radar image of the target is made to facilitate the identification as opposed to just analyzing the one-dimensional radar echoes. The fire control for close-range weapons like aircraft cannons requires the radar data so that the lead pursuit path to the target can be computed and displayed on the HUD (heads-up display). Also, the fire cross-hair will be displayed on the HUD to prompt the pilot to pull the trigger, again based on radar input on the speed, range, and angle of the target. For beyond-visual-range engagements using missiles like the AMRAAM, target update data from the aircraft radar can be transmitted to the missile should the target make sudden course changes after the missile launch. For terminal guidance, AMRAAM and other active-radar missiles use their own onboard radars to home in on the target.

Even longer-range searching and tracking can be accomplished by bigger radars installed on airborne platforms such as the AWACS, the EA-61 Prowler, and other electronic warfare aircraft. The ultramodern radar installed on the F-22 Raptor has estimated capabilities that in some aspects equal those on dedicated electronic warfare aircraft. Other important utilities of radars include high-resolution terrain mapping using SAR (described later), air traffic control, altimetry for low-altitude flights and terrain avoidance, precision velocity updates, and weather avoidance. Low-altitude flights are often used to avoid detection by the enemy radars; however, to maintain a low altitude without risking running into terrains precise altitude information is obtained from the time for the radar echo from the ground to come back to the sounding radar. To prevent disclosure by this radar operation, the altimetry radar is operated at very low PRF (pulse repetition frequency) and also using the radar frequency control—the radar power is spread over a very wide frequency ranges. For the precision velocity update, three thin radar beams are sent forward and down at shallow angles. The Doppler frequency of the returning signals then gives the speed of the aircraft with respect to the ground. Used extensively in meteorology and weather forecasting, Doppler radars detect the presence and speed of weather systems bearing rain drops that also reflect radar waves effectively. Again, the Doppler shift gives the speed of the storm fronts bearing rains. Using the same principle, wind shear (a sudden change in the horizontal wind velocity from one altitude to another) can be detected in a rain-bearing storm system by measuring the front velocity as a function of the altitude using Doppler radar.

Electromagnetic waves are generated as an electrical charge oscillates in time. The AM radio noise heard when an electrical appliance is turned on (e.g., fan) nearby is an example of radio waves being generated by the alternating current of the household electricity. By altering the current and frequency of the electrical oscillation, radar waves can be generated in different bands as listed in Table 4.3. Technically, these oscillators or "transmitters" are given names such as "klystron" and "magnetron," but the underlying principle of operations is the oscillation of electrical charges. For example, a magnetron is a circular tube acting as the anode (positive electrode) with a central cathode (negative electrode) core. A strong DC voltage is applied across the cathode and also to the central core to heat it up through electrical resistance. The latter effect is to generate electrodes from the cathode surface, which then would be drawn toward the positive anode and stream toward it under vacuum conditions inside the magnetron. The acceleration of electrons under permanent magnets that surround the magnetron induces circular motion of the electrons.

Similar to the way certain sound wave frequencies are amplified in a wind instrument, the frequency of the circular motion of the electrons is selectively amplified by the resonant cavities machined on the circular anode tube. The resonant cavities are equidistant circular holes on the anode tube. The klystron is another device that is used to generate radar waves. In contrast to the circular design for the magnetron, klystron has a linear geometry similar to a cathode ray tube where the electrons are generated from a heated cathode at one end and then accelerate toward the anode at the other end. Again, resonant cavities on both ends of the vacuum tube determine the frequency of the radar wave. As noted above, different frequency radar waves have certain optimum characteristics depending on the application. A key development in this regard is the gridded traveling wave tube amplifier (or TWT for short) in the 1960s. The use of the electron gun (cathode) in a vacuum under a high-voltage electric field is the same as the klystron; however, instead of resonant cavities TWT uses a helical microwave input that controls the frequency, phase, and amplitude of the output radar waves.

The radar source waves from the magnetron are linked to the antenna via a waveguide that directs the radar waves with minimum loss in the wave strength. The antenna is the component that sends the radar waves for scans, and typically the same antenna is used to receive the return signals. The returning electromagnetic waves can be converted to electrical signals through the reverse of the above principle, and the signals then can be filtered, processed, and analyzed.

A large amount of useful information can be obtained from the return radar signal. The distance to the target is determined by clocking the time delay between the transmitted and received signal. Since the propagation speed of radar waves can be precisely calculated knowing the atmospheric conditions, the distance to the target is the propagation speed times half the time delay between the transmitted and received pulses (accounting for the fact that the signal needs to travel to the target and back). For highly directional antennas such as the parabolic type, the angular location of the target can also be determined. Also, if the frequency of the transmitted and return signal is compared, the shift in frequency that occurs due to the relative velocity between the source and the target can be calculated. The altitude of the target is related to the angular location in the vertical plane and distance of the target. In addition, the strength and wave shape of the return signal can be analyzed to estimate the shape and size of the target, and therefore target identifications are made using a more detailed analysis of the signal. The above information can be synthesized and displayed, with the most common mode being the "plan position indicator (PPI)." In the PPI display mode, the targets are displayed in a polar plot with the radar position at the center. For 360-degree scan radars, the entire circular projection is displayed with the angle denoting the direction of the target and radius the range (distance). For forward-looking radars with less than full circular coverage, then a sector PPI display would show the same information except in a fan-shaped polar plot limited by the azimuthal angular range. For synthetic aperture radar used for ground mapping, a rectangular "patch map" of the ground terrains is displayed with the vertical axis referred to as the range and the horizontal cross-range.

The geometry of the radar determines the directional resolution and the also the outgoing radar beam profiles. The most familiar parabolic reflector geometry (the dish) generates a relatively tight beam with a good directional control. Slotted waveguides look like rotating bars, typically found in marine vehicles, and they have good directional resolution in the horizontal plane. Phased array radars involve more advanced technology where an array of individual antennas is controlled to shape the final outgoing radar beam. Because the direction of the outgoing beam is also controlled by the radar signals transmitted to the individual antennas electronically, the angular scan can be made quite rapidly, typically several thousand degrees per second. The scan speed is essential for detecting and scanning multiple targets, and therefore phased array configuration is now used as the fundamental military radar geometry.

Synthetic aperture radar (SAR) is used in high-resolution, broad-area mapping in all weather conditions. The principle of SAR is schematically illustrated in Fig. 4.22. The target grid area is to be scanned, but the radar primarily measures the range (distance) data from the return time for the reflected radar signal. In other words, only one data point for the range of the target area is collected in "real aperture radars." It was discovered as early as 1950s that the return signal from different parts in the target grid area contained a frequency shift due to the relative motion between the aircraft and the target point. Thus, to resolve the features in the azimuthal direction as shown in the figure, the Doppler shift of the return frequency is monitored. Due to the aircraft motion relative to the stationary features, the objects aft of the aircraft will be Doppler-shifted toward lower frequencies and those ahead toward higher frequencies. By mapping the return signal along with the frequency shift, the range information from multiple points in the grid area can be obtained by significantly increasing the resolution of the radar data. That is why this processing technique is named "synthetic aperture radar." The fine-resolution features can be mapped out much as a large-aperture radar with a much higher beam focusing may be able to generate. In actual operations, the signal processing and analysis to reconstruct the synthetic aperture mapping require sophisticated electronics and computing capabilities.

For advanced radar systems used in AWACS or JSTARS, further capabilities need to be embedded such as accounting for the atmospheric refraction (bending of the radar waves) and attenuation; processing of the relative motion between the aircraft, target, and the earth; having restrictions on the size and weight of the main radar antennas; and overcoming

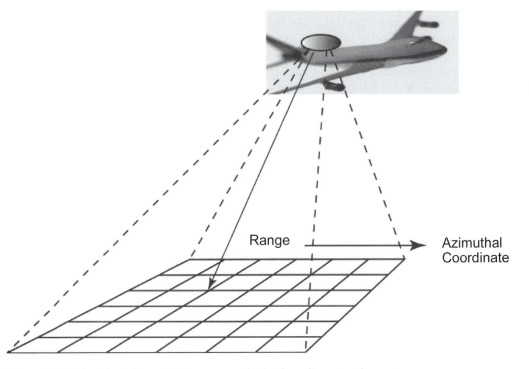

Figure 4.22. Principle of the synthetic aperture radar for three-dimensional mapping.

jamming and other electromagnetic interferences. With effective stealth technologies now being available, the radar technology must be improved to overcome the difficulties associated with detecting stealth aircraft as well as fast, low-altitude, low radar cross-section threats such as cruise missiles.

In addition to the radars, early warning systems now include other sensors and devices augmenting the radar scan and track capabilities. The IFF is a critical element in providing a radar-generated map of the battlefield situation. The IFF works by the land-based station, ship, or an aircraft (conventional or AWACS) sending an interrogating signal, typically at 1030 MHz, and the friendly aircraft responding with a coded reply at a shifted frequency, typically at 1090 MHz. The process is automated with the code input to the transponders and altered on a regular basis to avoid countermeasures. Any aircraft not responding with the correct coded reply is identified as opposing aircraft and duly displayed on the computer monitor. However, one fault in this system lies in the fact that it only identifies friendly aircraft with an IFF transponder operating at that time. Civilian or neutral aircraft, or even friendly aircraft with outdated codes, are all classified as foes under this system. A tragic incident in 1988 is an example of the possibility of a misidentification. An Iranian commercial airliner, an A300 Airbus, was shot down by a missile launched from the U.S. Navy Aegis-class cruiser Vincennes. The confusion apparently arose due to the two conflicting codes being detected, a military mode 2 and a civil mode A, and the fact that the Airbus was observed to descend toward the cruiser in an apparent attack pattern. Despite the circumstances, this incident throws some shadows on the lack of positive identification using this type of IFF method.

Electronic support measures (ESM) refer to scanning of a very large range of electromagnetic spectrum and using the data to identify and locate the source of the detected signals. Most military vehicles during normal operations (under non-radio-silence operations) emit a variety of electromagnetic emissions associated with radio communications, navigation, and also their own radars. By cataloging the electromagnetic characteristics used by major military forces and analyzing their signal strength and direction, much information can be added to that obtained from the conventional transmit/receive radars. ESM is by definition a passive intelligence method, with the receiver scanning across a wide range of electromagnetic frequencies.

The methods described above are used in various combinations and modes depending on the mission requirements. In the pulse Doppler non-elevation scans, all objects in the air down to the surface level area scanned for angular location and speed. The beyond-the-horizon mode is used for extended-range surveillance without the Doppler signal processing, with the beam pointing above the horizon to minimize the ground clutter. The pulse Doppler elevation scan refers to the radar operation in which the radar beam is scanned in the vertical direction to resolve the angular location, altitude, and speed of the targets. Finally, the passive mode is used as electronic support measure (ESM) by turning off the radar transmitters and monitoring for the incoming signals only.

For the ballistic missile early warning system (BMEWS), a combination of radar capabilities logistically located in and outside of the United States territory is used. The three sites (BMEWS) are located in (1) the U.S. Air Force facility in Thule, Greenland, (2) Clear Air Force Station in Alaska, and (3) a Royal Air Force facility at Fylingdales, United Kingdom, as discussed in Chapter 5 of this book. The site at Fylingdales operates an AN/FPS-49 surveillance and tracking radar, while Clear Air Force Station uses a group of radars—an AN/FPS-92, a FPS-49, and three AN/FPS-50 surveillance radars. At Thule, four FPS-50s and a phased array radar, the AN/FPS-115, monitors the space. The FPS-49 tracking radar's 82-ft dish is housed in a 141-ft diameter radome. It has a maximum scan range of 3110 miles in the UHF operating frequency range (see Table 4.3). The FPS-50 radar is even larger with a parabolic-torus reflector at a 400-ft width and a 165-ft height. Its scan range is approximately 3000 miles, and it has an angular coverage of 160 degrees with an elevation scan capability of 3.5 to 7 degrees. The FPS-115 phased array radar sends and receives signals from two faces with an approximately 90-ft diameter and a range that exceeds 3000 miles. As noted above, phased array radar has fixed orientation, but it can cover wide angles through electronic control of the phased array elements. For the FPS-115, the angular coverage is 120 degrees with elevation scans from 3 to 85 degrees.

Precision Acquisition Vehicle Entry Phased Array Warning System or PAVE PAWS is an integral component of the U.S. ballistic missile early warning network, with a primary function of detecting and tracking submarine-launched ballistic missiles. The U.S. PAVE PAWS carries the designation AN/FP-115, and the sites are located to monitor both the Atlantic and the Pacific Oceans: Cape Cod Air Force Station in Massachusetts, Beale Air Force Base in California, Robins Air Force Base in Georgia, and Eldorado Air Force Base in Texas. The PAVE PAWS in these installations have three faces with a 20-degree tilt from the vertical, and the enclosure building covers close to 77,000 square feet. The angular coverage of 240 degrees with an elevation scan from 3 to 85 degrees can be made using FP-115 radars with tracking capability up to 3455 miles.

ELECTRONIC COUNTER- AND COUNTER-COUNTERMEASURES

Electronic countermeasures (ECM) refer to methods to defeat the probing radar beams, while electronic counter-countermeasures (ECCM) attempt to defeat them (ECM). There is a large variety of ECM methods, but they can be classified under one of the following: chaff, jamming, false targets/decoys, gate stealers, and angle deception. Chaffs were used almost immediately after radars went into use during World War II. The radar technology was known on both sides of the Atlantic, and thus it was relatively straightforward to conjure up a scheme to interfere with the radar operation in detecting metal objects such as aircrafts. By dispersing strips of metal foils, the radar waves would be reflected off these chaffs, thus either giving false signals or shielding the actual aircraft. In modern chaff, literally billions of thin metal-coated fibers are stored in a casing the size of a penny, and when dispersed they tend to stay aloft in the air for persistent reflection of the radar signals. Although radar techniques such as the moving target indicator can discern actual targets from such stationary chaff elements, again they can be used for shielding purposes or at least provide an alternate reflector. The latter can be effective on less capable radars, such as those on air-to-air missiles, by introducing tracking noise that can cause a break in the radar lock during evasive maneuvers. An interesting effect is that the return signal from the chaff elements is the strongest in the probe radar frequency; however, due to resonance effect multiples of the source frequency are also scattered, which depends on the length-to-diameter ratio of the chaff fibers. To saturate the return frequency range, a set of chaff fibers with selected length-to-diameter ratios is used.

Jamming or noise jamming is a simple but effective method where a strong, broadband radar signal is broadcast to saturate the opposing radars. In modern applications, the noise jamming is tuned to the opposing radar frequency by occasionally monitoring the incoming radar frequencies and then using a frequency-tuning circuit to generate jamming noise. In spite of the fact that the jamming radar acts as a loud beacon to signal the presence of hostile intent, it does eliminate the ranging capabilities of the opposing radars. Thus, the range, number, and direction of the approaching force cannot be determined by the other side. They may be aware of something afoot, but cannot confirm, identify, or engage the approaching force using any of the radar-based weapons. For this reason, noise jamming is very effective in shielding large, multiple attacking groups, particularly if emitted by an independent electronic warfare aircraft or vehicle. Also, multiple aircraft can sequentially employ noise jamming so that even passive radar scans by the opposing side become useless. To defeat multiple radars operating in different frequencies, a number of jamming tactics are used. The entire radar frequency spectrum can be continuously swept by jamming radar noise to saturate the opposing radars, but this of course dilutes the amplitude and time. An alternate method is the "spot jamming" where the only observed radar frequencies are selectively jammed in sequence or simultaneously. However, even spot jamming takes a lot of radar power, which may result in leakage or consume too much of the radar power available. An advanced method called "bin masking" circumvents this difficulty. In the range bin masking method, the incoming probe radar signal is monitored, and jamming noise is generated only in the time interval that the probe radar is expected to receive the return signal from the jamming aircraft. This is particularly useful against low- to medium-PRF (pulse repetition frequency) radars. For high-PRF radars, velocity bin masking is used. As noted above, the velocity of targets is observed through the Doppler frequency shift of the radar return signal. Velocity bin masking again responds to the incoming probe radar signal, determines its frequency, and immediately shifts the frequency to emit that particular frequency through the jamming radar. The result is that the radar frequency range corresponding to the Doppler shifts of the target velocity becomes saturated.

False targets methods generate simulated return signals so that the hostile radar fails to correctly locate the aircraft. In the false target method, a compact electronic device first waits for the probe beam to arrive and then transmits a simulated signal after a desired time delay to simulate the false range and speed. This kind of false-echo device is called a transponder. In repeater–type devices, much more realistic echo signals can be generated by storing the incident radar waveform, generating the same waveform the computer memory, and then electronically amplifying and transmitting the reproduced radar waveform after a desired time delay. To add to the confusion, false time delays as well as Doppler shifts can be added to the transmitted beams in both the transponder and repeaters so that the observer may be induced into believing they are looking at a larger number of incoming objects spread out over a wide range and speed. If any of the false target circuitry is installed in either towed or expendable decoys, then the device is called an active radar decoy. In passive decoys, a spherical radar reflector is used to simulate the radar cross section of the deploying aircraft. The decoys are designed to match the speed of the deploying aircraft, at least during the initial phase of dispersal, so that the radar signature appears identical until the aircraft breaks off in an evasive maneuver leaving the decoy to attract the incident radar-guided projectiles.

As noted previously, probably the first electronic countermeasure, chaff, was invented based on the knowledge of the operating principles of radar. As the operating principles of the electronic countermeasures are also well known (to much greater detail than divulged in this book), people will always come up with ideas to defeat these ECM methods in a potentially never-ending cycle of one-upmanship at a grand scale. Standard electronic counter-countermeasures (ECCM) methods against sources of ECM are frequency agility and angle and range tracking on the jamming so that the jamming source can be engaged and destroyed. Constant changes in the radar frequency in the frequency agility approach prevent the ECM jammers from locking on to a particular frequency, in which case the only recourse may be an inefficient "barrage jamming" across broad frequency ranges. However, some pulse Doppler radars rely on persistent use of fixed-frequency radar signals, so they are prone to ECM measures, and other methods are needed to defeat the ECM source. In modern pulse Doppler radars using fixed frequencies, the angle-on jamming (AOJ) mode can be invoked, which displays the jamming radar signal as a bright line without the range data but showing the direction from which the jamming signal is coming. The AOJ mode is alternatively known as jam angle attack (JAM) or angle track-on jamming (ATOJ). This angular data allow the defender to point the anti-jamming weapons in the correct direction. There are missiles with home-on jamming (HOJ) guidance that seeks the "hottest" radar signature, and if these missiles are sent in the right direction they have a high probability of making a hit.

Although ECM jamming precludes active determination of the target range, there are passive ranging algorithms again so that the target location can be determined. For example, in the angle-rate ranging algorithm the ECCM aircraft (own aircraft) changes its heading, which then would alter the direction from which the ECM jamming radar signal is received. As noted above, using the AOJ mode the direction of the ECM signal can be determined. The rate of change of this angle, angle-rate, depends on the velocity difference between the own aircraft and the hostile aircraft, as well as the distance between the two aircraft. With the velocity of the own aircraft is known, the distance is calculated by continuously monitoring the angle-rate assuming that the hostile aircraft's velocity is constant. This method is limited by the latter assumption in that if the hostile aircraft changes its heading or speed then the distance calculation would be unfounded. Also, since the algorithm relies on angular data it is mostly effective at short ranges where the relative velocity will produce appreciable change in the angles. A related method is the classic "triangulation," where the aircraft again locates the angle of the incoming ECM signal at one position and takes another angular data point after traversing to another position as determined by inertial navigation or GPS. Triangulation also assumes that the hostile aircraft has not made course changes during the time it takes for the own aircraft to make the traverse. To circumvent this limitation, triangulation can be performed by two aircraft or in conjunction with a ground-based radar with similar angular resolution capabilities spaced at optimum distance to pinpoint the hostile aircraft. The radar signal strength decreases as the distance increases, or mathematically the radar signal strength is inversely proportional to the square of the distance. Thus, by monitoring the radar strength the range information can be deduced, except that other factors such as the change in the radar angle can drastically alter the radar signal strength.

STEALTH TECHNOLOGY

Stealth technology is a general term referring to methods to reduce the visibility and therefore the probability of detection by radar, infrared, or other probe beams. Although most prominently used in stealth aircraft, its application extends to all military vehicles and personnel. For stealth aircraft such as the F-117A and B-2 (shown in Fig. 4.23), a number of different technologies have gone into providing extremely low radar visibility. First, the geometry of the aircraft has a significant effect on the radar cross section, along with the aircraft size. The radar cross section refers to the strength of the reflected radar signal relative to the incident radar beam intensity. As the term "cross section" implies, a surface perpendicular to the surface or close to that orientation will tend to have the largest cross-sectional area as seen by the beam and will reflect the most of the incident radar energy. By slanting the surface, much of the radar energy can be directed to other angles. Most long-range radars will scan in the nearly horizontal directions, and therefore vertical protrusions will show up very brightly in radar scans. In addition, intersecting metallic plates and rotating elements such as propellers, fans, and turbine blades are associated with large radar cross sections. Intersecting plates form corners to effectively bounce the radar energy back in the direction that it came from, essentially acting like radar mirrors. In the F-117A, the combination of vertical and horizontal tails has been combined into a single

Figure 4.23. F-117A stealth aircraft (above) and B-2 Spirit stealth bomber (below). Photo courtesy of the U.S. Air Force.

set of tail surfaces at a low slant angle. In B-2 bombers, there are no rear stabilizers nor any aerodynamic surfaces above the main wing plane. In gas-turbine engines, there are usually rotating elements such as the fan and turbine blades that may be exposed to radar probe beams through openings in the engine intake or the exhaust nozzle. In Fig. 4.15, it can be seen that the air intake and the exhaust nozzles are shrouded in both the F-117A and the

B-2 Spirit. The weapons and other external devices that may by carried underneath the wing in non-stealth aircraft are all stored in internal bays to minimize protrusions and therefore radar cross sections. In some of the modern aircraft such as the F-22 Raptor, the thrust vectoring not only gives higher maneuverability, but it also circumvents the use of some aerodynamic surfaces that may form intersecting surfaces and therefore result in a large radar cross section.

In addition to the aircraft geometry, the material itself may be chosen or fabricated for minimum radar reflection. Metallic and carbon fiber surfaces reflect many of the incident radar beams. Composites with ferrite additives can be synthesized for low radar reflectivity and thus are good material for the aircraft wing-body for low radar cross section. Radar-absorbing paint contains micron- or nano-sized iron-based particles that oscillate under the incoming radar beam and dissipate the radar energy into heat. Urethane foam shaped into tiny pyramids can be layered beneath the aircraft skin, to again absorb the incident radar energy.

NIGHT VISION SYSTEMS

The ability to sense the surrounding and the enemy movements under adverse conditions enhances all phases of military operations, from aircraft-based long-range surveillance missions to army personnel seeking the enemy during a night ambush. The night vision system has been in existence since the 1950s, and now it has become standard equipment for U.S. soldiers during nighttime operations. Figure 4.24 shows a typical image as observed through

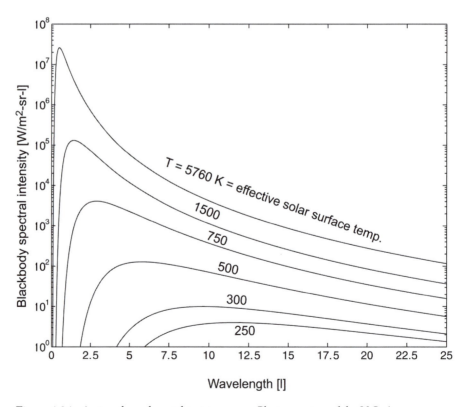

Figure 4.24. A view through a night vision scope. Photo courtesy of the U.S. Army.

a night vision scope or goggle. The low light level is amplified electronically, and one can see that any significant light such as the flashlight held by the soldier saturates the night vision scope and appears as bright white. The night vision display is usually projected in green because the human eye is most sensitive to green and is able to discern the fine shade differences. In theory, the display could be made in full color, but this may have little bearing on the actual color of the objects and therefore become confusing.

There are two principle methods through which night vision is enabled. One is electronic amplification of the light. Even under what may be perceived as total darkness, there is usually a weak but finite source of light such as stars, moon, distant lights, and other man-made sources. It is a matter of amplifying these light signals to a level where human eyes can easily discern shapes and objects. The second method is infrared imaging, sometimes also called thermal imaging.

Light amplification uses a device called image intensifiers sometimes called microchannel plates due to their internal geometry. Image intensifiers are used in military night vision, astronomical imaging, and other scientific applications where low-level light signals need to be detected and viewed. They work by generating electrons when the light goes through the object lens and hits a photocathode screen. A photocathode is a device that releases electrons in response to light. The electrons released from a given point on the photocathode travel through micron-sized channels (the microchannel plate) that are negatively biased (i.e., one side of an electrical power supply is connected to these channels). The negative bias means that there is an abundance of electrons, and when the electron released from the photocathode hits the channel surface multiple electrons spring from the surface. This process continues to occur along the channel until an avalanche of electrons are produced. Thus, in comparison to the photocathode by itself, a significantly greater number of electrons are produced in response to the light. The electron stream constitutes current that can be collected for each channel location and converted to an amplified, digital image (such as the one shown in Fig. 4.24) and displayed on an LCD or other devices for viewing. Although a gain of 1 million times or more can be achieved in some image intensifiers, for night vision applications gains of 20,000 times or above are typically used.

High gain using low power, sensitivity over a large wavelength range including infrared, large field-of-view, and good spatial resolution are some of the desired characteristics in night vision devices. A typical field of view may be about 40 degrees whereas the normal human peripheral vision covers 190 degrees. Also, due to the microchannel design the number of pixels that can be used in image intensifier devices is much less than that for normal digital imaging systems. Unlike digital cameras, image intensifiers have a lifetime on the order of 10,000 hours due to the microchannels deterioration over extended usage.

The name "thermal imaging" originates from the fact that all objects at different surface temperatures emit light in the infrared by a different amount and at different wavelengths. In fact, if the surface temperature is high enough we start to see this emitted light in the visible wavelength range, first in the red color, thus leading to the English expression "red hot." If the object is heated to a yet higher temperature, yellow, green, and blue components of the light will be radiated from the surface. All of the rainbow colors combined will tend to appear white, and thus the English phrase "white hot." In fact, there is a precise relationship between the wavelength (color) and the amount of radiation emitted from the surface and its temperature, as shown in Fig. 4.25. It can be seen that below a temperature of 1000 K or 727° C, the amount of radiation (called the "blackbody spectral intensity" in Fig. 4.17) is small and occurs only in the infrared from a wavelength of 1 to 25 microns and beyond. One micron is one-millionth of a meter or one-thousandth of a millimeter. It is only when the temperature exceeds 1000 K that we start seeing at least a portion of the emission in the visible range. Indeed, at higher temperatures much of the

Figure 4.25. Plot of the emitted light at different temperatures. The vertical axis is the amount of emitted light, while the horizontal axis is the wavelength at which the light is emitted. Photo courtesy of the U.S. Department of Defense.

Figure 4.26. An infrared night vision pod for navigation and targeting, attached to F-16 Fighting Falcon. Photo courtesy of the U.S. Air Force.

radiation may occur in the visible. For sunlight that originates from the sun's surface temperature of 5760 K, the radiation peaks in the visible, or more precisely in the green wavelength of about half a micron. It is no coincidence that human vision and also that of other mammals is most sensitive at green.

The difference in the thermal radiation from surfaces with different temperatures can be used as the basis for thermal imaging. Cold surfaces will appear darker while warm surfaces will appear bright. The ground, any forestation, buildings, vehicles, and humans will all exhibit different temperature due to different cooling and heating properties. Vehicles will tend to be hot, particularly near the engines and exhausts; humans will usually exhibit intermediate temperatures under nighttime conditions, while buildings and grounds will tend to be at lower temperatures. For this reason, thermal imaging is most frequently used in larger night vision systems such as FLIR (forward looking infrared) sensors. FLIR systems are capable of forming images not only under low-light conditions but through fog, smoke, or dust as infrared attenuation through them is much less that that for visible light. FLIR systems operate either in the mid-infrared (3 to 5 micrometer wavelength) or in the far infrared (8 to 10 micrometers). As we can see in the Fig. 4.17, far infrared allows lower temperature objects to be observed at the expense of decreased range due to infrared absorption by the water vapor. Fig. 4.26 shows a FLIR pod attached to an F-16 Fighting Falcon aircraft.

An example of a combined sensor system used on aircraft is the AAQ-13/14 LANTIRN (low-altitude navigation and targeting infrared system for night). LANTIRN allows the fighter aircraft to fly and acquire targets at low-light conditions. Due to the limited resolution at high distances, LANTIRN effectiveness is limited to low-altitude missions. The AAQ-13 combines a J-band (10 to 20 GHz) terrain-following radar (TFR)

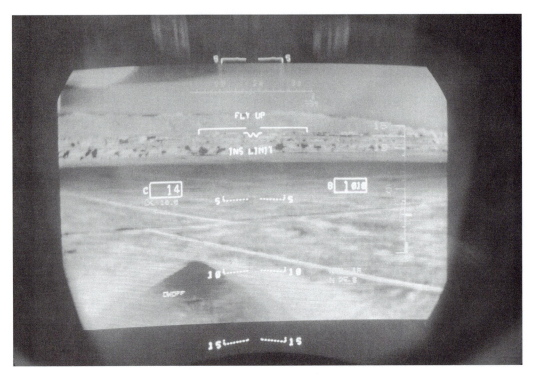

Figure 4.27. An infrared imagery from LANTIRN displayed on the head-up display. Photo courtesy of the U.S. Department of Defense.

and a navigational FLIR. The TFR has five selectable modes: (1) manual preset altitude flight from 100 to 1000 ft; (2) very low clearance mode; (3) weather (rain, fog) mode; (4) low probability of intercept (low radar energy); and (5) electronic counter-countermeasure. The FLIR also has options in operations, from a wide 6-degree field of view to a 1.7-degree narrow field of view. The direction of the FLIR view can also be shifted 11 degrees to either side for sweep scans in the forward direction. The AAQ-14 is a targeting sensor with a gimbaled FLIR and a laser designator rangefinder.

DETECTION OF IMPROVISED EXPLOSIVES

For both battlefield and domestic anti-terror uses, the detection and disposal of improvised explosives have become an important topic. The phrase "improved explosives and devices (IED)" existed from the 1960s. The American military was exposed to many of these devices during the Vietnam War, where mundane materials such as empty cans were used by the irregular North Vietnamese soldiers. An example of the simplicity and lethal effectiveness of IED is a hand grenade (often U.S.-made obtained either through the black market or from the field) placed with the safety pin pulled off in a cut-off can. Detonation occurs only when both the safety pin and safety handle are released, and the can holds the safety handle in place. A thin trip wire is tied to the grenade, and if this wire is tripped then the grenade is pulled out of the can releasing the safety handle. Approximately one-quarter of the troop losses during the Vietnam War are attributed to anti-personnel explosives such as IEDs. Since 2003, during the American presence in Iraq some 40 percent of the losses were caused by IEDs. By this time, there were many more electronic gadgets that could be used in IEDs—digital clocks, walkie-talkies, cell phones, and so forth to trigger the explosives.

The explosive material itself could be from unexploded bombs or homemade chemical concoctions. The military explosives are typically TNT, RDX, PETN, and related chemical compounds designed for large heat release, low smoke, and stability under diverse storage conditions. Explosive compounds, however, can be synthesized from chemicals that are not difficult to obtain through commercial or natural sources. It may be recalled that the early explosive black powder was discovered while experimenting with various mixes of materials, including saltpeter, sulfur, and charcoal carbon. Several hundred combinations exist where a crude mix of common materials, even some household chemicals, can yield substantial explosive characteristics. Many of these combinations may not exhibit some of the required properties such as long-term stability and handling safety, but then for some unconventional uses such issues are of minimal concern. Rather detailed information on production of these dangerous chemicals appears to already have been placed in public domains, but without adding any unneeded details improvised explosives can be categorized as follows:

1. Mix of combustible hydrocarbons (with carbon-hydrogen links) with oxidizing salts (i.e., substances that contain oxygen, nitrate, chlorate, or perchlorate that release oxidizer when heated).
2. Mix of combustible hydrocarbons (with carbon-hydrogen links) with commercial-grade organic substances that contain nitro-, nitroxy-, or nitramine compounds.
3. Peroxides (e.g., hydrogen peroxide) at high concentrations.
4. Combustible fuels (gasoline, methanol, etc.) with ventilation to provide air or oxygen.
5. Mixture of nitric acid and aromatic hydrocarbon compounds.

Of course, if military-grade explosives are available, they can be incorporated into the IED as has been done frequently. Most of the above materials, except for some peroxides, are not easily detonated and require a primer or primary explosive to set off the main explosives. The same material that has been used as the primer for small arms ammunition can be used for this purpose (e.g., lead azide, mercury fulminate, etc.). A typical IED consists of the explosive material, detonation device, and casing. The casing can be anything from steel or plastic pipes, bags, vehicles, or containers. The detonation device may involve simple electronic gadget, mechanical trigger (pull or tension release connected to a suicide bomber or a booby trap), or environmental trigger (pressure, light, temperature, magnetic field, etc.). For most of the explosive and casing combinations, a typical range of damage is 45 m for 2 kg of explosive, 80 m for 10 kg, 100 m for 25 kg. Such large variations in the shape, size, and materials in IEDs represent a significant challenge to machine or other detection means. The detection of IEDs can focus on the casing, the detonation device, or the explosive material itself. X-ray imaging systems can be used to identify the shape and type of materials under layers of surrounding materials. Either a compact single-energy transmitted X-ray imaging can be used, or devices that use two-energy X-rays. A single-energy X-ray device can be made small and portable but can only be used to visualize the internal or external mechanisms of IEDs. Two-energy X-ray devices can determine the shape and the "nuclear charge" of materials, so that the materials can be classified as metals (large nuclear charge), organics including explosives (low nuclear charge), and other materials with intermediate nuclear charge. X-rays have high penetrability through up to one inch of steel, and a very detailed picture of the material content can be made down to micron-level resolution. In the hands of trained experts, X-rays can be used to identify high-risk items among layers of hiding materials. Subsurface radars can also determine the material content based on the microwave reflection at image resolution of 1 to 2 cm. Radar is particularly sensitive to metals, even in very thin foil forms. Detonation devices can in theory be detected if they involve electronic circuitry. Non-linear junction detectors can sense junctions between metals and semi-conductor materials and are quite sensitive, with detection ranges of tens of meters. These detectors thus can detect in real time any trigger mechanism that involves any kind of electrical circuitry, however since many common electronic devices also contain electrical circuits they are not very useful for applications for homeland security.

The detection of the explosive material itself can target the vapor or the bulk content. Explosive materials have varying levels of volatility, meaning that even a normally solid material will release some vapor to air in minute but detectible amounts (typically measured by "vapor pressure" in parts per trillion or ppt). For example, at a temperature of 25° C the vapor pressure of RDX is 6.0 ppt, PETN 18 ppt, TNT 7700 ppt, and nitroglycerine 400,000 ppt. The vapor pressure deceases with temperature, and also if the IED is sealed, as is often the case, then the explosive vapor needs to be collected to a higher concentration. Once the explosive vapor is sampled, however, there are various chemical analysis methods such as calorimetry, gas chromatography, mass spectroscopy, and other methods to determine the explosive vapor content. Of course, more classical methods like using trained dogs essentially trace the smell associated with these vapors. Calorimetry is a method that relies on chemical reactions of the explosive compounds with an added reagent. In the ELITE coupon method developed by the Lawrence Livermore National Laboratory, for example, a small piece of swipe material called the "coupon" collects the sample, and complex agents are sequentially wetted to the swipe. A large number of explosive compounds undergo chemical reactions with complex agents that produce fluorescent reaction products (i.e., materials that will emit color under normal lighting conditions). Explosive compounds such as nitroglycerin, PETN, TNT, RDX, HMX, TATB, potassium nitrate, and many others at 100-ng (nanogram, one billionth of a gram) levels can be detected using the ELITE coupon method. Both the gas chromatography (GC) and mass spectrometry (MS) are chemical analysis methods useful for analyzing a large number of samples. The samples are injected into the gas chromatograph machine, and the different diffusive velocity in the GC medium results in separation of chemical compounds. The diffusive velocity of explosive compounds can be compared with reference values for detection. Mass spectrometry works by ionizing the samples using electron beams or other means and deflecting the ions in a magnetic field to determine the sample mass per molecule, which again can be compared against reference data.

Magnetic or quadruple resonance methods are used to detect the bulk explosives. Both methods use the nuclear magnetic resonance that is also used in medical imaging. Nuclear magnetic resonance involves placing the samples in a very strong magnetic field and using probe electromagnetic waves in the MHz range (radio waves). The strong magnetic field induces two separate nuclear energy states, one at lower energy and the other at higher. The probe electromagnetic wave can send the molecular nuclei to the higher energy state, and on transition back to the lower energy state a photon or radio frequency electromagnetic wave is emitted that can be detected. The frequency of the emitted electromagnetic wave is specific to different compounds. The quadruple resonance method can be used for identifying a wide variety of plastic explosives such as RDX, PETN, HMX, tetryl, TNT, ammonium nitrate, peroxides, and many others. QRSciences is one of the major manufacturers of the quadruple magnetic detectors for explosives, and in some instances the quadruple resonance detector is combined with dual-beam X-ray imaging devices to check baggage at airport security points. These detectors operate at high speeds of up to 200 bags per hour, based on automated software analyses of the signals.

REFERENCES

Blackwell, James. *Thunder in the Desert, The Strategy and Tactics of the Persian Gulf War*. New York: Bantam Books, 1991.

Crickmore, P.F. *Lockheed SR-71 Blackbird*. New York: Osprey Publishing Limited, 1986.

Day, Dwayne A., John M. Logsdon, and Brian Latell (eds.). *Eyes in the Sky*. Washington, DC: Smithsonian Institute Press, 1998.

Laur, Col. T.M., and S.L. Llanso. *Encyclopedia of Modern U.S. Military Weapons*. New York: Berkeley Books, 1995.

Long, M.W. (ed). *Airborne Early Warning System Concepts*. Norwood, MA: Artech House, 1991.

Morchin, W.C. *Airborne Early Warning Radar*. Norwood, MA: Artech House, 1989.

Peebles, Curtis. *GUARDIANS: Strategic Reconnaissance Satellites*. New York: Presidio Press, 1987.

Shubert, Hiltmar, and Andrey Kuznetsov (eds.). *Detection and Disposal of Improvised Explosives*, NATO Security through Science Series. New York: Springer, 2004.

Stimson, George W. *Introduction to Airborne Radar*, 2nd ed. Raleigh, NC: SciTech Publishing Inc., 1998.

For further information on radar, see Web page en.wikipedia.org/wiki/Radar.

SPACE WARFARE: NUCLEAR ARMAMENTS AND MISSILE DEFENSE

THE U.S. STRATEGIC COMMAND (USSTRATCOM) maintains a triad of land-, sea-, and aircraft-based launch capabilities for strategic nuclear weapons, along with global surveillance and missile intercept systems with the latter part under development. The land launch involves the use of the intercontinental ballistic missiles (ICBM). Submarines and long-range bombers make the other two components of the strategic triad. Although long-range ICBMs are stored in hardened silos, smaller "tactical" nuclear weapons can be delivered using a variety of means including Tomahawk cruise missiles and artillery shells.

In the event of a launch, or detection of any object bearing the suspicious speed and radar signature, the radars and satellites deployed by the ballistic missile early warning system will track the object. The radar signal–processing computer programs and human judgments will be busily employed to verify the identity and orbit of the object. If the object is indeed a ballistic missile, within three to five minutes of the launch it will have reached at altitude of several hundreds of kilometers (1 km is 0.625 miles) and a speed of 7 km/s (about 4.5 miles per second). At this point, the thermal signature of the missile nearly disappears because the missile has burnt out its rocket propellants and is subject only to gravitational and aerodynamic forces to determine its final impact point. The momentum at burnout carries the missile to a peak altitude of over 1000 km (well into what we would call "space"). In comparison, the U.S. space shuttle orbits at an altitude of 300 to 400 km. During this mid-course phase, lasting about twenty minutes or so, the missile may disassemble into multiple objects including decoys and actual warheads, the latter being called the multiple independently targetable reentry vehicles (or MIRV). Now, the possibility of tracking and intercepting the targets has become multiply complicated. At an altitude of about 100 km, the atmosphere begins to take effect on the objects. The high speed of the reentry objects, exceeding Mach 20, severely heats the surfaces. Pushing through the air causing shock waves and trailing a vapor trail, these objects will impact the ground at speeds exceeding 4 km/s. But of course the kinetic energy of the impact is the lesser of the destructive forces in light of the total devastation rendered by the nuclear warheads. The entire tragedy of this drama lasts only about half an hour from one side of the earth to the other and obviously is a terrifying scenario to all.

EFFECTS OF A THERMONUCLEAR EXPLOSION

The forces of a nuclear explosion are exerted through the blast wave, intense heat, nuclear radiation, and fallout. The blast wave is a shock wave resulting from the sudden energy release. The energy release heats up the air temperature at the point of explosion to 10 billion degrees Celsius (not that it gives a better feel for how hot that is, but in Farenheit this would be about 20 billion degrees), which is comparable to the temperature in the interior of the sun. The heated air expands rapidly and builds a supersonic pressure wave, which is called a blast wave. This is what causes the loud bang of any explosion, except in a nuclear explosion the pressure surge is extreme. The blast wave expands outward at supersonic speeds (about 1100 feet per second or 0.2 miles per second). An overpressure of only 6 psi is sufficient to level most residential buildings and their occupants. The normal atmospheric pressure is 14.7 psi, and an overpressure of 6 psi corresponds to the pressure exerted by a wind of approximately 170 miles per hour. To give an idea, a 1-megaton bomb exploded at an altitude of 10,000 ft will generate a 6 psi overpressure out to a 4-mile radius. Because this blast wave expands as a near hemisphere, the overpressure is proportional to the cube root of the bomb yield (e.g., a 1-kiloton [1/1000 of a 1-megaton] bomb will have ten times less overpressure). To get into a rather unpleasant subject, humans suffer sever lung damage at an overpressure of 25 psi and will have 50 percent mortality rate in the 50 to 75 psi overpressure range. At 100 psi overpressure, the lethality is 100 percent. Table 5.1 shows the overpressure effect as a function of the distance from ground zero for a 1-megaton blast at 4000 feet. As shown in the table, it does not take the full blast effect to incur human losses. Significant lethality occurs as residential buildings and their content become secondary projectiles toward occupants. As an example, an overpressure of only 4 psi can shatter a glass window and cause the fragments to fly around at up to 120 miles an hour.

A yet even more unpleasant topic is the effect of the thermal radiation. Despite the technical wizardry of the machines we are discussing, all of them result in tragic effects on humans. Nuclear weapons only magnify the scale and intensity. As noted previously, at ground zero the temperature can reach 10 billion degrees Celsius. At such high temperatures, there is intense radiation, similar to the sun radiating so much energy. This radiation alone can cause "flashblindness" or retinal burns out to distances of 20 miles, again for a 1-megaton blast at 10,000 feet. The heat emanating from the blast and its damage is

Table 5.1. Blast Effects of a 1-Megaton Detonation at an Altitude of 4000 ft.

Distance from Ground Zero, in miles	Overpressure, in psi	Equivalent Wind Velocity, in mph	Effects
0.53	100	1415	100% lethality from the pressure effect alone.
1.53	20	502	Severe lung damage, reinforced concrete buildings demolished.
2.35	10	294	Lung damage, commercial buildings destroyed.
3.6	5	163	Residential buildings destroyed, 50% lethality for occupants.
6.3	2	70	Moderate damage to houses.
9.5	1	37	Light damage.

typically measured in terms of energy density in calories per square centimeter (cal/cm²). A 4- to 6-cal/cm² energy density is sufficient to ignite a newspaper and also causes second-degree burns. Third-degree burns are inflicted at an energy density of 10 cal/cm² or more. Table 5.2 shows the thermal damage effects of a 1-megaton blast at an altitude of 6000 feet.

Nuclear radiation is another destructive effect of these weapons, mostly in the form of gamma rays and neutrons. Gamma rays are a form of electromagnetic radiation, like light, except that they are much more energetic than visible light, even more powerful and penetrating than X-rays. For example, one light quanta (particle) of gamma ray carries 1 million times more energy than that of visible light. The gamma rays are produced from atoms in the extreme high-temperature plasma caused by the thermonuclear explosion. Gamma rays penetrate and damage biological tissues at the molecular level. Gamma rays released from a 1-megaton bomb will be lethal out to about 3000 yards from ground zero and will cause radiation sickness beyond that point. However, material like concrete or metal can shield much of the gamma rays. For example, gamma ray radiation from fission bombs will become half its initial strength through a 3.5-inch concrete wall. Neutron particles are released during the thermonuclear explosions and can also cause radiation damage to humans. Again, neutron radiation can be blocked by solid structures. An underground shelter 3 feet below the ground can block more than 99 percent of either the gamma ray or neutron radiation. Similarly, a 9-in concrete wall can block 80 to 90 percent of the gamma rays and 50 to 70 percent of the neutron radiation.

The neutrons in turn can cause other material to become radioactive. Radioactive materials emit high-energy electrons and gamma rays and can thus damage life forms for extended periods of time. The soil, weapons debris, and the products of the nuclear reactions become radioactive during a thermonuclear explosion and are collectively referred to as nuclear fallout. Nuclear fallout may consist of 300 different radioactive materials, with varying lifetimes for radioactivity. Some fallout material like Krypton 85, Strontium 90, and Samarium 57 have a radioactive lifetime measured in tens of years, while some plutonium fission products last several thousand years in their radioactive longevity.

A large-scale nuclear exchange, if it should ever happen, would wipe out 80 percent of the population in the targeted areas due to the initial blast and thermal radiation alone. Estimates vary from several hundred million to 1 billion for the number of fatalities resulting from the prolonged, global environmental and radiological effects of such nuclear war. The long-lasting devastation arising from the aftereffects of global-scale nuclear attacks

Table 5.2. Thermal and Blast Damage Effects of a 1-Megaton Detonation at an Altitude of 6000 ft.

Distance from Ground Zero, in miles	Overpressure, in psi	Thermal Energy Density, in cal/cm²	Effects
1.8	20	150	All combustible material incinerated.
2.7	10	80	All combustible material ignited.
4	5	35	Clothing ignited, wood chars without being ignited.
7	2	9	Moderate heat damage.
10	1	3	Retinal burn, light heat damage to materials.

has been termed by some as "nuclear winter." It involves persistent radiation, an altered environment, and an eco-system that would make the earth uninhabitable, at least by humans. The irreversible course of history must be steered to prevent the use of nuclear weapons. A cursory examination of the history of armed conflicts shows that the number of deaths in wars has escalated in proportion to the available military technology. During the classical period, where conflicts involved clashes of swords, lances, and volleys of arrows, the total number of those lying dead at the end was limited by the human strength to wield these weapons in spite of the perceived cruelty and gore of such warfare. In contrast, during World War II, Russia alone lost 20 million people. Humanity may not be able to survive the next increment in this disturbing trend. Technology does not necessarily win wars (both the Germans and Japanese had superior technology and strategy at the outset of World War II), but history has shown that it brings to our disposal a means to take much higher tolls in human losses.

THE WORLD NUCLEAR ARSENAL

Humankind has yet to be judged for its ability to find a way to live with, or better yet without, this technology of ultimate destruction. In the meantime, the United States, Russia, the United Kingdom, France, China, India, Israel, Pakistan, and North Korea each maintain an arsenal, large and small, of nuclear weapons, as shown in Table 5.3. From 1985 to 2002, the United States and the former Soviet Union went through a series of nuclear arms reduction pacts; however, this process did not completely dispose of the weapons but only disassembled or deactivated them to reduce the total active warheads. The numbers for the active and total nuclear weapons are listed in Table 5.3. The list of course does not include those with current and past intentions and abilities to develop nuclear arms.

The insanely large number of the nuclear stockpiles held by the United States and Russia is the remnant of the nuclear arms race during the Cold War. It takes about 1000 psi of overpressure or more to knock out hardened silos for the ICBMs holding nuclear warheads, requiring a close hit within a few hundred feet for a preemptive 1-megaton bomb. The more of these silos built, the larger the number of the nuclear warheads needed to potentially knock them out. One positive trend, if there could be anything positive about

Table 5.3. Current Estimates on the Number of Nuclear Warheads in the World.

State	Number of Nuclear Warheads (Active/Total)	Total Megatons
United States	4663/9938	1229
Russia (former Soviet Union)	3340/15,000	1587
United Kingdom	160/200	14.4
France	348/348	46.8
China	145/200	273
India	50/50	0.6
Pakistan	60/60	0.7
Israel	80/80	1.6
North Korea	1–10 (estimate)	0.01 (estimate)

nuclear weaponry, is that at least as of the 2002 Treaty on Strategic Offensive Reductions the United States is pledged to reduce its nuclear arsenal down to 2200 warheads by 2012. However, the current estimate is that United States holds a total of estimated 3500 megatons in nuclear warheads, while Russia has two to three times that tonnage. The total number of warheads peaked during the mid-1960s and are now reduced to about 10,000 between the United States and Russia. The warheads are divided among three deployment carriers. For the United States, out of the 5735 warheads, 1050 are mounted on land-based ICBMs (Minuteman missiles) while the rest are roughly equally deployable on bomber aircrafts (mostly B-2s) and submarines. There are approximately 500 "tactical" (meaning it could be used in battle situations) warheads that can be delivered using Tomahawk cruise missiles or bombs.

THE DEVELOPMENT OF THE NUCLEAR ARSENAL

As Americans and Japanese are well aware, the first nuclear bombs were developed by the United States and used against Hiroshima and Nagasaki, a few days before the end of World War II. Some have argued that the use of the bombs lessened the number of casualties that would have been incurred on both sides had the war continued or that the number of civilian casualties from conventional bombing in both Europe and Japan far exceeded those of the nuclear strikes. That is somewhat akin to arguing that those killed by single-fire rifles would have eventually equaled those felled by rapid-fire machine guns during the trench warfare of World War I. Technology changes the content and outcome of warfare, and the nuclear bomb completely altered the concept of national security for the United States and the rest of the world. As we can see in Table 5.3, the number of nuclear weapons not only has proliferated in total number but is in danger of being proliferated among yet more states, some with intentions to use them.

Soon after the Japanese attack on Pearl Harbor, the United States government started a massive program to develop an atomic bomb. Several billion dollars were spent, which was huge by the standards of that time, and the nation's top intellectual resources (at least in physics) were concentrated in a dreary town in New Mexico called Los Alamos. The group of physicists that at least at first participated with patriotic zeal reads like the Who's Who of the great American and European scientists—J. Robert Oppenheimer, Enrico Fermi, Neils Bohr, Richard Feynmann, and many others. The project was codenamed the Manhattan Project, and as is well known, the scientists and engineers involved in the project were able to design, test, and build the first atomic bombs by the summer of 1945.

The principle of the nuclear bomb is contained in the relationship between the mass and energy.

$$E = mc^2$$

where E = energy, m = mass, and c = speed of light = 300,000 km/s

Because the speed of light is a large number and its square, c^2, even larger, the above relationship means that a small mass can be converted to a very large amount of energy. However, mass is conserved in most natural processes that we are familiar with, except in nuclear reactions. In nuclear fissions, certain types of heavy elements such as uranium and plutonium break into smaller fragment elements with a total mass that is not equal to the original uranium or plutonium mass. This mass is converted to energy. An isotope (variant) of uranium, written with the symbol $^{235}_{92}U$ (meaning it has 92 protons and

143 neutrons to make its atomic weight 235), can split into barium and krypton when bombard by a neutron. The fission reaction products, barium and krypton along with extra neutrons, have a minute mass difference from the original uranium isotope, and this mass difference is converted to thermal energy. The mass difference between the original uranium and the final fission products is extremely small, about 1/1000th of the original uranium mass. So within, say, 57 grams of energy, only 0.057 grams of mass is converted to energy by $E = mc^2$. 57 grams is a little over 1/10th of a pound. However, multiplying this mass by c^2 results in an energy of 4.2×10^{12} (10^{12} is the same as a million times a million) joules in scientific units, or the equivalent of 1 kiloton of TNT. 1 kiloton is 1000 ton, and 1 ton is 1000 kg, so this means 1 million kilograms or about 2 million pounds of TNT.

The uranium that occurs in abundance in nature, $^{238}_{92}U$ is heavier, much more stable, and does not undergo fission reaction. The more rare isotope, $^{235}_{92}U$, or plutonium is used as the fission material due to their tendency to disintegrate into smaller atomic fragments and generate fission energy. Once the fission reaction starts, it produces in addition to the atomic fragments two or three extra neutrons that in turn can be absorbed by other uranium nuclei to start a fission reaction of their own. These chain reactions produce in sequence barium, krypton, rubidium, cesium, strontium, yittrium, zirconium, and a host of subatomic particles and radiation. So once the fission reaction is initiated, it becomes self-sustaining until all of the nuclear fuel is disassembled into fission products, energy, and radiation.

For the above principle to proceed to an explosion, the number of trigger neutrons that are released must exceed the number of neutrons that are lost from the fission material. Neutrons can simply escape out into the air or be absorbed by impurities. To maintain the avalanche exponential growth of the number of nuclear reactions, an atom bomb requires a sufficient mass of the fissionable material, called the "critical mass." For uranium, a baseball-sized sphere weighing 10 kilograms contains more than the critical mass. It also means that an atom bomb will typically carry at least 20 kilotons of TNT-equivalent destructive power. The first atom bomb detonated (ironically named "Little Boy" dropped on Hiroshima, on August 6, 1945) was a 13-kiloton bomb using uranium, so it had just over the critical mass. This bomb capacity was just a fraction of modern megaton nuclear warheads, and yet it killed an estimated 80,000 to 140,000 people, almost all civilians, on impact.

Nuclear fission material below the critical mass is safe, and in an atom bomb the material is separated until detonation. The detonation involves bringing together these material masses so that its total mass exceeds the critical mass. There are two ways to bring this about: One is called the "gun-type" and the other an implosion bomb. In both instances, conventional explosives are used to merge the subcritical masses of the fission material, as shown in Fig. 5.1. The gun-type is used for uranium bombs, such as the Little Boy, and the implosion method is used for plutonium fission bombs (e.g., "Fat Man," the second atom bomb used on Nagasaki; its effect is seen from a safe, far distance in Fig. 5.2).

The limitation of the atom bomb was that its total size could not be large because the fission material needed to be kept separate and under the critical mass, then brought together simultaneously at detonation. The complexity of bringing together many such subcritical masses grew rapidly as the total size increased. 500 kilotons is about the maximum capacity of fission bombs. In addition to fission, however, nuclear energy can be released through fusion, combining two hydrogen isotopes to form helium. This is the same nuclear reaction that fuels the burning of the sun. The hydrogen atom is written in scientific notation as ^1_1H, similar to $^{235}_{92}U$ for the uranium isotope. This notation simply means that hydrogen, H, has 1 proton (subscript) in the nucleus and a total atomic weight of 1 (superscript). However, in nature there are some isotopes of the hydrogen atom that have one or two additional neutrons in the nucleus to make the atomic weight higher, like deuterium, ^2_1H, and tritium, ^3_1H. Chemically, they are nearly identical to the normal hydrogen except they

Gun-Type Fission Bomb

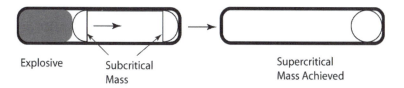

Explosive   Subcritical   Supercritical
              Mass   Mass Achieved

Implosion Fission Bomb

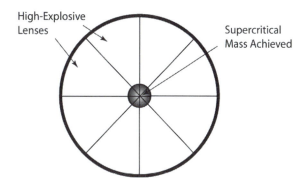

High-Explosive   Supercritical
Lenses   Mass Achieved

Figure 5.1. Gun-Type and Implosion Fission Bombs.

Figure 5.2. The huge smoke after the atomic bomb explosion at Nagasaki. Photo courtesy of the U.S. Air Force.

are much heavier and contain extra neutrons. One major difference is that they can undergo nuclear reaction to form helium with a minute loss in mass that is again converted to energy.

$$^2_1H + ^3_1H \rightarrow ^4_2 + He + neutron + energy$$

The above nuclear reaction indicates that deuterium and tritium combine to form a normal helium atom with a nuclear energy release. If this were to occur under normal conditions, the earth even with a small amount of these hydrogen isotopes would be at a temperature close to that of the sun. Fortunately in this regard, fusion reaction only takes place under extreme temperature conditions, to the tune of 100 million degrees Celsius. This is why the peaceful use of fusion reactions, for power generation for example, is much more difficult than fission reactions. The way to achieve this extreme condition was devised by Edward Teller and Stanislaw Ulam, again of the Manhattan Project group. It involved using the atom bomb detonation and resulting gamma ray energy to focus it toward hydrogen isotopes. Thus, hydrogen bombs include an atom bomb as its detonation device! Since the hydrogen isotopes are much lighter than fission material, H-bombs can achieve their destructive power with much less fusion material. It requires 57 kilograms of uranium or plutonium to produce a 1-megaton bomb, while the requirement for H-bomb is 14 kilograms of deuterium and tritium for the same tonnage. With fewer limitations on its maximum size and the light weight of the fusion material, the largest of the fusion nuclear warheads is close to 10 megatons, or about twenty times the strength of the largest fission bombs.

Having first developed and used nuclear weapons, the United States had a clear dominance in nuclear power through the 1950s, while the Soviet Union awakened to its status as a superpower later as the former European powers were concentrating their resources in rebuilding their war-torn economy and infrastructure. The initial American stand was tough, with Secretary of State John Dulles under the Eisenhower administration stating that the United States would respond to acts of aggression through massive retaliatory means "at a time and place of our choosing." By this time, even more powerful hydrogen bombs were being developed, and the implication of course was that use of such weapons was not beyond the scope of means. However, through the 1960s the Soviet Union also developed a sizable nuclear arsenal as well the means to deliver them at intercontinental range. This situation soon escalated into a race to build ever-increasing numbers of nuclear warheads and delivery vehicles of longer range and better accuracy in a misconceived notion that such weapons could preemptively knock out enough of the other side's launch capabilities and other assets. This stand-off, with massive nuclear arsenals aimed at one another, became appropriate known as MAD, mutually assured destruction. Some of the NATO allies had also developed modest nuclear arsenals of their own. Thus, a unilateral decision or even implication to use nuclear weapons, regardless of its scope, had the potential to affect the entire world as each repercussion of the decision could rapidly be amplified into an unforeseen escalation of events. The MAD scenario could be averted by a "rational decision maker" who, realizing that the initiation of the nuclear exchange leads to loss of all and zero gain, seeks other channels of solution to prevent MAD. A new phrase, "nuclear deterrence," was also coined during this period: If both sides possess sufficiently large arsenals of accurate nuclear missiles then this will deter them from ever using it. Still, the assumption that the other side would have a rational decision maker or that there even was a common basis of rationality was tenuous during the Cold War, given the level of mistrust among the two superpowers. Also, there were other factors, such as regional conflicts where the interests of the two superpowers may differ, rogue commanders who may have ulterior motives, and the possibility of malfunctions and misreads of early warning data to raise false alarms on nuclear launch from the other side. None of the above factors is very comforting to people of all levels if there is a constant possibility of complete destruction.

The U.S. response was to gain the upper hand through technological advances. First, the accuracy of the strategic nuclear weapons was improved to a point where they could score direct hits of hardened ICBM silos in preemptive strikes through the use of MIRV (multiple independently targetable reentry vehicle). MIRVs take separate trajectories as shown in Fig. 5.3. Also, as described in Chapter 9, a completely independent, mobile, and hidden platform for delivering counterstrikes was developed in ballistic missile nuclear

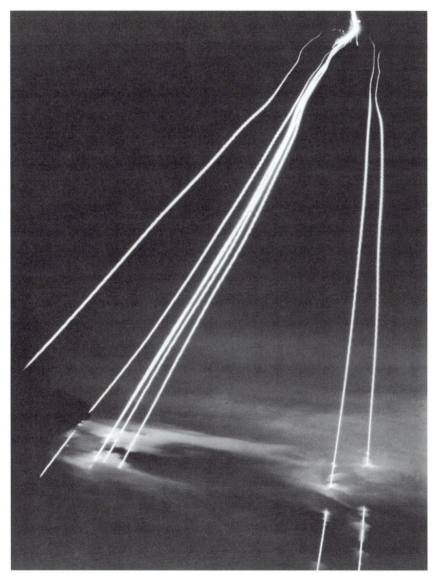

Figure 5.3. Unarmed MIRVs hitting separate targets during testing. Photo courtesy of the U.S. Department of Defense.

submarines. Finally, methods were sought in defending against incoming ballistic missiles. The controversial anti-ballistic missile (ABM) program originates from the late 1960s. On the Soviet side, they caught up in most of the above advances in MIRV and SLBM (submarine-launched ballistic missiles) and also accelerated the pace of the increase of the number of warheads. By the early 1980s, both sides had about 10,000 warheads each. This number peaked in the early 1990s, after which the number was reduced through mutual agreements following the break-up of the Soviet Union.

WEAPONS DELIVERY

The strategic nuclear weapons are maintained in a number of different ways, specifically designed to make preemptive strikes on nuclear capabilities difficult or nearly impossible. Land-based ICBMs are stored in fixed sites or on mobile platforms. Depending on the range, the land-based missiles are classified as either ICBM for 5500-km range or above, IRBM (intermediate-range ballistic missiles) or IBM for 2400 to 5499 km, MRBM (medium-range ballistic missiles) for 800 to 2399 km, or SRBM (short-range ballistic missiles) for 150 to 799 km. Missiles with less than 150 km range are considered tactical, battlefield weapons and do not come under strategic arms limitations in negotiated agreements. Nuclear submarines carrying SLBMs (submarine-launched ballistic missiles) are highly effective in maintaining a constant strike threat from unknown locations close to the target. Due to the stealth and high survivability of SLBM submarines, a large fraction of the total U.S. nuclear arsenal is maintained in a fleet of SSBN (ballistic missile submarines). However, a portion of the weapons is still designed to be delivered through gravity bombs from strategic and stealth bombers. The strategic bombers (B-52 Stratofortress and B-2 Spirit stealth bombers) are assigned to the U.S. 8th Air Force at Barksdale AFB, Louisiana, Minot AFB, North Dakota, and Whiteman AFB, Missouri.

Different ways of storing and delivering the nuclear weapons were devised and developed to counter the preemptive attacks on fixed sites. The strategic bombers, placed on constant short alert status, enable "launch on warning" capability, while nuclear submarines carrying SLBMs can remain in unknown locations, in many instances close to the target, for months. These mutual counterattack capabilities served as a strong deterrent during the Cold War, because both the United States and the Soviet Union maintained a similar level of nuclear destructive potential. Tactical weapons with kiloton-range warheads can be deployed in devices ranging from artillery shells and land mines to torpedoes. Tomahawk cruise missiles can be loaded with tactical nuclear warheads and can be launched from land, aircraft, and naval vessels including submarines. However, due to their typical subsonic speeds they take hours to reach targets.

Most nuclear states also possess long-range delivery capabilities via ICBM, SLBM, or IRBM. These missiles are characterized by larger boosters able to carry the payload to extreme altitudes (up to 1000 km). On reentry, the payload can separate into multiple warheads (MIRV) to strike multiple targets from a single missile and also to make missile defense intractable. Three to twelve MIRVs can be carried by a single booster rocket and can also release decoys. As of 2007, the United States uses Minuteman III (military designation, LGM-30G) missiles as the primary land-based ICBM for strategic nuclear weapons delivery and Trident (UGM-93A/B) for submarine-launched missiles. Minuteman III consists of a three-stage booster (Fig. 5.4), capable of delivering the MIRV payload to targets 6000 miles away. It reaches a speed of approximately 15,000 mph at burnout and undergoes gravitational reentry from that point. The current version of the Minuteman missile, LGM-30G, uses the Mk12 reentry vehicle that contains the payload mounting platform penetration aids, three reentry vehicles, and an aerodynamic shroud. The payload mounting platform serves as the platform to launch the reentry vehicles independently using hypergolic thrusters. Several hundreds of these missiles are maintained by the U.S. strategic missile squadrons, mostly in the upper Rocky Mountain states (North Dakota, Montana, and Wyoming). Figure 5.3 shows the unarmed MIRVs hitting separate targets. Each of the MIRVs can represent nuclear warheads up to several hundred kilotons. Trident missiles are also three-stage, all-solid propellant rockets capable of carrying eight 100-kiloton MIRVs. A photograph of a test launch of the Trident missile is shown in Fig. 5.7. Details of the Trident SLBM development and characteristics are described in Chapter 9.

Other known ICBMs by other states include the R-series (the NATO designation SS-series) in Russia, the Dong Feng ("East Wind") series in China, and the worrisome Daepodong series of the North Koreans. The latter is worrisome due to the North Korea's willingness to sell these missiles to other nations of dubious intentions. The early Soviet ICBMs were characterized by the use of nitric acid as the oxidizer, as opposed to liquid oxygen in American missiles. Nitric acid is highly toxic and corrosive but does have the advantage of stability in storage because it does not require cryogenic cooling as in the case of liquid oxygen. The kerosene/nitric acid fuel-oxidizer combination in Soviet ICBMs for this reason allowed for shorter time to fire, because the nitric acid could be pumped into the rocket and kept there for a longer period of time. Nowadays, the U.S. Minuteman III and similar counterparts in other nations use solid rocket boosters for long-term, constant readiness. The missiles undergo maintenance and upgrade programs, including a propulsion replacement program to replace the lower stages with new "environmentally friendly" solid-propellant boosters. The most advanced ICBMs, the MX "Peacekeeper" missiles, are currently not deployed in accordance with the START (Strategic Arms Reduction Treaty) II. Table 5.4 shows some of the main characteristics of U.S. ICBMs, including the MX missile.

Figure 5.4. Minuteman III ICBM in a test launch. Photo courtesy of the U.S. Air Force.

Figure 5.5. The Trident SLBM. Photo courtesy of the U.S. Department of Defense.

The ground-based launch sites consist of a central command base and a number of launch control centers. Launch control centers are small, underground capsules adjacent to the hardened ICBM silos, and a two-officer crew operates the communications and missile launch/control equipment in these isolated, hardened, self-sufficient bunkers. In the event of a launch, the ICBMs are launched directly (called a "hot" launch) from these silos using the first-stage rocket. A Minuteman missile in a silo is shown in Fig. 5.8. A test fire of the MX Peacekeeper missile is shown in Fig. 5.9. For the Minuteman III, the first-stage booster burns for about one minute, and the second stage for another sixty seconds. After approximately three minutes of thrust, the missile ends its boost phase as shown in Fig. 5.5, and the payload consisting of the warheads and post-boost vehicle are separated and deployed from the remaining booster. The Minuteman III post-boost vehicle contains a thrust device to further guide the warheads. This post-boost thruster is controlled by an inertial guidance system that

Figure 5.6. The SLBM tubes with the hatches open on Ohio-class SSBN. Photo courtesy of the U.S. Department of Defense.

Figure 5.7. Test launch of the Trident III missile from a submarine. Photo courtesy of the U.S. Department of Defense.

Table 5.4. Main Characteristics of U.S. ICBMs (Adapted from "The Future of Land-Based Strategic Missiles").

Launch Vehicle	Minuteman II	Minuteman III	Minuteman IIIA	MX
Length (m)	17.7	18.3	18.3	21.6
Diameter (m)	1.7	1.7	1.7	2.3
Weight (kg)	33,000	35,000	35,000	87,000
Range (km)	11,000	11,000	11,000	11,000
Number of stages	3	3	3	3
Number of warheads	1	3	3	10
Reentry vehicle	Mark-11C	Mark-12	Mark-12A	Mark-21
Warhead	W56	W62	W78	W87
Warhead yield (megaton)	1.2	0.17	0.35	0.3
CEP (m)	370	220	220	90
Silo maximum pressure (kPa)	133 ~ 200	133 ~ 200	133 ~ 200	133 ~ 200

tracks the missile acceleration and trajectory throughout the missile flight and maneuvers the final flight toward the targets using gimbaled liquid-fueled (monomethyl-hydrazine with nitrogen tetroxide) rocket motors. These gimbaled motors consist of six pitch and yaw motors, along with four roll motors, so they control the trajectory by adjusting all attitude angles of the delivery vehicle. The current level of accuracy achieved through this guidance is within 100 m of the target. During reentry into the atmosphere, the warheads along with decoys and chaff to mislead the radar surveillance are released in trajectories toward separate targets (MIRV). Shortly after reentry, the warheads are armed and may be detonated as air or ground bursts depending on the mission.

Figure 5.8. An ICBM in a hardened silo. Photo courtesy of the U.S. Department of Defense.

The ground-based ICBMs constitute a part of the nuclear arsenal in most states, they have the following characteristics:

Survivability: Low for silo-based ICBMs. Current accuracy of strike weapons make fixed-site ICBMs susceptible to pre-emptive strikes.

Accuracy: The accuracy of a ballistic missile is measured by its circular error probability (CEP). CEP is defined as the radius of a circle centered at the target that the missile will strike with a probability of 50 percent or better. Minuteman III has a CEP of 220 to 275 meters depending on the reentry vehicle that is used. This is considered a high-level accuracy capable of knocking out hardened missile silos. Russia's "Iskander" missile is believed to have a CEP of less than 100 meters.

Time on target: ICBMs are ballistic missiles, meaning that they attain a very high velocity during boost phase and mostly maintain that velocity until impact. Thus, the transit time to target is measured in minutes.

Figure 5.9. Launch of MX ICBM from a silo. Photo courtesy of the U.S. Department of Defense.

Figure 5.10. B-83 nuclear bomb. Photo courtesy of the U.S. Department of Defense.

Figure 5.11. Airborne launch control system on an EC-135 Stratolifter aircraft. This control panel decodes the launch instructions and remotely sends launch sequence commands to a ground-based Minuteman III missile from the air. Photo courtesy of the U.S. Department of Defense.

The latter two factors favor the use of the ICBMs, though the low survivability has led to the development of alternate strike or counterstrike capabilities through airborne or submarine-launched nuclear weapons. For this reason, the submarine launch capability is an important asset in the nuclear arsenal.

The naval nuclear arsenal now involves tactical nuclear-tipped cruise missiles and strategic SLBMs. Due to the size and launch requirements for SLBMs, it is not hard to imagine that such concepts initially met with much resistance, both inside and outside the U.S. Navy. The first proposed SLBM was called a "Jupiter" rocket, and it was 90 feet long and 95 inches in diameter. Adding to its size was the fact that Jupiter rockets were liquid-fueled. However, by the late 1950s a number of factors started to favor the development of a viable submarine launch capability. The most important one was the realization was that with the buildup rate of nuclear arsenal in United States and Soviet Union both states would have sufficient nuclear strike capabilities to wipe out major targets, including the land-based launch sites, many times over. As noted previously, the airborne delivery capabilities must be delivered on "launch on warning" basis to avoid being destroyed on the ground. However, submarines submerged deep in the ocean with a communication link to the command base could in principle provide a means to deliver counterattacks. Technologically, guidance systems have been developed that are more accurate, reliable, and compact in size and weight (by the MIT Instrumentation Laboratory). Also, reliable, high specific-impulse solid propellants were becoming available. These developments led to the "Polaris" SLBM program with an initial goal of developing a delivery capability for 1-Mt (megaton) warhead over 1500 miles. During development, these goals were slightly downgraded, resulting in the Polaris A-1, with a 600-kt warhead (W-47) and a range of 1200 miles.

The development work for the launch submarines was performed in parallel, and existing submarines were modified to allow for housing, protection, and launch of the Polaris missiles. The method to eject the SLBMs out of the missile tubes on submarines involves a "cold" launch. A high-pressure compressed air system is used to punch the missiles out of the tubes and to the surface of the water. Prior to the launch, the hard hatches covering the tubes are opened exposing only a thin diaphragm between the water and the missile tube. The missile tube is pressurized to the water pressure outside, then at launch the diaphragm is explosively removed, and the missile is out of the tube with the high pressure air. To minimize the shock from the launch, the missile tubes are suspended on top of oil-filled shock absorbers. The first submarine to carry nuclear SLBMs was the George Washington, originally an attack submarine modified for this purpose.

The Polaris missile program went through several rounds of improvements before the Poseidon missiles replaced them by 1972. The Poseidon C-3 had a length of 34 feet, a range of up to 3200 miles, and had a larger payload capability (up to 10 MIRVs with a 40-kt warhead each). The modern SLBM deployed by United States and also the British Royal Navy is the Trident series, carried by Ohio-class submarines. Trident missiles are made by U.S. Lockheed Martin Space Systems under contract with the U.S. Department of Defense but have been made available to the Royal Navy under an agreement dating back to 1960s. Exchange of strategic missiles of this level of capability and sensitivity is an indicator of the close political and military relationship between the two nations. The Trident missiles cover a range up to 7000 miles with a total yield of 3.8 megatons carried by up to eight MIRVs. The missile guidance is again via inertial tracking, but while the missile is in outer space it is also able to use celestial reference to correct its trajectories. Celestial reference is comparing the apparent positions of reference stars to locate the missile latitude, longitude, and altitude. GPS guidance used in some versions improves the accuracy to a CEP (circular error probability) of 90 m.

Table 5.5. Major Characteristics of Ohio-Class Ballistic Missile Submarines (Source: www.navy.mil)

Builder	General Dynamics Electric Boat Division
Propulsion	Single nuclear reactor, single shaft
Length	560 ft
Width	42 ft
Displacement	19,000.1 metric tons when submerged
Speed	23 mph
Crew	15 Officers, 140 Enlisted
Armament	24 tubes for Trident I and II, Mk-48 nuclear-tipped torpedoes in 4 torpedo tubes
Base	Bangor, WA, and Kings Bay, GA
Fleet	USS Henry M. Jackson (SSBN 730), USS Alabama (SSBN 731), USS Alaska (SSBN 732), USS Nevada (SSBN 733), USS Tennessee (SSBN 734), USS Pennsylvania (SSBN 735), USS West Virginia (SSBN 736), USS Kentucky (SSBN 737), USS Maryland (SSBN 738), USS Nebraska (SSBN 739), USS Rhode Island (SSBN 740), USS Maine (SSBN 741), USS Wyoming (SSBN 742), USS Louisiana (SSBN 743)

Currently, the U.S. Navy operates a fleet of eighteen Ohio-class SSBNs (ballistic missile submarines), each carrying twenty-four Trident missiles with MIRVs. An estimated 50 percent of the U.S. nuclear strike capabilities are entrusted to this fleet, due to the high survivability of SSBNs. When their locations are under deep sea and not known, it is difficult to knock them out. Table 5.5 shows some of the major aspects of Ohio-class SSBNs. The SSBNs obviously carry the Trident SLBMs but also have a capability to launch nuclear-tipped torpedoes. We will look at the details of these ships in a later chapter in this book.

NUCLEAR EARLY WARNING SYSTEM

Since the end of the Cold War and recent developments in the Middle East, the focus of the nuclear strategy (both on offense and defense) has somewhat shifted. This of course does not negate the need to maintain vigilance and capability to monitor the entire globe for signs of nuclear missile launch. Due to the high speeds attained by ICBMs and SLBMs, the amount of time available to respond to a nuclear attack is in terms of minutes (typically twenty-five minutes for ICBMs and fifteen minutes for SLBMs). This makes it imperative that any potential missile launch events be immediately detected, identified, and communicated to the top levels. Because nuclear weaponry is in constant danger of being proliferated, the requirements become more severe and expansive to monitor the entire world for potential use of nuclear weapons, particularly through avenues other than the traditional delivery methods discussed previously. The missile defense program against conventional missile attacks has been controversial from the start, and a huge economic and technical investment has been and is being made. The missile defense technology will be discussed later in this chapter, and it begins with an ability to detect and track missile launches around the globe.

USSTRATCOM is entrusted with a daunting task of coordinating the nuclear strike capability as well as global monitoring and developing ballistic missile defense technologies. Its mission statement reads:

> USSTRATCOM is a global integrator charged with the missions of full-spectrum global strike, space operations, computer network operations, Department of Defense information operations, strategic warning, integrated missile defense, global C4ISR (Command, Control,

Communications, Computers, Intelligence, Surveillance, and Reconnaissance), combating weapons of mass destruction, and specialized expertise to the joint warfighter. (Source: www .stratcom.mil)

One of the functional components of the USSTRATCOM is the JFCC-ISR (Joint Functional Component Command for Intelligence, Surveillance, and Reconnaissance). This is the group responsible for monitoring the globe for any signs of hostile missile launch. The U.S. early warning network started in 1959 with a group of three installation sites with radars. The three sites were located in (1) the U.S. Air Force facility in Thule, Greenland, (2) Clear Air Force Station in Alaska, and (3) a Royal Air Force facility at Fylingdales, United Kingdom. The original radars were L-band radars, and depending on the antenna size and geometry these radars could cover a wide area or focus on a smaller section to identify and track airborne objects. Radars use microwave radiation (electromagnetic waves with frequency from 100 MHz to several hundred GHz) reflected from objects to identify the position, velocity, and in some cases approximate shapes. Depending on the exact frequency bands within the microwave range, radars are designated as L-, S-, C-, X-, or K-band in the order of increasing frequencies. Different radar bands have different propagation characteristics through the atmosphere and also require different wave generators and antennas. L-band is used for long-range surveillance due to its propagation properties.

Since the early installations of the above facilities, at least four known sites have been added at Eareckson Air Station in Alaska, Beale Air Force Base in California, Cape Cod Air Force Base in Massachusetts, and Cavalier Air Force Station in North Dakota. The phased array radar at the Cape Cod site is shown in Fig. 5.12. The Alaska locations monitor the activities in eastern Siberia, Russia, including part of the Antarctic region, while Beale AFB can monitor the Pacific region, including the sea off the coast of North Korea.

Figure 5.12. Pave Paws phased-array radar at the Cape Cod missile early warning station. Photo courtesy of the U.S. Department of Defense.

Table 5.6. Russian Radar Stations for Ballistic Missile Early Warning.

Location (Site Designation)	Radars	Operational Date
Olegngorsk (RO-1)	Dnestr-M/Dnepr, Daugava	1976
Mishelevka (OS-1)	Dnestr-M/Dnepr	1976
Balkhash, Kazakhstan (OS-2)	Dnestr-M/Dnepr, Dnestr	1976
Svastopol, Ukraine (RO-4)	Dnepr	1979
Mukachevo, Ukraine (RO-5)	Dnepr	1979
Pechora (RO-30)	Daryal	1984
Gabala, Azerbaijan (RO-7)	Daryalt	1985
Baranovichi, Belarus	Volga	2002
Lekhtusi	Voronezh-DM	2006
Armavir	Voronezh-DM	2007

The sites in Greenland and on the U.S. East Coast monitor the Atlantic and European region. The advanced radar systems called phased array radars are used in all of these installations with a range close to 3000 miles radius. The global monitoring capability is significantly enhanced by the military surveillance satellites. Satellites use a spectrum of visible and radar frequency waves to detect ground and air activities and also have the advantage of being directly above or close to the areas of interest. In fact, there are several known incidents of false alarms for nuclear attacks that have been corrected using satellite-based data. The exact details of the technology in radar and satellite surveillance have been discussed in Chapter 4.

During the Cold War, the Soviets were not negligent in the race to build up their nuclear arsenal or in developing an equally functional early warning system. Along with a suite of satellites in various orbital configurations (geostationary, high elliptical), the Russians also have installed a group of radar bases. Table 5.6 shows the known radar installations operated by Russia.

MISSILE DEFENSE

The nuclear early warning system was initially put in place to initiate counterstrikes based on the launch scales of the opposing side. This network of radars will have another use, if the missile defense program produces viable anti-ballistic missile weapons, in setting off launches of projectiles to shield the United States against incoming missiles. The concept of a comprehensive missile defense encompasses huge scales (a former distant early warning line in North America stretched 3600 miles) and yet if successful can provide a safety net for the side that possesses it. On the other hand, the margin of error in the technology is minimal, where even a leakage of one or two ballistic missiles may be considered as a failure of the system given the consequences. The anti-ballistic missile capability on one side may prompt the other to attempt to saturate the defense system by increasing the number of available nuclear weapons. In spite of these constraints, the United States, Russia, and several other nations possess some form of operational defense against short-range, tactical missiles (nuclear or conventional). The United States, in particular, has invested a significant amount of economic and human resources to develop defensive capabilities against long-range ICBMs. The origin of this effort goes back many years. Several years after both the United States and the former Soviet Union amassed a sizable nuclear arsenal, the United States initiated a program to develop ballistic missile defense in 1958. During the last decade of the

Cold War, the Reagan administration unveiled a renewed plan to realize the missile defense capability in a comprehensive and expensive research and development program publicized as the "Strategic Defense Initiative (SDI)" or by its nickname "Star Wars." In spite of the administration changes since then, it still lives on amidst astronomical costs, political debates, technical controversies, and also in continuous tests and demonstrations of the technology at limited but increasing scales. It seemed to be an ideal countermeasure for then-growing nuclear threats in the previous era of mistrust and uncertainty between the two superpowers. If the only certainty of a massive nuclear exchange was mutual assured destruction as well as the global collapse of the survivable environment, then what would be better than being able to provide a shield against horrific weapons and yet be capable of wielding counterattack weapons under this umbrella? One element of the missile defense program that cannot be ignored is that the Kremlin policy makers were greatly disturbed by this threat of missile defense, which may have led to changes in their military and political philosophy. The imbalance caused by one side being able to defend against the nuclear attack must have been a powerful destabilizing force.

One of the questions that emerge then is what exactly is the purpose of the missile defense? Many controversies concerning its technical feasibility, impact on economy, and priorities in national defense in the changing global scene continue. Indeed, as one may have seen thus far in this book, many of the issues surrounding military technologies in national and global defense have become so complicated that an individual or a group of individuals may have a really difficult time synthesizing all of the effects and nuances of these systems. As organizations grow, military or civilian, they develop a life of their own in the form of bureaucracy, philosophical fixations, or visions. It takes a true visionary, and on top of it much training and thought in technical and political issues, to be able to guide an organization and on a large scale the nation and the world to an acceptable path. It is a luxury to be able to read and debate the blatant mistakes made by past empires resulting in huge human suffering. We now play at much higher stakes. To quote Albert Einstein, "I do not know with what weapons World War III will be fought. But World War IV will be fought with sticks and stones."

In Chapter 2 of this book, it is noted that the first guided missile, the German V-2, flew in 1942. By the early 1960s, both the United States and the Soviet Union had multi-stage, long-range, ballistic missiles armed with nuclear warheads. This is indeed a quantum leap in human capability to destroy at a scale far surpassing any of the previous means. The ability to shield against this capability would not be so rapid. In spite of the massive publicity associated with the Ronald Reagan administration and the SDI, there were lesser-known research programs in both the United States and the Soviet Union to develop this logical response to the missile threat. The U.S. Defense Advanced Research Projects Agency (DARPA) had a $1 billion project from 1958 to 1969 on various defense concepts and testing, as did the Soviet Union on a much smaller scale. The some of the technical challenges became quite evident from the start. First, how do you identify a missile launch from a distance more than 3000 miles away with a fair amount of certainty? Indeed, there are several incidents of false alarm concerning nuclear missile launches that were judiciously averted. Second, by the end of the boost phase, which lasts all of three minutes or so of the missile trajectory, these missiles are ballistic—meaning that they are flying at speeds close to 15,000 mph. How do you track these missiles and also guide your own projectiles to meet these objects in outer space or in the upper atmosphere? In the subsequent development of the nuclear missile technology, multiple independently targetable reentry vehicles (MIRV) became the standard in the ICBM warheads. A single missile now could become multiple targets, and to hide their target trajectories the warhead platform could release decoys and chaff in addition to the MIRVs. So on top of being an extremely high-speed guidance game, now it becomes a numbers game. Can you put up enough of these defense systems to counter a shower of these incoming objects from the sky? By the latter statement, it also brings about the dollars issue. In many instances, using a $500,000 cruise missile on an isolated radar installation, for example, may be justified due to the lives it may have saved in not having to risk piloted missions to knock out the radar. However, when a program is sustained over several decades with astronomical expenditure, one has to weigh the implications of the technology development again on military, economic, and political grounds.

The anti-ballistic missile defense is to be distinguished from tactical missile defense for which operational systems currently exist, as in the U.S. Patriot, the U.S. Standard SM-3, and the Israeli Arrow missiles (see Fig. 5.13). The Patriot is a tactical missile defense system for short- to intermediate-range missiles that made its debut during the 1991 Gulf War and progressively has gotten better in its reliability. The Navy's Standard SM-3 also

Figure 5.13. A test launch of the Arrow anti-ballistic missile. Photo courtesy of the U.S. Department of Defense.

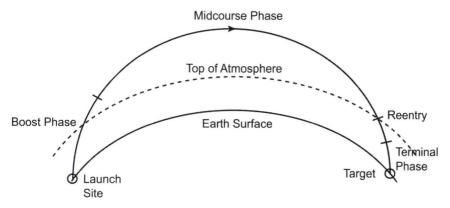

Figure 5.14. Flight phases of an ICBM.

defends against medium-range tactical missiles by providing a shield for the carrier-based task groups. The Arrow missile system is a joint project between the United States and Israel that has the potential for intercept capabilities at longer ranges.

As shown in the Fig. 5.14, ICBMs trajectories are characterized by three phases: (1) a boost phase where the rockets are firing and thus give off easily detectible infrared signatures; (2)

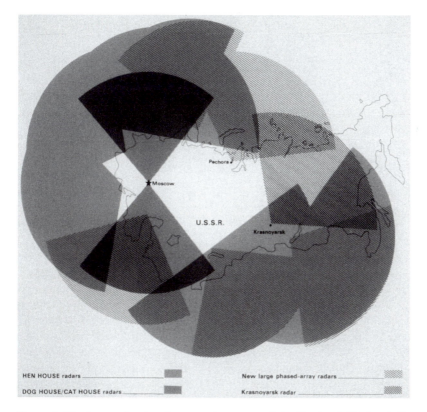

Figure 5.15. A map showing the general coverage of the Russian ballistic missile early warning system. Photo courtesy of the U.S. Department of Defense.

Figure 5.16. An artistic rendition of the Russian GALOSH anti-ballistic missile. Photo courtesy of the U.S. Department of Defense.

the mid-course phase, the longest duration of the missile trajectory involving a free flight in the outer space; and (3) the short re-entry phase where the missiles and decoys are deployed in their flights to the targets. The defense system can in theory be deployed during any phase of the missile trajectory, and the system itself can be ground-based or something that is operating in the air or even outer space from a satellite platform in orbit. The system must contain components of an early detection/identification and ballistic missile interception/kill. A number of kill methods have been proposed for knocking out ballistic missiles in flight: (1) laser-beam weapons; (2) particle-beam weapons; (3) kinetic-energy projectiles or rail guns; and (4) guided missiles. Lasers are used in devices ranging from CD players and barcode readers to optical diagnostics and industrial machining. The word "laser" stands for light amplification by stimulated emission of radiation. It is a method through which lasing molecules contained in a "laser cavity" are made to act in unison to produce intense, monochromatic (single or few wavelengths) light. Laser beams are light waves, so they travel at the speed of light. Particle beams are ions (atoms with plus or minus an electron or two) or neutral atoms accelerated to extreme speeds so that their combined kinetic energy can penetrate missile enclosures. Kinetic-energy projectiles are essentially bullets, except larger and much faster (as in 1000 times faster than rifle bullets). One type of gun proposed to attain this kind of projectile speed is the rail gun using electromagnetic forces for metal projectile acceleration. Finally, the guided missile is like other guided missiles except it will have to have much higher speed and much more accurate guidance to have any realistic probability of intercepting and destroying a target moving at 15,000 mph.

After the ambitious declaration by the Ronald Reagan administration to develop and deploy a missile defense system capable of dealing with a massive missile attack, the project objectives went through some revisions. By the time the Clinton administration took office, the program was mostly focused on developing a ground-based mid-course defense system (or GMD). To give an idea as to the Clinton-era budget on the missile defense program, $3.76 billion was allocated from GMD along with $500 million for boost-phase and $200 million for terminal-phase research and development in the fiscal year 2002. Prior to this date, the budget for the missile defense program ranged from $1 to $5 billion/year. Within the lifetime of the "Star Wars" program from 1984 to the present, the total expenditure is estimated at $120 billion, and by the target deployment date the estimated total amount to be poured into it is over $1 trillion. As a side note, some of the past great empires have weakened themselves by over-expanding and spreading their military resources thin. The initial objective of the ground-based mid-course defense (GMD) system was to develop the capability of destroying five ICBMs with five warheads and low-tech decoys. Then the goals become progressively more extensive: to have the capability to destroy 25 ICBMs that deploy 25 low-tech decoys or 5 ICBMs + 5 warheads with 20 high-tech decoys before 2010. By 2010 to 2015, the goal increases to 50 ICBMs with 50 warheads with low-tech decoys, or 20 ICBMs with 20 warheads + 100 high-tech (as of 2007) decoys, far short of the initial concept of defending the United States against an all-out nuclear attack.

The system that has received the most funding thus far is the ground-based mid-course defense system, with the initial objective of providing an effective defense against one or a few missiles launched against the United States. The anti-ballistic missile (ABM) defense system being tested in installations at Fort Greely, Alaska, and Vandenberg Air Force Base in California is an example of a GMD system. Thus far, the most recent threat of missile launch against the United States by a rogue state has been that of North Korea. They had the crude idea of bolting together a set of old Russian SCUD missiles and giving it their own name of "Taepodong-2." The boosters were designed to ignite in sequence, much like multi-stage rockets. North Koreans, given to exaggeration, claimed a range of 9300 miles, making the U.S. mainland well within its reach. However, during a publicized test firing of this missile on July 4, 2006, it crashed after a forty-two-second flight. In the meantime, the U.S. GMD tests have been ongoing with varied results. To be fair, the final assessments should not be made of the program as of yet. The missile defense agency does claim that since 2005 sixteen out of the seventeen flight tests have been successful and that the program has accumulated twenty-seven successful intercepts out of thirty-four test launches since 2001. However, the public is probably more aware of the failed tests like the "no test" in May 2007 when the target ICBM failed to arrive at the test area or the failed launch of the intercept missile itself in December 2004 at the Marshall Islands in the Pacific and again in February 2005 due to "software error." As of now, the tests of anti-ballistic missiles have involved limiting the number of operational variables and gradually relaxing these constraints as confidence and technology is gained from the test. For example, initial tests involved the use of homing devices or electronic beacons installed on the test target missiles, with the reason being that a complete surveillance system of satellites and radars to actually track target missiles is lagging in development. The Missile Defense Agency did report a successful hit-to-kill launch against two short-range missiles at an altitude of 100 km in April 2007 using a guided kinetic-energy missile. This demonstrated the tracking capability on isolated missiles (two of them in this case), although the speed and altitude of the target missiles are far short of those of ICBMs. It was reported by the Missile Defense Agency that the target missiles were destroyed three minutes after the launch at a range 250 miles downstream of the launch site.

The GMD consists of an array of interceptor missiles launched from the ground, and a comprehensive surveillance network involving spy satellites and ground-based X-band radars (microwave at the 2.5- to 4-cm wavelength range) for accurate tracking. The signals from the satellites and radars are transmitted to a command-and-control center, where massive computing facilities and software analyze the combined set of signals to determine the identity and trajectory of any objects flying toward the United States. The GMD intercept missile itself is a conventional rocket with a two-stage booster and a final liquid-fueled rocket engine used for intercept. Liquid-propellant rocket engines offer much more controllability in the thrust, simply by metering the fuel and oxidizer flows. These missiles will also reach a speed close to 15,000 miles per hour. Currently, the intercept missiles are not equipped with warheads. Instead, they are designed to impact on the incoming missile and in that regard can be considered as a guided kinetic-energy projectile. As noted above, the main delay even in GMD appears to be in the lack of a reliable surveillance-identification system and in missile guidance involved in meeting a 15,000 mph missile in space with another 15,000 mph missile. A photograph in Fig. 5.18 shows the so-called "exoatmospheric reentry vehicle interceptions system" under development. It is based on the

Figure 5.17. The GALOSH mobile launch vehicle. Photo courtesy of the U.S. Department of Defense.

Figure 5.18. An exoatmospheric reentry vehicle interceptions system under development. Photo courtesy of the U.S. Missile Defense Agency.

infrared target acquisition, and the cylinder at the top of the device is perceived to be a kill enhancement device.

The mid-course intercept option is considered to offer the largest window of opportunity for the missile defense. Both the boost phase and terminal phases are very short, and rocket propulsion technology is advancing to a point where the boost phase can be shortened to less than two minutes. Also, to knock out a missile in its boost phase requires the intercept missiles to be in at least some proximity, and this is not always possible for ground-based systems given the geopolitical constraints. The terminal phase also lasts two minutes at most, and current surveillance and analysis capabilities simply cannot complete their tasks in this amount of time. Of course, by the terminal phase any error in analysis or intercept will lead to immediate consequences. The original goal of the missile defense serving as a massive umbrella against large-scale missile attack was somewhat far-fetched either out of misinformation or by design. The fact of the matter is that it is simply much cheaper for the attacking side to devise decoys or other devices to defeat the missile defense system than try to put together a comprehensive missile defense system. It is believed that Russia has warhead deployment schemes capable of overwhelming any conceivable missile defense as of today. The Russian Topol-M ICBM, commissioned in 2005, has high specific-impulse solid-rocket boosters, which shorten the boost phase to a point where the boost phase defense is nearly inconceivable. Along with hardened casing and reflective coating to deflect laser beams, the warhead consists of MIRVs and four high-tech decoys. The missile even has mid-course evasive capability. Other methods of target discrimination include particle beams to check for the presence of fissionable material, laser beams, and kinetic-energy particle probes. The latter method checks the deviation of the object trajectory after the particle impact, to estimate the mass of the target.

One advantage of the boost-phase missile defense, however, is that it is deployed during a phase where the missiles are relatively slow, and there will be clear infrared signature due to the rocket plumes. In addition, the decoys or other diversionary devices are not yet being deployed. At least these are the justifications for proponents of the boost-phase intercept. Of course, one big question is how to tell whether the missile launch is for a benign placement of satellites or for a hostile attack involving nuclear warheads. One concept, out of many, that has been proposed for the boost-phase defense is the use an airborne anti-missile laser placed on a modified Boeing 747-400F. To penetrate through the missile casing, the required power was first estimated at 1 million watts of laser energy focused on essentially a fixed spot on the missile. So not only must a laser beam of this magnitude be generated on board the aircraft and penetrate the atmosphere, but also the beam needs to be directed and tracked to follow the target missile. As we know on hot summer days, light gets refracted by hot air over the road surface or the backyard grill. The same thing happens through the atmosphere. Any density or temperature change will alter the beam trajectory, in spite of the fact the beam may be propagating at the speed of light. Any dust or cloud particles will trap some of the laser energy as well. With current laser technology, several SUV-sized laser modules need to be aligned to produce one gigantic beam, and this grouping of heavy lasers is estimated to test the limits of the Boeing 747-400F aircraft's lift capability. Finally, such heavily-laden 747s will be indefensible.

An alternate concept is to place chemical lasers emitting infrared beams in low earth orbits at an altitude above 100 km. For these chemical lasers, the required laser output rises to the 1 gigawatt range or 1 billion watts. Also, to cover the large expanse of Russia alone with a missile launch capability of up to 3000 ICBMs, a whopping 500 satellites carrying heavy lasers would be required at a cost of over $1 trillion just for these satellites. Other types of laser beams are also being researched, like short wavelength X-ray lasers, ultraviolet excimer lasers and geosynchronous orbiting mirrors, but all with equal or greater fundamental difficulties, at least insofar as a comprehensive anti-ballistic missile defense is concerned.

As noted previously, particle-beam weapons use accelerated ions or neutral particles. These particles can penetrate deeper into the missile shields than photons generated by lasers. However, electrically charged ions are subject to forces of the earth's electromagnetic field and its fluctuations. So the trajectory may become completely warped in unpredictable ways, more so than atmospheric turbulence may deflect laser beams. To defeat this effect, one concept that has been proposed is to first accelerate the electrically charged ions in an electromagnetic accelerator and attach electrons back to the ions as they exit the accelerator, making them electromagnetically neutral. This then has the unwanted effect of being unusable in any atmosphere, as the collisions of these particles with atmospheric molecules will knock out the electrons and turn them back to ions. In any event, the electromagnetic accelerators tend to be again bulky and require a lot of power. It is again estimated that to cover the Russian ICBM threat about 100 billion watts of electrical power concentrated in time intervals of 50 to 100 seconds are needed.

A method called "Brilliant Pebbles" has also been proposed, which is an updated version of the spaced-based interceptor idea back studied by the United States Air Force back in the 1970s. In a project called "High Frontier," it was proposed to place large satellite "trucks" that circle in orbit over the Soviet ICBM launch sites. Each truck was to carry forty-five kill projectiles. At the level of technology in 1970, however, the interception would require 350 seconds while the Soviet boosters of this period, the SS-18s, only had a boost phase lasting 300 seconds. The 432 trucks proposed to be sent into the orbit with forty-five kinetic projectiles each had the capability to shoot down only 12 percent of the Soviet ICBMs. This satellite-based projectile method was resurrected as "Smart Rocks" in the 1980s and evaluated at the Lawrence Livermore National Laboratory in northern California. It again involved a large number, thousands, of small launch satellites dispersed in shallow earth orbits to aim and fire rocket-propelled projectiles. In a series of computer simulations, a group of scientists and engineers from the laboratory was able to convince the Reagan administration that this constellation of interceptor satellites, if realized and implemented, had the capability to provide an umbrella against the full-scale nuclear attack. In 1988, the concept was upgraded to reflect some advances in the technology and renamed "Brilliant Pebbles." Through intermittent funding following the demise of the Soviet Union, it is still considered as the most cost-effective method in comparison to other kill methods described above. Although most of the missile defense work in recent years has been on ground-based (GMD) interceptor missiles, the Brilliant Pebbles idea continues to intermittently receive evaluations based on current level of technology. Brilliant Pebbles involved a small satellite of approximately one meter in length that could operate autonomously with independent sensor, inertial guidance, attitude/aim control thrusters, and a rocket canister for firing the kinetic-energy projectile. At the time these concepts were proposed, the focus was on defense against full-scale nuclear missile launch by the former Soviet Union. To defend against 1000 nuclear missiles, it was estimated that some 80,000 of the Brilliant Pebbles satellites would be needed. Since these killer satellites would be in low earth orbit and have minimal temporal and spatial coverage, a large number would be needed to fully cover the missile launch sites. Perhaps as the shift has changed to theater defense against a much smaller number of threat launches, this concept may be revisited by the missile defense program.

COUNTERMEASURES TO ANTI-BALLISTIC MISSILE DEFENSE

One of the fundamental problems of the anti-ballistic missile defense is that effective countermeasures can be installed at a tiny fraction of the cost of any technology designed to defeat them. One obvious countermeasure is the use of decoys. Current ICBM payloads contain decoys and balloons (to aid the reentry of the warhead), along with multiple warheads. In outer space, there is close to zero resistance to object motion, so all these objects will follow the trajectory as set by the missile at the end of the boost phase. Modern ICBMs can carry up to 10 MIRVs per missile, and this capability can be enhanced to yet larger number of MIRVs without too much technical difficulty although current agreement is toward reducing the number of MIRVs. To assist during the atmospheric reentry, up to twenty balloons are enclosed per each reentry vehicle. These balloons have aluminized mylar surfaces to reflect radar and appear as reentry vehicles on the radar. This means that for a large-scale missile launch involving 1000 missiles, there could be as many as 350,000 objects in the sky to track, identify, and shoot down. Since trying to shoot down all of these objects is futile, a key component of a missile defense is the target discrimination between warheads and non-warheads.

One method proposed is to use the infrared signatures of the warheads, as they will absorb some of the heat of the boosters to an extent greater than the balloons. The heated warheads emit infrared radiation that may be sensed from long ranges. Again, the showstopper is that balloons can easily be equipped with small heaters to give off thermal infrared radiation equal to that of the warheads. Moreover, the warheads themselves can be insulated to block out any thermal emission. A small amount of spray released from the missile can also shroud the infrared signature. Finally, for an infrared detector placed on a satellite, there would be a substantial amount of background infrared emission from the earth surface that could drown any perceivable signals.

The radar tracking of the warheads can also be eluded using a number of simple countermeasures. Aluminum chaff and smoke clouds are used in aircraft anti-missile systems because they reflect the incoming radar beams or absorb and scatter them. These can be easily carried and deployed by ICBMs. The missile surface itself can be coated with either ablative or reflective material to absorb the anti-missile laser beam or reflect it away. Even a small amount of protective coating will translate to a many-fold increase in the power requirements for the anti-missile defense devices, because they must overcome these barriers to ensure destruction of the warhead or the missile.

To defeat the boost-phase anti-missile systems, fast-burn boosters can be used to simply shorten the boost time during which there will be quite a strong infrared signature from the rocket plume, and all of the warheads are contained within the missile. With improvements in the booster design and propellant, boost time can be shortened to less than a minute. This will severely limit the effectiveness of guided interceptor missiles against these objects. Fast-burn boosters can attain 80 km altitude in sixty seconds, by reducing its payload mass slightly. Some solid-propellant boosters can reach 100 to 160 km heights in less than two minutes. In contrast, guided missiles move at a speed of about 10 kilometers per second, and it will take them more 100 seconds to reach a target 1000 kilometers away. For this reason, a mathematical analysis gives that the maximum kill area (the area that the guided interceptor missile can cover to score a kill) is proportional to the square of its velocity and also to the square of the time available: $A_{max} = \pi v^2 t^2$. So if the burnout time of the target ballistic missile is reduced by half, then the maximum effective area for the interceptor missile diminishes to one-quarter of the original. Also, after the boost phase is over, if the guidance missile relied on thermal emission then it will be flying mostly blind. As shown in the above equation, one way to compensate for these fast-burn times of target missiles is to increase the interceptor missile velocity proportionately. However, to increase the speed of guidance missiles requires more propellant mass, actually quite a lot more. To gain a two-fold increase in the maximum speed, a whopping twenty-eight times increase in the propellant mass, and therefore the missile rocket size, is required. In spite of these difficulties, there are efforts underway to devise interceptor missiles with substantially higher speeds, to the tune of Mach 10 or above.

Alternatively, the missiles can be launched to follow depressed trajectories below the horizons of the early warning radars or satellite sensors. More thrust is required because the missile will fly against higher atmospheric drag and also at a trajectory that does not make the optimum use of the gravity, but SLBMs can compensate for the larger required thrust by moving closer to the target. The so-called minimum-energy ballistic trajectories follow a path to achieve the needed altitude to fall to the target at a given range, and typical ballistic missiles are programmed to follow this path. For example, for a 1500-km range target the missile boost phase may last about sixty seconds, at which time the missile altitude would be 58 km. For the missile following a minimum energy trajectory, it will have to travel for another 482 seconds (8 minutes and 2 seconds) to reach the target. If the trajectories are depressed, then this flight time can be 40 percent less. If an interceptor missile to defeat this ballistic missile had a speed of 2.0 km/s (1.25 miles/s) and range of 500 km from its point of launch, then it would require approximately 313 seconds to reach the target. For the minimum energy trajectory, the window of opportunity exists assuming that all goes as projected, but for the depressed path the time window is minimal or nonexistent.

The critical time factor is further encumbered by the fact that missile intercept must follow a series of protocols. The sequence of events leading to the launch of the intercept missile begins from the satellite, radar, or airborne sensor detecting the launch of a threat missile. A number of radar hits by a single or multiple radars are needed to confirm the direction and characteristics of the threat missile. Next, the optimal interceptor missile type and launch site are assigned based on the threat missile identification, at which point the radar track data are downloaded to the launch computer. The fire control radar at the selected launch site then takes over the tracking and proceeds to launch the interceptor missile. The trajectories of the threat and intercept missiles are tracked for possible mid-course corrections and for kill confirmations. The time available for the above sequence is two to fifteen minutes depending on the missile range. For the minimum energy trajectories mentioned earlier, a 3000 km range is covered in 14 minutes, 2000 km in 11.48 minutes, 1000 km in 8.23 minutes, and so on, with the depressed trajectories again taking much less time.

Another imbalance in this numbers game is that the missile defense can be overwhelmed by an increased number of missiles and accompanying decoys. In addition to the infrastructure cost to build the surveillance and target discrimination hardware and software, it costs much more to build the missile defense satellites or other systems than to increase the offensive weapons arsenal. A conservative estimate is about $25 million to add a new ICBM against $1 billion for one missile defense satellite. Finally, putting the missile defense systems in place does not ensure their continuous operation. Satellites, aircraft, or ground-based missile defense systems themselves can be attacked, and a nuclear attack on sky or ground targets cannot be ruled out. In fact, there is a perception among some experts that the missile defense systems either by design or by deceit may be put to much more effective use against satellites. It would require quite an advanced technology to knock out indiscernible objects traveling in outer space at 15,000 miles per hour, but in comparison satellites or ground-based radar and communication systems, whether they are linked to the nuclear offensive capabilities or not, would be sitting ducks against knockout punches delivered by some of the concept weapons discussed above. This is perhaps the true battleground for the future space warfare technology.

ANTI-SATELLITE WARFARE

Satellites are now closely linked with the way civilized society operates. Live TV broadcasts of events occurring anywhere in the world, even real-time battlefield reporting as in the Iraqi War that began in 2003, are now taken for granted. Flow of information and financial, diplomatic, and global news occurs through satellite links. Earth-observing satellites monitor surface meteorology, pollution, land use, water, and other resources. The global positioning system, first developed for military use including missile guidance, is becoming a daily necessity in navigating an automobile on less familiar roads.

The satellites may be categorized by their functions or by their orbital altitude. So-called low earth orbit (LEO) satellites up to an altitude of 2000 km include mobile communication satellites like the Globalstar, Gonets, Iridium, and Orbcomm. Other civil, military, and commercial imaging satellites also fall in this category. There are also an estimated fifty or so military early warning satellites in this orbital range, like the FSW, Helio, Jump-sea, Lacrosse, and Tselina series for intelligence and photoreconnaissance. Other military applications of LEO satellites include defense meteorology, navigation, tactical communications, and technology development. The medium earth orbit (MEO) refers to the range of altitude above 2000 km but below the geosynchronous orbit of 22,236 km. The NAVSTAR GPS system of twenty-four satellites operated by the U.S. Air Force operates in the MEO range. Finally, at an altitude above 22,236 km the satellites can be induced to move at the same speed as the earth rotation and thus the name geosynchronous or geostationary earth orbit (GEO). Commercial communication satellites are sent to these orbits for telephone, broadcasting, video, and data transfer functions.

As discussed in Chapter 4, sensors on the satellites for military purposes have become highly sophisticated. A large part of the electromagnetic spectrum, ranging from visible and infrared to microwave, is used to detect and identify military activities. A large magnification imaging system looking down on earth, aided by computer image processing, allows identification of objects less than 1 m. Missile defense itself is closely supported by satellite surveillance. A large fraction of these military and civilian operations nowadays will be rendered blind if these satellites were put out of commission. Moreover, some of the missile kill devices under development are designed to be placed in orbit, in the same altitude range as most of these satellites. It would be a relatively simple matter to point and shoot at the relatively slow-moving satellites in the vicinity.

Military operations are more and more dependent on satellites. Surveillance, communication, and guidance are provided by satellite signals. Unmanned aerial vehicles (UAVs) like the Predator and the Global Hawk require satellite-guided navigation for their flights. The U.S. military operates over 500,000-plus GPS receivers linked with signal-generating satellites on cruise missiles, precision-guided bombs, and battlefield management devices. GPS consists of twenty-four or more satellites in medium earth orbit (12,600 to 14,760 miles above the earth), and these satellites send out time signals based on onboard atomic clocks with high accuracy. The receiver reads and compares the time signals from at least three satellites, whose positions as a function of time are in the data base. Knowing the distances to these satellites at known positions allows the calculation of altitude, latitude, and longitude to within about five meters or better.

In all, more than 800 satellites are used for military and commercial purposes according to an estimate made in 2005. Nearly half of these are operated by the U.S. government or private sector. The functions of these satellites range from meteorological observations, earth surface remote sensing, and audio-video communications to military surveillance. A communication satellite in a geosynchronous orbit moves around the earth in a twenty-four hour cycle at an altitude of 22,237 miles. This orbital motion translates to a speed of 1000 miles per hour, just a fraction of the ICBMs 15,000 mph speeds. Other satellites may be moving at higher speed but at a much lower altitude down to a few hundred miles, like the military surveillance satellites at 100 to 240 miles above the earth. Moreover, for the satellites to be useful they must follow a precise, predictable orbit around the earth. Any one of the missile defense weapons can be used to track and knock out these satellites, numbering in the hundreds, to cause serious disruptions.

BEAM WEAPONS

The entertainment media and the public have had a long history of fascination with laser or beam weapons. Numerous comics and comics-like movies have shown ray guns or beam weapons, probably the most notable ones being the light sabers and an assortment of blasters in the *Star Wars* series. This notion was actually used in earlier science fictions like "The War of the Worlds" by H.G. Wells in the 1890s, in which Martians were armed with "heat rays." In it, the Martians are described as "able to slay men so swiftly and so silently" using a device "to generate an intense heat in a chamber of practically absolute non-conductivity." An actual use of directed beams may have been used way back in 212 BCE. Archimedes, the Greek genius mathematician and engineer who did everything from figuring out the density of metals to inventing siege and anti-siege machines, used large, curved mirrors to focus sunlight onto the invading Roman ships perhaps to ignite the sail and other combustible material on board. Although this was insufficient to stop the invasion, and in fact Archimedes was killed during this attack when he refused to disengage from a mathematical problem according a legend, this is perhaps the earliest known use of beam weaponry.

The discovery of lasers in the 1950s was made nearly simultaneously by American and Soviet scientists, Charles H. Townes and Arthur Schawlow of Columbia University and Nikolai G. Basov and Aleksander M. Prokhorov of Lebedev Physics Institute in Moscow. Laser works by electronic energy in high-energy atoms or molecules being released when the atoms or molecules return to low-energy state. The energy release occurs through giving off photons or light, which is made much more effective when this light is induced to bounce back and forth in a cavity. This sweeping motion of photons induces yet more release of photons of the same energy (or wavelength), resulting in amplification of the light emission. In fact, this is where the term "laser" originated; as previously mentioned, it's actually an acronym for light amplification by stimulated emission of radiation. A large number of materials can be used to generate lasers, and the energy states of the constituent atom or molecule then determines the output wavelength of the laser. An external energy source is needed to send the laser material atoms or molecules to higher energy state, and this is accomplished by using flash lamps or in some cases another laser!

The utility of lasers was not lost to the military, and the commercial sector soon caught on as well. From industrial lasers used for laser machining and welding and laser range-finder scopes down to CD players, lasers are ubiquitous in modern engineered products. The United States military has had an interest in lasers as beam weapons from early on. A carbon dioxide laser was developed under a Pentagon contract to reach a power level of 60,000 W. Chemical lasers were discovered in the early 1960s, and this type of lasers had a potential for a much higher power output. Chemical lasers excite the lasing molecules from internal chemical reactions, not external light sources like the flash lamps. If we burn fuel and oxygen, the net thermal energy increases, raising the temperature. This type of chemical reaction is called an exothermic reaction. For some reactants, such exothermicity can generate heat *and* high-energy atoms or molecules that can again be used as lasing material. For example, in an oxygen-iodine chemical laser, the laser cavity is fed with gaseous chlorine, molecular ions, and a mixture of hydrogen peroxide and potassium chloride. The ensuing chemical reactions produce excited oxygen and iodine, and it is iodine that emits photons through stimulated emission at the 1.315 μm wavelength (infrared). The chemical lasers had the advantage of being easy to scale up and continuous feeding of the reactants to replenish the lasing material. A large-scale chemical laser was built and tested by the Rocketdyne Division of the Rockwell International Corporation at a remote site that delivered a laser output of 100,000 watts in 1977. As early as 1978, the U.S. Navy used a chemical laser to shoot down a small anti-tank missile in a test range, perhaps serving as a precursor to the later rush to develop anti-ballistic missile lasers.

A class of lasers called "excimer" lasers contains xenon or krypton with halogen atoms like chlorine and fluorine. When these atoms combine to from xenon chloride, krypton fluoride, and so forth, they become electronically excited. Krypton is not a magic element (as in "kryptonite" in the Superman comics) but a naturally occurring element. The energy to form the above excimer compounds come from electrical discharge or electron beams. Since the excimers are electronically excited, they are unstable, and during a reverse reaction into separate atoms they release photons or laser light. The unique aspect of excimer lasers is that they are capable of high-power output in the ultraviolet range. A concept that has been entertained was using a ground-based excimer laser at a mountain-top site and using satellite mirrors in orbit to reflect and direct the beams to targets. However, atmospheric effects such as beam refraction and absorption by ozone layer make such a realization difficult.

A far-fetched concept of generating powerful laser beams involves a nuclear bomb and X-ray lasers. This concept uses the energy of a nuclear bomb explosion to power X-ray laser rods. The energy is sufficient to generate something like fifty extremely powerful X-ray laser beams to be centered onto multiple targets. Once the nuclear bomb is exploded, the X-ray laser rods of course become a single-use component. In fact, the resulting X-ray will be on its path as set by the initial alignment of the laser rod, followed by the debris of the nuclear blast.

These beam weapons use photon beams (i.e., light beams). Other particles can also be accelerated to carry sufficient kinetic energy. Electrically charged particles like electrons or ions (atoms with one or more deficit or surplus electrons) can be accelerated in electric or electromagnetic fields. Opposite charges attract, and therefore positive ions for example will be drawn to the negative electrodes (cathodes) in an electric field. In contrast to the relative ease with which charged particles can be accelerated, their kinetic energy can also be rapidly dissipated through collision with other particles, like the atmospheric molecules. That is why electron-drive devices like the old-fashioned TV screens operate in a vacuum. In addition, charged particles are subject to the earth's magnetic field and other electromagnetic disturbances, making their flight control extremely difficult. To circumvent the latter effect, neutrally charged particle beams have been considered. The ions (e.g., positive hydrogen ions) are accelerated in alternating electric fields. First, the electrode is charged to negative bias, attracting the hydrogen ion, and as the hydrogen ion passes through the electrode, it reverses its charge to positive to repel the ion. The next set of electrodes will undergo the same precisely timed sequence. The total voltage used in this accelerator may exceed 1 billion volts, and the resulting velocity of the ions is close to the speed of light. The ions are then passed through a chamber filled with a small amount of gas. During the passage of the accelerated ions in this chamber, the electrons are drawn to the positive hydrogen ions to make the particles electrically neutral. The ion particles then proceed on their paths toward the target at extreme velocities and in neutral charge states.

REFERENCES

Hecht, Jeff. *Beam Weapons: The Next Arms Race*. New York: Plenum Press, 1984.

Levi, B.G., M. Sakitt, and A. Hobson (eds.). *The Future of Land-Based Strategic Missiles*. New York: American Institute of Physics, 1989.

Pahl, David. *The Space Warfare and Strategic Defense*.Winnipeg, Canada: Bison Books, 1987.

For further information on Reagan's "Star Wars" program, see www.fas.org/spp/starwars/program/nmd.